Helping Stop Hitler's Luftwaffe

The Memoirs of a Pilot Involved in the Development of Radar Interception, Vital in the Battle of Britain

Air Marshal Sir Arthur McDonald
KCB AFC FRAes DL

First published in Great Britain in 2020 by
Pen & Sword Air World
An imprint of
Pen & Sword Books Ltd
Yorkshire – Philadelphia

Copyright © the estate of Sir Arthur McDonald 2020

ISBN 978 1 52676 478 2

The right of the estate of Sir Arthur McDonald to be identified as Author of this work has been asserted by them in accordance with the Copyright, Designs and Patents Act 1988.

A CIP catalogue record for this book is
available from the British Library.

All rights reserved. No part of this book may be reproduced or transmitted in any form or by any means, electronic or mechanical including photocopying, recording or by any information storage and retrieval system, without permission from the Publisher in writing.

Typeset by Mac Style
Printed and bound in the UK by TJ Books Limited, Padstow, Cornwall.

Pen & Sword Books Limited incorporates the imprints of Atlas, Archaeology, Aviation, Discovery, Family History, Fiction, History, Maritime, Military, Military Classics, Politics, Select, Transport, True Crime, Air World, Frontline Publishing, Leo Cooper, Remember When, Seaforth Publishing, The Praetorian Press, Wharncliffe Local History, Wharncliffe Transport, Wharncliffe True Crime and White Owl.

For a complete list of Pen & Sword titles please contact

PEN & SWORD BOOKS LIMITED
47 Church Street, Barnsley, South Yorkshire, S70 2AS, England
E-mail: enquiries@pen-and-sword.co.uk
Website: www.pen-and-sword.co.uk

Or

PEN AND SWORD BOOKS
1950 Lawrence Rd, Havertown, PA 19083, USA
E-mail: Uspen-and-sword@casematepublishers.com
Website: www.penandswordbooks.com

Contents

Acknowledgements		vii
Introduction		ix
Chapter 1	Growing up in the West Indies, 1903–1912	1
Chapter 2	Antigua School Days, 1913–1916	11
Chapter 3	Relocation to England, 1916–1920	20
Chapter 4	The Antigua Sugar Factory and the Motor Boat *Isa*	26
Chapter 5	Return to England and Entry into the RAF. Flying the Mono Avro 504K, 1923–1925	35
Chapter 6	The Dangers of Anoxia, 1924	52
Chapter 7	Problems with Navigation, 1925	60
Chapter 8	23 Squadron, Henlow: Night Exercises, 1925	65
Chapter 9	Engineering at Henlow: a Smashed Propeller, 1927–1928	75
Chapter 10	Cambridge University and Imperial College London, 1929–1932	82
Chapter 11	The Singapore Experience, 1933–1935	88
Chapter 12	Water Sports at RAF Base Seletar and Return to England	111
Chapter 13	Return to Competitive Sailing, 1936	118
Chapter 14	Biggin Hill, 1936–1937	133
Chapter 15	Andover Staff College and The Dowding Experiment, 1938	148
Chapter 16	**Outbreak of War, 1939**	158

Chapter 17	The Duxford Invisible Flight Path, 1941	163
Chapter 18	Across Africa to Ceylon: The War in the Far East Against Japan, 1942–1943	179
Chapter 19	The War in the Far East Against Japan, 1943–1945. Air Officer for Training, India	184
Chapter 20	Photo Reconnaissance, 1945–1946	188
Chapter 21	The 1948 Olympic Games, Torquay	191
Chapter 22	Later Career, 1948–1962	196

Appendix I: The Battle of the Saintes, 1782 — 200

Appendix II: Ian Donald Roy McDonald MC DFC, Arthur's First Cousin and First World War Air Ace — 203

Appendix III: The Prelude to the Biggin Hill Experiment, the men who made it possible: H.E. Wimperis, Tizard, Watson-Watt and Dowding — 207

Appendix IV: The Biggin Hill Experiment: Further background information written by Arthur — 209

Appendix V: The Battle Re-Thought: A Critique on the Symposium on the Battle of Britain in 1990, by Arthur — 214

Appendix VI: Background Information on Ceylon During the War and Documents Relating to Arthur's Time in Ceylon and India — 220

Appendix VII: Table of Aircraft, compiled by Arthur's Great Grandchild Joe Jameson — 227

Appendix VIII: Commander-in-Chief, Pakistan Air Force, 1955–1957 — 230

Appendix IX: RAF Service History — 270

Appendix X: Address Made at the Celebration of Sir Arthur's 90th Birthday, 16 June 1993 — 272

Appendix XI: Sailing Highlights in Retirement, Royal Lymington Yacht Club — 276

Bibliography — 278

Index — 279

Acknowledgements

We would like to thank the following people and organisations who have helped in completing this project:

The National Archives in Kew for providing documents relating to the Biggin Hill Experiment and other documents which helped fill in gaps about Arthur's later service history in Ceylon and India during the war.

The Imperial War Museum, for its excellent photo library, which produced some new photos.

Duxford Museum, particularly the helpful volunteer tour guide Graham Rogers, who gave the family a wonderful tour, and its historian Carl Warner.

Our editor, Richard Doherty, for being so knowledgeable about the historical details.

Arthur's wife, Mary, for her informative letters about Arthur's time as Commander in Chief of the Pakistan Air Force.

The book, *Tizzard* by Ronald W. Clark, which gives a helpful account of the events leading up to the Biggin Hill Experiment.

Graham Clarke, the historian of the Royal Lymington Yacht Club, for taking the time to send us details of Arthur's sailing achievements.

Phil Listemann, who runs the excellent website, RAF-in-Combat, who spent time looking through his vast photo collection to find photos of relevant planes.

Particular thanks also go to Robin and Ian McDonald for their help in providing photos and information for the Antigua sections of the book.

We would also like to thank family members in the UK, particularly Jean, John, Peter, Ian, Alison, Simon, Joe and Jez who all helped provide extra details for the book and helped with proof reading.

The family also gained useful information visiting the new museum at Biggin Hill and the excellent Battle of Britain Bunker at Uxbridge when researching the book.

Unless otherwise stated, all images have been provided from Arthur's own collection. Many of the RAF photos contained in Arthur's collection were taken by official RAF photographers and were under Crown Copyright until this expired.

These memoirs were completed by Arthur's oldest daughter Ann and granddaughter Jackie.

Introduction

This 'Biographical Sketch' was dictated by Arthur into a tape-recorder at his home in Lymington, Hampshire, during his nineties, long after he retired from the RAF. When settling in Lymington he asked the estate agent for a house within cycling distance of the Royal Lymington Yacht Club. As someone who represented his country in sailing in the 1948 Olympic Games, his passion for yacht racing continued throughout his long and happy retirement. He was still racing regularly at the yacht club well into his late eighties.

As well as describing how and where his love of sailing began, Arthur's memoirs give a fascinating insight into life as a pilot in the early days of the RAF. He talks about the, then unknown, dangers facing pilots in the early days of flying, the risks of anoxia and of carbon monoxide poisoning.

The memoirs outline the significant achievements in his career that led to him receiving his knighthood in 1958 and rising to the rank of Air Marshal before retiring in 1962. Such achievements include being involved in the little-known Biggin Hill Experiment, which played a vital part in the development of our radar defences by ground to air control just before the Second World War. There is also a detailed explanation of the invisible flare-path he developed for his pilots returning to base at Duxford during the war, so that none of them were shot down while landing at night.

In the early chapters of the book, Arthur shares what it was like to grow up in Antigua, one of the Leeward Islands of the West Indies, and explains how his interest in engineering started as an apprentice in the Antigua Sugar Factory.

In the appendices we have included background information to some of the events mentioned in the book. As Arthur was not able to complete his memoirs, we have included brief descriptions of some of his later postings from other sources.

These memoirs have been compiled directly from Arthur's tapes by his eldest daughter, Ann, who was present during the recordings, and his granddaughter Jackie, with help from his family in the UK and Antigua.

Chapter 1

Growing up in the West Indies, 1903–1912

My earliest memories were of living in a small wooden framehouse with my parents on a sugar estate in the island of St Kitts in the West Indies; this would have been around 1908 to 1909.

The house had been built for the manager of the estate, but several estates had been merged and the joint manager of the group had been accommodated elsewhere. The house had, therefore, been made available for my father who was a doctor and had been appointed by the Colonial Office to be the doctor for the northern side of St Kitts.

Arthur's parents, Hilda and William McDonald on their wedding day 1902, Port Elizabeth, South Africa. (*Photo courtesy of Robin McDonald*)

My father and mother both came from families which had lived in Antigua for several generations. On my mother's side I can trace my ancestry back to the 1670s or 1680s to a man by the name of Lydeat, who is on record as having been there when the first British government was formed in 1667 after Antigua had been recovered from French rule.

The first McDonald emigrated to Antigua in the 1820s. He set up in business as McDonald and Company, Import Export Merchants, in 1830. My father had been educated in Edinburgh and had received his medical training in St Bartholomew's Hospital in London. He had then practised medicine for some years in Antigua, after which he volunteered to join the British Army in the Royal Army Medical Corps for the duration of the South African War.

When he left for South Africa he must have been engaged to my mother for she followed him there. They were married in South Africa and I was born in Klerksdorp in the Transvaal on the 14th June 1903, or so I have been told.

Arthur's Uncle Harry and Aunt Winifred (Holmes) with Archie and Arthur, sitting next to his mother Hilda, on the steps of Mills House, St Kitts. (*Photo courtesy of Robin McDonald*)

Arthur on a visit to St Kitts in 1978, standing outside his childhood home, Mills House.

The house we lived in in St Kitts was within sight and sound of a steam-driven sugar-cane crusher and mill, and during the sugar-cane cropping season the *chuff, chuff* of the steam engine was audible all over the house during daylight hours, but it was shut down during the night. As a small boy I was extremely interested in the mechanical details of the mill and had free access to wander round and inspect it at any time.

The vintage of the steam engine must have been about early- or mid-nineteenth century. It was a beam engine of a type now only to be seen in museums, with a horizontal beam supported on pedestals about eight or ten feet high. This had a single vertical cylinder, and piston rod at one end which pushed that end of the beam up and down. A connecting rod on the other end was connected to a crank on a crankshaft at about ground level. This was joined to a gear wheel about ten feet in diameter. That was followed by a train of gear wheels which reduced the revolutions from about sixty a minute at the engine itself to about three revolutions for a group of cast-iron crushing rollers. The configuration of the group of rollers was the traditional form which was used throughout the West Indies for all sugar crushing mills during the whole history of the sugar industry there.

This grouping consisted of a single roller at the top turning in one direction. This pressed down on two rollers close together below it, which turned in the opposite direction. This meant that the cane which was fed in at one side was crushed as it entered the mill between the top and one of the bottom rollers and then a second time as it exited from the mill on the other side. The juice from the crushers was run down into a series of open-topped boiling pans, which were set into masonry on top of the flue of a furnace. The juice was ladled from one to the other as the water was boiled off until it had reached a syrupy consistency, after which it was pumped into a boiling pan heated by coils using the exhaust steam from the engine. The fuel for the furnace consisted of the pithy inside of the cane. After the juice had been squeezed out of it, this was taken from the crushers and spread on the ground to dry in the sun. Then it was moved by hand on a contraption looking like a giant stretcher. This had a man at each end with two long poles with fabric in between. They carried it to the furnace doors where it was fed into the furnace.

Next to the sugar mill and the buildings containing the whole arrangement, about twenty or thirty yards away, there were the massive remains of a windmill tower, but the vanes and all the machinery from the windmill had disappeared.

Arthur's son John standing next to a sugar crusher in Antigua.

The development of the sugar industry in the east Caribbean Islands started with windmills in the eighteenth century and at that time wind power was the only power available which could have enabled that quantity of cane to be crushed. This was the reason for the enormous wealth-creating ability of the east Caribbean Sugar Islands in the eighteenth century and the reason why the French and British fought over them bitterly for over a hundred years.

This fact seems to have escaped the notice of British historians. When I was at the Antigua Grammar School from 1913 onwards, my Antiguan form master, teaching from English textbooks, informed me that the 'Trade Wind' was so called because it propelled the ships that carried the trade.

As a result of what I now know about the sugar industry and its development, I am now convinced that the Trade Wind was originally described as such because it was the wind that created the trade in the first place. If there had been no Trade Wind there would be no trade to carry and those Islands would have remained in the condition in which they were for 150 years after they were discovered by Columbus – in other words practically uninhabited.

During the windmill era, the islands of Barbados, St Kitts and Antigua were the principal sugar-producing islands. At that time they contained hundreds of windmills. There are records of 500 in Barbados and 175 in Antigua and, from books which I have obtained from the Public Library in Lymington after retirement, I have discovered that each of those windmills was powered by a steady breeze of over twenty knots day and night for about 360 days of the year. They could crush about 200 tons of cane a week each, so that the 500 mills in Barbados could have crushed 500 multiplied by 200 which is 100,000 tons of sugar cane a week. Nowhere else in the world in the eighteenth century could sugar cane have been crushed at that rate in an area of that size, or in any area.

This gave the Eastern Caribbean Sugar Islands a complete monopoly in the mass production of cane sugar, and before the days when beet sugar production had been developed in Europe it gave them a world monopoly in the mass production of sugar. It was for this reason that the French and British fought over those Islands for so long, and that the Naval Dock Yard at English Harbour was constructed and the British maintained a West Indian Battle Fleet of thirty-three ships of the line and the French had a West Indian Battle Fleet of almost the same size based on Martinique.

The decisive battle which ended that long period of conflict was the Battle of the Saintes (see appendix), which took place in 1782.[1] This is a forgotten battle because it is seldom mentioned in the history books. Every tourist is now taught when he visits Antigua that the Naval Dock Yard was Nelson's Dock Yard, but the decisive battle, which was fought by a fleet based at English Harbour, was the Battle of the Saintes. This took place two years before Nelson arrived in Antigua as a young post captain in charge of a frigate.

To return to the mill at St Kitts, everything was very primitive there. The water supply for the whole estate, including the McDonalds' house, came down the hill in a single 1.5-inch-diameter pipe which poured continuously into an open-topped cistern about thirty or forty feet across. Overflow pipes from this cistern took water down to the mill and to the cattle troughs. As far as the McDonalds' house was concerned there was no water supply and all water used had to be brought in buckets from the cistern and carried into the house or into the kitchen. The kitchen was outside the house in a lean-to at the far side of the backyard. There was, of course, no flush sanitation. All the cooking was done on locally produced charcoal on little burners called coal pots. These would be placed in a window of the lean-to kitchen facing the Trade Wind so as to get a sort of forced draught. This could be adjusted by moving the position of the coal pots. Lighting in the McDonalds' house and in the mill was either by kerosene oil lamps or by candles.

Despite these primitive arrangements, the McDonalds actually had the use of an enclosed private swimming pool. Everything was primitive. When the swimming pool had to be emptied, the drain pipe was simply a pipe lying on the grass outside with a wooden plug driven into the end of it. The plug was removed, knocked out, and the pool emptied itself and was then scrubbed out and the plug replaced. The water to fill the pool was obtained by knocking another wooden plug into the end of the pipe which poured continuously into the cistern. This forced the water in the

---

1. Arthur's great-great-great grandfather, William Spry, has written a first-hand account of the battle, included in Appendix 1.

supply pipe up over an inverted U-shaped pipe and thus it filled the pool. When it was full, the supply pipe was removed. It was all as simple as that.

One of my most vivid memories of my time at the mills in St Kitts was the sight of Halley's Comet in 1910. Those who may have tried to see it in 1985 can have no idea what Halley's Comet looked like when it looped round the sun on the same side as the Earth happened to be in its orbit. It was a brilliant display, brighter than the full moon with a tail stretching across about 20 degrees of arc. This lightened up the landscape as brightly as a full moon. No wonder that the shepherds 'who watched their flocks by night', were astounded when they saw it around about AD 1. When I saw Halley's Comet in 1910 it rose about midnight and my parents woke me up and also my younger brother aged four (I was then seven) and took us to an east-facing window to see this bright star rising in the east. I can only remember one remark that was made on that occasion, but that I do remember very clearly, it was made by my grandmother who was with us and who said, 'Well one thing is certain, none of us adults can possibly ever see that again, but you boys, if you are very lucky, mind if you are very lucky, might possibly do so.' My younger brother has one memory of that occasion, but his memory is of being woken up in his cot, a very unusual occurrence in the middle of the night, and told that he was going to see something called Halley's Comet, but he doesn't remember seeing it, so he must have gone to sleep in my mother's arms before he was taken to the window. The remark of my grandmother that we might possibly see Halley's Comet again I regarded as a challenge and I was determined, given all the necessary luck, that I would see it again; so when it was due in 1985 I took a lot of trouble to do so. I think that it is very unlikely that many other ordinary people in this country, or anywhere in the world, saw it in 1985 as there was almost nothing to see. This was because the Comet on that occasion looped round the sun on the far side of the Earth's orbit and all that was visible was a very faint white fuzz in one of the constellations. I took the trouble to read up the papers and to discover in which constellation it would appear, and even then I had to go down to the marshes at Pennington near Lymington, as the marshes were at least a mile away from any house lighting or street lighting. I also had to use binoculars to see anything at all. On the first occasion, I saw this little white fuzz which might have been Halley's Comet but I couldn't be sure, but, when

I went back two or three days later, there it was again, but it had moved across the constellation in the anticipated direction; so, I am in no doubt at all that I have seen Halley's Comet twice.

The other memorable event which occurred during my time in St Kitts was the sinking of the *Titanic* in 1912. We got news of this on the cable, I suppose probably on the next day, 16 April 1912 1 can very distinctly remember a conversation which occurred in which young Arthur, aged nine at that time, explained to his parents how such an extraordinary thing could have happened. My mother kept saying, 'But it couldn't have, the ship was unsinkable. She had all these watertight bulkheads. If one or two compartments were holed she would not sink.' So young Arthur had to explain to them, having read extensively in a children's encyclopaedia, that the bulk of an iceberg is mainly under the water so that they are much wider below the water line than they are above it, so if a ship scraped along the side of an iceberg it was highly likely that a shelf of ice would scrape along the bilge and cut a long gash along the side of the ship, thus flooding many compartments.

As an aside, quite recently, in 1995 I picked up a book, which gave a blow-by-blow account of the *Titanic* disaster and I found it fascinating to read in 1995 a description of an event which coincided exactly with what I had told my parents in 1912. There was only one factor which I had not appreciated on the first occasion and that is that there was a design weakness on the *Titanic*, which I had not known about on the first occasion, in that had the watertight bulkheads extended one deck higher they would have saved the ship, because four compartments were holed and flooded the tops of the watertight bulkheads which were far above the normal water level on the ship, but, with four compartments flooded, the bow dropped so that the water went over the top of the fifth bulkhead and that is what finally caused her to sink.

I was interested to learn in 1985, seventy-three years after this discussion in 1912 with my parents about the sinking of the *Titanic*, that a young French boy aged ten had also had a discussion with his parents in France. I learned this at a symposium held at the Institute of Electrical Engineers in 1985 to celebrate Fifty Years of Radar. The symposium took place fifty years after the first British experiments in radar.

Those took place in 1935, when Robert Watson Watt used reflected radio waves to detect approaching aircraft, first at Daventry, and then at Orfordness and, later, at Bawdsey.

I was invited to speak at the symposium because I had taken part in the Biggin Hill Experiment. At Biggin Hill in 1936 to 1937 we developed the system of ground-to-air control of fighter aeroplanes, which was vital to the RAF in the Battle of Britain in 1940. In a later chapter I discuss the importance of this work at Biggin Hill and how we overcame the difficulties which we faced.

At the symposium in 1985 I was asked to give an account of what had happened at Biggin Hill in 1936 to 1937, and I did so, but I listened with interest to the rest of the contributions from other people at the symposium.

In 1936, and probably for years after that, I had believed that radar was a British invention. At this symposium it was made perfectly clear that this was not the case and that radar had been discovered quite independently in six or eight different countries at different times, in some cases before the 1930s.[2]

One of the representatives of the other countries who spoke at the symposium was a Frenchman who went on to explain how radar was invented in France. He went on to the dais and called for the first slide, and an enormous cartoon picture appeared of a four-funnelled liner, upended, plunging to its doom in the Atlantic with its stern, rudder and propellers in the air. It had a little blurb of a band playing 'Nearer My God To Thee' and showed people on the quarterdeck slithering down the side and so on. He said nothing for a few moments. Everybody of my generation knew perfectly well, of course, that that must have been the *Titanic*. He still said nothing, and I couldn't help wondering what on earth the sinking of the *Titanic* in 1912 had to do with the discovery or invention or radar, but the Frenchman then continued:

> 'Yes, that is the *Titanic*, he said, 'Young Monsieur Dubois was ten years old when this dreadful thing happened. He was very much affected by it, took it to heart, and discussed it with his father. He said to his father, "That was a dreadful thing all those people freezing to death in the Atlantic." He said, "When I grow up I am going to invent a device which will prevent transatlantic liners running into icebergs in fog or darkness." His father replied, "Yes my boy, of course you will," and never thought anything more about it again.'

---

2. Arthur learned at the symposium that a German, Christian Hülsmeyer discovered radar in 1904.

But young Monsieur Dubois never forgot. When he grew up he got himself a degree in electrical engineering and developed a radar set for use on ships to give them warning of obstructions in conditions of darkness or fog. This was fitted to one of the French transatlantic liners, I think it was the one which was called *Ile de France*, but I can't remember the name of the particular one. This was before the Second World War. The skipper of the ship was very sceptical about this and thought it was a lot of nonsense, and installation was not complete when the ship was due to sail for New York with a load of passengers. So Monsieur Dubois, with his crew of mechanics, went with the ship to finish the installation during the voyage. The completion took place about halfway through the voyage. Monsieur Dubois told the captain when it was ready. They switched the set on but, of course, the screen was completely blank because the ocean all round them was empty. There were no ships in the vicinity and, of course, no icebergs or anything else. So the captain said, 'I told you so, we'll never get anything out of this.' Mr Dubois said, 'When we get fifty miles from New York the skyscrapers at Manhattan will show up very well on this thing.' So they waited until they got fifty or sixty miles from New York and switched it on again.

Unfortunately, in the meantime, the ship had gone through a tremendous storm and salt spray had been thrown all over the place and all over the conductors and insulators and antennae of this installation. The one thing Monsieur Dubois had not done was to cover them all up as in the case of modern radar sets fitted to ships. Salt water is a good conductor of electricity so when the set was switched on there was a series of blue flashes and white smoke and nothing else. The captain was furious. He said, 'You've wasted our time, I told you it was a load of rubbish, throw it over the side.' He was the captain, his orders had to be obeyed, so the first radar set ever made in France was thrown over the side into the Hudson River. Subsequent investigation showed that, but for the salt spray, that radar set would have worked perfectly well. So, on the day or the second day after the sinking of the *Titanic* the same subject had been discussed by two boys of nine and ten, one an English boy in St Kitts and the other a French boy in France.

Chapter 2

Antigua School Days, 1913–1916

In 1913, my father was posted by the Colonial Office back to Antigua to take up the appointment as Medical Officer of Health for the Leeward Islands and Superintendent of the Holberton Hospital in Antigua. He was also permitted to do private practice and to keep what he made from that for himself. This was fortunate for the people of Antigua but it did nothing to support the McDonald family, because a fairly high proportion of the white people in Antigua were related to the McDonalds and my father would never have thought of charging any relatives for his services, nor would he have considered ever charging the families of the other two doctors in Antigua. He could and did provide his services and answer the call outs of the black inhabitants of Antigua, but he made nothing out of that because none of them had any money. Antigua at that time was a very poverty-stricken community, so if the McDonalds had had to rely on what my father made in private practice the family would have starved to death.

Although Antigua and St Kitts are within sight of each other and the passage time for steamers was only about six hours, nevertheless the move of the McDonald family and their possessions was quite a complicated business. We decided to take with us our buggy and one of our horses, Nellie the mare. Shipping these was fairly complicated because in neither St Kitts nor Antigua was there a harbour or quay where ships could go alongside. In St Kitts there was no harbour at all. As with many other eastern Caribbean islands, ships lay off in a roadstead on the south or the south-west side of the island. They anchored about half a mile offshore and connection between the ship and the shore was by rowing boat or barge, there being a jetty on the beach to facilitate this sort of operation. So, Nellie the mare had to be hoisted in a canvas sling into a barge, taken off to the ship, hoisted up into the hold and the buggy treated likewise. In Antigua, there were several harbours as it had a heavily indented coastline. The one used for landing goods and passengers was at St John's. There was another harbour called English Harbour at the other side of the island, but this had been constructed as a naval dockyard in the eighteenth century and was not used for commercial shipping. Landing in St John's was an even more tedious business than landing at St Kitts, because although there was a harbour there, and I dare say that the old sailing ships used to enter it, there was a bar across outside the entrance which was too shallow for steam ships to enter, so they had to lie off three miles at least from the landing quay in St John's. Communication between ship and shore was by means of the Antigua Government steam launch. This carried passengers and hand luggage and towed behind it a barge carrying heavier articles such as Nellie our horse and the buggy. All these difficulties, however, were overcome and we arrived in Antigua.

The Government quarters allocated to my father were very pleasantly situated on the eastern, or upwind side, of St John's on a ridge, or hill, where we had the full benefit of the Trade Wind blowing through the open windows and doors all day and all night, so it was delightfully cool. The house was situated less than half a mile from the Antigua Grammar School, so my brother and I were enrolled there and could walk down to the school or bicycle down, when we eventually achieved bicycles, very easily.

One of the reasons why the McDonalds had welcomed the move to Antigua was that there were only two schools in the eastern Caribbean which had a reputation for excellence: Codrington College in Barbados and Antigua Grammar School. The latter was so popular that it ran a boarding house, or at least a dormitory, for fifteen or twenty boys who came to Antigua for boarding-school education from other islands as far away as the Virgin Islands to the north. Some of the boys from the Virgin Islands were Danes because some of the Virgin Islands had belonged to Denmark and had eventually been sold to the United States somewhere about the turn of the century and Danish families were still living there. Anyway they considered it worthwhile to send their sons to Antigua for a boarding-school education.

The Antigua Grammar School was an excellent school in every way: it would compare favourably with many of the state schools in this country at the present time. It never turned out a boy who was in any way illiterate, who couldn't read, write and speak English grammatically and fluently and handle numbers. In addition, the headmaster took the view, very unfashionable at the present time amongst professional expert educators, that civilisation and civilised behaviour have to be taught, that they do not come naturally to human beings. So, the boys at the Grammar School were taught something about how our Western civilisation had developed from the classical days of Greece, with the discussions on philosophy between Aristotle, Socrates and others of that age, via the Roman Empire, the Roman occupation of Britain and so on to the present day.

He taught boys that there really was a difference between right and wrong, and it was not for them to decide on issues of that kind. Experience did count for something and the study of history was important. As a result of this the discipline at the Antigua Grammar School, and in fact in society as a whole in Antigua, was far better than in many parts of this country at the present time. There was virtually no criminal activity that I can remember in any sections of society. No boy from the Antigua Grammar School considered it conceivable that a gang of young men should knock an old lady to the ground and steal her handbag. No crimes of that kind ever occurred.

Discipline in Antigua Grammar School was enforced when necessary by the use of the cane, this of course would have laid the Headmaster open to prosecution if he'd done such a thing at the present time in this country, but it was taken for granted there and those experts and professionals who say that corporal punishment does not have a deterrent effect can only be people who have never experienced it. I have experienced it and I know that it certainly deterred me and my other young friends.

Corporal punishment, use of the cane, was not used very often at the Grammar School but there was one hilarious episode when a new boy just joining the school was actually caned before he had enrolled in the school on his first day after arrival.

The background to this was that this young boy, whom we may call Alex, was very worried about going to school for the first time. His little friends tried to put the wind up him by trying to tell him that terrible things happened at the Grammar School; boys were sometimes caned if they didn't do the right thing or say the right thing, and he expressed serious apprehension about his first day at school. His mother sought to reassure him and told him that it would be alright because she would send him to school in the care of another little boy, who in fact did have the curious name of Tooney, who would show him what to do. Provided he followed Tooney's example and did exactly what Tooney told him to do, he would escape trouble. The two boys arrived at school a little bit early and at that moment two other boys, brothers from one of the sugar estates arrived, as they always did in a donkey cart. They unharnessed the donkey, tied it to a tree, provided it with water and fodder and left the donkey cart on the gravel outside the window of the headmaster's office. The window was, of course, wide open for coolness in a tropical climate.

It so happened that the week before this event one of the very early Hollywood blockbuster films had arrived in Antigua and had been shown at Antigua Cinema in St John's. All the boys of my generation will recollect the film I am referring to if they hear the words 'Ben Hur and the chariot race'. I can't remember who Ben Hur was, but the most exciting scene in the film was a chariot race in the Circus Maximus at Rome, round narrow sharp corners with chariots colliding, wheels coming off, chariots rolling over, cracking of whips, shouting of the spectators, all very exciting and enjoyable. The boys all remembered this and one of them looked at the donkey cart and said, 'If we had two donkey carts we could organise a chariot race between them, between teams of seven, two boys on each shaft, makes four, two pushing behind, makes six, and one in the seat cracking the whip and urging the others on.'

This sounded a splendid idea but, unfortunately, there was not a second donkey cart available. However, one boy had a watch with a second hand. He may have been the only boy in the school who had a watch but anyway he did have one, and he pointed out that if it was not possible to have an actual race they could at least have a timed trial between two teams. He could start the first team off when his second hand was at the top and measure the time it took to get round the tree at the end and back again to the starting point within about one second. It was agreed that this was a good idea; teams were assembled and at the word 'go', off the first one went. There was much crunching of iron-shod wheels on the gravel, shouting of encouragement from the spectators, cracking of the whip by the driver and so on. By the time they got back to the starting point the headmaster came out absolutely furious, and said in a very angry voice. 'Will you boys stop that noise immediately, I can't hear myself think. Now this is your final warning. Stop that noise!' He went in.

Of course, young Alex had taken no part in this activity at all. He had looked on in amazement; it was not the sort of behaviour he had expected to find at the Grammar School, but the others stopped for some time and then started to mutter and say, 'Well what a pity that was. Perhaps if we did it again without all the shouting and tried to keep it quiet we could get away with it.' So they staged a second team to do the same operation but, in the course of the chase, they rather forgot and the noise built up, so that by the time the donkey cart returned for the second time, there was almost as much noise going on as there was on the first occasion. The headmaster came out extremely angry and said, 'What did I tell you? I gave you a warning. Will the boy or boys who disobeyed my explicit instruction come to my office immediately!'

There was only one boy present who didn't know what that summons meant, that was young Alex. All the others knew that an invitation to the headmaster's office meant six strokes of the cane. So they looked at each other and wondered what to do and Tooney pointed at young Alex who was still standing there absolutely bemused at the whole situation and said, 'He means you. He means you.' Now young Alex's mother had told him, the last thing she said as he went off was, 'Now remember to do everything that Tooney tells you.' So he followed the headmaster into his office, the headmaster, without looking up, reached for the cane hanging up on a hook on the wall and said, 'Bend down.' He then turned round and gave him six of the best on the buttocks. Young Alex stood up rubbing his backside, the headmaster looked at him and said, 'Oh! Who are you? I don't remember seeing your face before.' And young Alex said, 'No. Sir, I don't think you have, I haven't enrolled in the School yet.' This was regarded as the best joke that occurred at the Grammar School in that particular year.

But there were one or two other occasions when things happened, which to say the least, would be unusual in this country. Two other brothers from a sugar estate used to arrive at school riding ponies, one pony each. The first day they arrived barefooted, wearing shorts and a shirt and no boots or shoes. They did this because they never wore shoes and considered it soft or effeminate. None of the local Antiguans wore boots and shoes; the soles of their feet had developed hard horny pads like the pads on a camel and they could walk all day on gravelled roads or anywhere else without discomfort, and these planter's sons reckoned that they should do what everybody else did and at home they went about without boots or shoes. But the headmaster, when he saw them coming in barefooted, said, 'I will not have barefooted boys in my school. Now this is the last time. Next time you must wear boots or shoes.' So the next day the boys arrived, barefooted as usual, but each one with a pair of boots tied together by the laces, hung over their saddlebrows. They then dismounted, unsaddled their ponies, tied them to a tree, put on their boots – I don't think they had any socks – and walked into the school. Honour was satisfied and, when the school day was over, the first thing they did on coming out was to take the boots off and tie them together and ride home again barefooted.

Games were played every afternoon at the Grammar School. It was usually cricket all through the year except that for a brief period in the slightly cooler weather after Christmas we were allowed to play soccer. This meant that boys there either became very keen and very good at cricket or they became very bored with it. I was one of the ones who became very bored and was never any good at it but, later on, after I had left there was a boy there by the name of Vivian Richards who in later life became one of the greatest cricketers in the world. He had started with every advantage from that point of view. His father had been a warder at the jail at St John's; the jail was just across the road from the main cricket ground on which international matches were played from time to time, so he was exposed to the sight of international cricket being played from a very early age. The jail was only about a quarter of a mile from the Grammar School, so he was enrolled there at a young age and went on from that and became a great cricketer. In his retirement, recently in the early 1990s, he returned to Antigua and announced he might go into politics but I do not know exactly what has happened to him.[3]

---

3. Vivian Richards never entered politics but he was knighted and has a stadium in Antigua named in his honour.

Another memorable event which occurred about that time, on 4 August 1914, was the announcement of the outbreak of the First World War. I got the news in a slightly unusual situation; 4 August 1914 must have been the August bank holiday that year, because there was quite a large swimming party organised on a beach off my sugar-planter uncle's house at a place called High Point. I had been in the water for some time when one of my young friends beckoned to me from the beach and, when I came ashore through the surf, he informed me, 'We are at War with Germany.'

Not many weeks after this there was a scare in Antigua because an unexpected ship appeared on the south-west horizon and, as it approached, it became obvious that it was a warship and we knew that there was a German squadron of heavy cruisers loose in the Atlantic, engaged in commerce raiding. It was thought that it might be one of those which was approaching, so the local militia were called out. They were armed with bolt-action Lee Enfield .303 rifles and what they could have done against an 8-inch gun cruiser I don't know, but anyway a gesture had to be made and so they proceeded down to one of the forts that had been constructed in the seventeenth and eighteenth centuries to protect Antigua against the French.

At the time when the forts were built, the eastern Caribbean Islands were such a valuable source of wealth because they had a monopoly in the mass production of cane sugar. This was conferred on them by the fact that they were the only place in the world where there was a constant and regular supply of mechanical power. In other words the Trade Winds, which were harnessed by means of many large windmills. It was this which attracted the French in 1666 when they captured and occupied Antigua for a year, but the island was handed back to the British under the terms of the Treaty of Breda in 1667.

It was as a result of this experience that the Antiguans learnt the lesson that it was no good defending a naval dockyard from frontal attack from the sea if one left the back door open. What had happened in 1666 was that the French had landed on the opposite side of the Island, walked across and taken the dockyard in the rear. As the result of this experience the Antiguans learnt their lesson and constructed all these forts.

But to get back to the warship, when she came closer to the island she identified herself as being the *Good Hope*, the flagship of a British squadron which was searching for the German squadron loose in the Atlantic.[4] I don't know why Admiral Craddock, who was in charge of the British squadron, should have called in at Antigua, but I suspect that he was keeping wireless silence and he wanted to communicate with the Admiralty in London. This could be done very quickly and easily through the cable station in Antigua, which was in communication with England via Barbados. At any rate, after a short stay the *Good Hope* turned round and steamed away again.

It may well be that we were the last British people ever to see the *Good Hope* because the next news we learned of her was that she and the other ships of the British squadron had all been sunk at the Battle of Coronel off the west coast of Chile. The British ships were obsolescent whereas Vize-Admiral Maximilian Graf von Spee's squadron was composed of modern warships. Moreover, it appears that when the squadrons came into contact with each other, it was sunset, the British ships were to the west of the Germans, which were close in under the shadows of the land and invisible to the British gun-layers who had nothing to aim at except the flashes of the German guns. The German gun-layers, however, had brilliantly illuminated targets as the British ships were outlined against the western sunset sky.

Shortly after the Battle of Coronel, the Admiralty sent two battlecruisers into the South Atlantic to round up the German squadron. These ships were faster and more powerful than any of the German ships and, provided they could make contact with them, they should have been able to destroy them.

The two battle cruisers called in at Port Stanley in the Falkland Islands to refuel and while they were doing this a man came galloping across the island from one of the sheep farms on the southern coast with a message that a squadron of warships had been seen approaching from the south. It was immediately assumed that this was the German squadron, the

---

4. At the time the German squadron, under Vize-Admiral Maximilian Graf von Spee, was still in the Pacific Ocean on its journey home from China via Cape Horn.

British battlecruisers at once started to raise steam for full speed and as the German ships came round the point the British battlecruisers were starting to move out of the harbour. In the stern chase battle which followed, all of the German ships were sunk.[5]

---

5. The Germans had been shadowed by a British ship and the ships in Stanley were waiting in ambush. As well as the battlecruisers *Inflexible* and *Invincible*, there were three armoured cruisers, two light cruisers and an armed merchant cruiser. Not suspecting the presence or strength of the British force, Admiral von Spee's squadron of eight ships attempted to raid the base at Stanley but were forced to flee. Pursued by Admiral Sturdee's squadron, all but one of the German ships were sunk. The sole survivor was the SMS *Seydlitz*. The anniversary of the battle, 8 December, is a public holiday in the Falkland Islands. Admiral von Spee went down with his ship. His two sons were also serving in the squadron and were also lost.

Chapter 3

Relocation to England, 1916–1920

In 1916, my father, for the second time in his life, volunteered to join the Army in the Royal Army Medical Corps. This time it was for the duration of the First World War. He joined the West Indies Regiment, which was being formed at that time, and it was assumed that he would find himself located somewhere in France or in England.

The family had to move out of the house in which they were living because this was a government quarter required for my father's successor. My mother could, I suppose, have found other accommodation in Antigua, but she did not fancy the idea of not being able to see my father for an indefinite period. She also thought that, if she moved to England, he might be stationed either in England or in France and she might see him occasionally on his leaves. She must have been a very courageous woman because she then decided to move to England by ship with her four children, my brother and I, aged ten and thirteen, and my two young sisters aged two and three. In 1916, at a very critical stage of the war, we embarked for the voyage in a small cargo ship with accommodation for twelve passengers.

I had forgotten the name of the ship but my sister, who was one of the infants in the party, is still living in Lymington at the time of writing and has reminded me that the name of the ship was the *Arzilla*. One of the extraordinary things which I remember about that trip was that the first-class fare from Antigua to London, including the cost of three weeks' board and lodging, was £15 for an adult and half fare for children.

The *Arzilla* had no wireless or radio communication, so from the time we left Antigua, where we were in communication with the war situation in Europe via the cable bulletins every day, we had no news at all for the duration of the voyage, which was very nearly three weeks.

The *Arzilla* was a small ship of 3,000 or 4,000 tons. She was coal-burning and very slow, with a cruising speed of 8 or 9 knots. She was not armed, had no wireless, no convoy protection; she was probably too slow to keep up with a convoy.[1] She did not zig-zag to avoid submarines, there would have been no point in it, she just went straight from Antigua to London and hoped that she would not by chance encounter a German submarine. If she had done so we would all have been lost. It was at about that time that the Germans engaged in a sink-on-sight policy, in which they sank ships (without trace). The *Arzilla* could have been sunk without wasting a torpedo as a German submarine could have overtaken her from behind, come up alongside and fired one round from its deck gun into her hull below the waterline and that would have been it; and according to reports, they might then have machine-gunned the crew in the boats and left no trace of what had happened to her.

At any rate we were lucky and nothing of this kind occurred. We had, of course, to steam blacked out, with no navigation lights. One extra precaution was taken. As a coal-burning ship the *Arzilla* had to dispose of the cinders from her furnaces once a day. If they had been thrown over the side in daylight the ashes might have floated and indicated to a passing submarine that a ship had passed that way. So all the ashes and cinders for twenty-four hours were saved up and dumped over the side as soon as it got dark in the evening. The idea was that by first light next morning they would be so much dispersed so far astern of the ship that they would give no useful information. There was an added precaution that some of the cinders from the furnace might have been glowing red, not quite extinguished. As this might have given away the position to a submarine, a wooden chute down the side was constructed, which projected above the rail and inboard at the top end, so that the cinders could be shovelled in to the top of the chute.

Our luck held and in due course the *Arzilla* arrived at London docks. On the way up the Thames I caught sight, for the first time, of an aeroplane. This was my first sight of an aeroplane at the age of thirteen.

My mother found accommodation for the family in rooms in a rather scruffy area of London – Parsons Green, if I remember rightly. We settled down there for the time being.

---

1. In fact, convoys were not introduced in the Atlantic until spring 1917.

During the voyage she had discussed, with a clergyman who was a fellow passenger – I think he may have been a bishop, the problem of education for my brother and myself. She had no idea at that time what kind of schooling she might be able to obtain for us. However the bishop, if that is what he was, happened to know a man who ran a preparatory boarding school at Southbourne near Christchurch. He promised to write to this man, whose name was Alfred Meakin, and ask whether he would take my brother and me on as boarders. In due course, this was arranged and at the beginning of the September term 1916 my brother and I took a train from Waterloo to Christchurch to join the school. This was the first mainline train journey we had done since 1909 when the family had come over to England for a holiday.

On arrival at Christchurch we were met by the headmaster and taken to the school. There were about twelve or fifteen boys on the train and we were conveyed to the school in a horse-drawn vehicle, petrol being very scarce during that stage of the First World War. I think the vehicle was called a dray; it had a number of seats round the side. Whether it was pulled by one or two horses I cannot remember, but anyway it was horse-drawn.

There were other unusual, or least unusual to us, methods of transport to be seen in the streets. A number of people had converted their petrol engines on vans or buses to run on gas. Most of the gas was, of course, coal gas, which was the standard gas at that time. It was used for illumination, cooking and, to some extent, heating. The gas used on the vehicles was stored in a large bag of balloon fabric, like an elongated balloon fastened down to the top or back of the vehicle. In the morning, when the vehicle started out, this balloon was fully inflated and ended up with folds of floppy material flopping about on the top or back of the vehicle.

There was another ingenious method of running vehicles. This was called producer gas. The producer gas was produced in a sort of furnace on the back of the vehicle burning coal. The air supply through the little furnace was restricted so that the flue gas consisted of a fairly high proportion of carbon monoxide or coal gas. How this contraption ever worked I have never understood, but they were to be seen and the vehicles did run on them; I daresay the power available was only a fraction of what it would have been in the original form using petrol.

At the start of the September term in 1916, there was a fine spell and old Meakin used to take us boys on a scramble down the cliffs at Southbourne on to the beach where we changed into swim suits in the open and plunged into the sea. This experience came as a considerable shock to my brother and myself because the temperature of the water was about 20 degrees lower than the sea bathing we were used to in Antigua. However, we survived it and in fact found it quite bracing after a time. We found life at the prep school what might be described as claustrophobic, after what we had been used to. We had to change our shoes or boots every time we left the building. Our indoor shoes or slippers were exchanged for outdoor shoes in a locker room before we ever went out of doors. This was in marked contrast to what we had been used to, when the headmaster of our previous school had simply had to insist that boots were put on when entering school and we were free to remove them when we left the school building.

The games played at Pembroke Lodge, which was the name of the school, were association football, which I enjoyed in the autumn term, and the following term, the January term, we played rugby football which I also enjoyed.

Christmas 1916 we spent in the rooms at Parsons Green. It was not a particularly festive Christmas. My father by that time was working in a military hospital in Egypt, and the family were not likely to see him for a long time in the future. We had no relations in England.

In January 1917, we took the train again for our second term at Pembroke Lodge and on the way down to Christchurch we saw, for the first time, people engaged in ice skating in the open on frozen ponds alongside the line. The winter of 1916/17, or rather January and February 1917, was one of the cold winters which occur about every twenty or thirty years. There was skating on ponds near the south coast for weeks on end. Meakin kept a number of clip-on skates in the attic of the school, sufficient to issue each boy with a pair. We screwed these on to our boots and I learnt to skate on an open pond near Southbourne in January 1917.

Sometime during the spring term 1917, my mother rented a house in Southbourne on the Tucton Bridge Road where she lived with my two sisters (and we boys when we were home on holiday) until my father returned from the war, when they both returned to Antigua with my two sisters.

In September 1917, at the age of thirteen, I left the preparatory school and at the age of fourteen I entered Epsom College, where I stayed until 1920. In later years I realised that I had really wasted my time at Epsom, from the point of view of obtaining academic qualifications which would fit me for one of the professions or for any other worthwhile job. At the time, however, there seemed to be a reason for this, inasmuch as in September 1917 the First World War was going very badly for the Western Allies. The Russian government was in a state of revolution. The enormous Russian army was disintegrating, and the Germans were moving very large forces from the Eastern Front over to the Western Front. At the same time, the impact which the American entry into the war would make was not yet apparent. Under these circumstances it seemed to me that my future was already mapped out and that nothing I could do would change it. That is to say that when I left school I would follow the example of the boys who had left Epsom during the past two years or so. I would go into the armed forces, probably the Army, and proceed from there to France, from where, if the war went on long enough, one was almost bound to be killed. So all one could do, in my view, at that time was to prepare oneself for gaining a commission in the Army in the hope of making a sort of career there up the rank ladder.

To this end I joined the Officers' Training Corps and took part in its activities with enthusiasm. I joined the technical section of it, the Signals Section. I learned to operate signals equipment and handle Morse Code transmission and reception at up to eight words a minute. Apart from that, I kept myself fit and became dedicated to rugby football. I became captain of my house, and before I left Epsom in 1920 I was captain of the school rugby team.

In March 1918, only six months after I arrived at Epsom, the position of the Allies in the war seemed to be in a really desperate situation. The Germans were putting in an enormous offensive on the Western Front and it seemed that the British Army in France might be on the point of being overwhelmed. It was at that time that Haig issued his famous order of the day (known as the 'back to the wall' order) that there could be no more retreat for British forces, that British army units in France must remain where they were, dead or alive. None of this was encouraging to us boys or encouraged us in the thought that the war might soon be concluded satisfactorily.

However, six months later, on 11 November 1918, the headmaster summoned all boys to the assembly hall at Epsom and announced that the First World War was over. The Germans had sued for an armistice.

It took some time for the effect of this on our lives to sink in. It meant, of course, that a career in the armed forces, from being the obvious programme for us, was hardly an option at all. The armed forces were being demobilised as fast as possible and there was much talk of universal disarmament.

The war was spoken of as a war to end wars and to make the world safe for democracy. Under those circumstances it was a bit late for me to change my approach to education and to strive to obtain academic qualifications which would have fitted me for a career in the professions, such as medicine. In any case, my father would not have been able to afford to keep me in education for long enough to qualify as a doctor. And it was apparent that I would, in the not too distant future, be returning to Antigua.

There were several reasons for this. One was that I had no relatives in England at all; I had no home in England and in the holidays I was dependent on the headmaster of my prep school, who was kind enough to take me into his home in Staffordshire, so I was not keen to stay on at Epsom any longer than I had to. Accordingly, in February 1920, I left Epsom and returned to Antigua, aged sixteen and a half.

Chapter 4

The Antigua Sugar Factory and the Motor Boat *Isa*

On arrival in Antigua I started an apprenticeship in the central cane sugar factory. Cane sugar production was the main and, in fact, the only export industry in Antigua and the whole economy of the island depended upon it. The idea was that I would do three years' apprenticeship in the machine shop of the central sugar factory and then complete the whole course by doing two years in the works of the firm that manufactured the machinery used in the factory. The firm was Merilees Watson and, as far as I know, it was in Glasgow.

The start of my apprenticeship came as somewhat of a shock to me. I arrived in Antigua on a Friday and was due to start work at the sugar factory on the following Monday morning. At the time the factory was not in production. It was between one crop and the next, and I assumed that there would not be very much to do there except just to polish up the machinery ready for the next cropping season. So I enquired at what time I would have to clock in the morning and was told 6.00am. This was a little bit of a shock, even after the rigours of an English boarding school. It meant that I would have to get out of bed at about 5.00 in the morning which, in the tropics is a time when it is pitch dark. Then I would have my breakfast, dress and pedal three miles against the Trade Wind to be at the factory by 6.00am. I then asked what time I would be knocking off and I was told 10.00. Thinking that perhaps there wasn't very much to do there at that time, I assumed that this was 10.00am and I said 'Well that is a nice short working day for breaking in on this job.' I was told that I didn't understand, it wasn't 10.00am, it was 10.00pm. The overhaul of the machinery prior to the following cropping season was behind hand and overtime was being worked sixteen hours a day.

I was on productive work at the factory and received a salary or pay packet, but I couldn't have lived on it because it was less than £1 a week … £1 a week!

The period during which overtime was worked didn't last for very long. The cropping season eventually started, the factory went into production and the work force reverted to what was regarded as normal working hours. This was a sixty-six hour week for, in my case as I have said, pay of under £1 a week.

At that time, the Antigua Sugar Factory was a very successful business. In words frequently used today, it was very competitive. It had to be highly competitive because, at that time I can remember very clearly, the world price for sugar was only £15 per ton. As it takes almost ten tons of sugar cane to produce one ton of sugar this meant that money available to pay the sugar-cane planters and the sugar factory worked out at only £1.50 per ton for growing sugar cane, if all the money had gone to the planters, but of course the central factory had to take some of that, though what proportion they actually took I do not know, but it was a very small amount of money for processing ten tons of sugar cane into one ton of sugar.

The company owning the sugar factory therefore had to keep labour costs as low as possible and one of the measures they took to achieve that was a very simple one of running a continuous process, on two shifts instead of three. Twelve hours on and twelve hours off.

Antigua sugar factory, Arthur worked here as an apprentice engineer at a starting wage of £1 a week. (*Photo courtesy of Robin McDonald*)

The crushing mills ran continuously from 6.00pm on Sunday afternoon until midday on the following Saturday, day and night. The interval at the weekend was used for cleaning up any minor repairs and so on. So the working hours were extremely long.

In spite of the very long hours, I enjoyed the work and found it most interesting. None of it was repetitive. A new problem had to be faced every week or every month. The complexity of the work and the amount of work required of the machine-shop staff was increased during that time by the fact that the company had decided to add on a refinery to their production factory. The factory had been constructed in 1904, and until 1920, when I became an apprentice, it had been producing sugar, known as yellow crystals, or now described as demerara. This was shipped back to England to Tate and Lyle, who refined it, or most of it, into white sugar for worldwide distribution. Some of this white sugar was exported back to the West Indies and it was very sensibly thought that it might be more economical to do the refining of this proportion of the output on the spot for sale locally.

The building of the refinery was a complex process and involved all sorts of modifications and alterations to the original layout. The method used was to complete the process of producing the yellow crystals and put them into hessian bags. Then, instead of shipping the whole lot back to England, a proportion of the bagged sugar was taken to the adjoining refinery, where it was dissolved in water and put through the refining process. After this, of course, the excess water had to be boiled off for the second time and the whole process of drying the sugar in spin-dryers had also to be gone through for the second time.

Probably the biggest problem which had to be solved when the refinery was built was the problem of obtaining the extra heat energy required for operating the refinery to produce the refined white sugar, in addition to the original factory in which the yellow crystals were produced.

Ever since the central factory had been built in 1904 the heat energy required to operate it had been obtained by burning the solid part of the sugar cane after the cane juice, or sucrose solution, had been squeezed out of it in the crushing rollers. It would not have been economical to operate a cane-sugar production unit if imported fuel had had to be used.

But the refinery meant that a lot of extra heat energy would have to be obtained from the same limited amount of the solid part of the cane. This part used as fuel was called bagasse. This involved major modifications to the whole of the furnace system in the factory. An extra boiler, a fourth boiler, in addition to the original three, had to be installed. A second 150-foot steel chimney had to be constructed, and many other modifications had to be made. The whole of the changeover to a refinery in addition to the original production factory took place during my time as an apprentice. It added very greatly, not only to the amount of work that we apprentices and the other maintenance staff had to do, but also to the variety and complexity of that work. We were engaged in the erection of quite a large and complex unit.

There were four of us white apprentices at the factory when I started work there, and during my three years one of the four caught typhoid fever and then there were three. The three of us remained working at an enormous variety of different tasks until I left three years later.

The manager of the sugar factory took the view that as we apprentices were there to learn we should be employed on as wide a variety of problems and tasks as possible. We were never to be engaged on repetitive work. This made the job extremely interesting for us. We were all the time engaged in tackling problems which were new to us. Because of this I learnt a lot of lessons about practical engineering, which have been of much benefit to me throughout my life.

One particular lesson I learned a few weeks after I started work at the factory. I was working in a gang, the foreman of which was the senior apprentice. The senior apprentice was six months younger than I was. The reason why he was senior was that he had left school at fourteen and he had had two years to absorb the ethos of the place. What happened was that I was given a job to do which appeared to me to be totally impossible. I was told to collect a petrol engine which had been lying on a scrapheap in the sun and rain for months, if not years, because an engine of that type was required for some particular purpose and the problem of buying a new one would have been too time-consuming. We simply couldn't wait, so that the one that was there had to be made to work.

I came to the conclusion that the job was totally impossible because the engine was rusted solid from end to end. Every nut was rusted on to every bolt, the pistons were rusted solid in the cylinder bores, nothing could be made to move, and I reported this to my boss, the foreman, aged sixteen, and he took me to task in no uncertain terms. He said, 'Impossible; that word is not in the vocabulary of this establishment. The motto of this establishment is that the difficult is done at once and the impossible takes slightly longer.' He then proceeded to demonstrate to me how the job could be done. We did, in fact, recondition that engine and made it work to at least 90 per cent of its original efficiency.

I was reminded of this recently when a senior politician said that something was impossible. I remembered the lesson taught to me all those years ago, which is, that when people say that something is impossible, as often as not, what they really mean is that the will to do it is missing, or the skill is missing, or both are missing.

Our opportunities for recreation outside the factory were not very great. There was no question of us joining the Tennis Club and going for a game of tennis at five o'clock, which was the custom of many people in Antigua, because we didn't knock off work in time. But at the weekends, on Saturday and Sunday, there were opportunities.

Off the north-east coast of Antigua there was a stretch of sheltered water enclosed by coral reefs and a string of mini desert islands just asking to be explored. At that time in the 1920s there was no means for the young people of Antigua to explore them. There wasn't a single sailing dinghy, sailing yacht, motor-boat or any craft used for recreational purposes in the whole island.

The area of enclosed water was about the size of the Solent and, whereas on a sunny summer Sunday there are probably more than a thousand small boats engaged in recreational activities in the whole of the Solent area, in Antigua there wasn't a single one. It is difficult to explain why this should have been so. I suppose tropical lethargy had something to do with it. Too many people in Antigua endorsed the view expressed by Noel Coward many years later that it was only mad dogs and Englishmen who went out in the midday sun. One couldn't explore this stretch of water in the short interval between 5 o'clock when the sun lost its strength and power and 6 o'clock when the tropical dark descended suddenly. There was also another reason and that is that society in Antigua could only be described as poverty-stricken; nobody could afford to spend money on yachts or motor-boats or any recreational activities of that kind.

However, we apprentices felt that we should build ourselves a boat to explore this area of the north coast and we set about getting hold of one. We discovered an old hull of an 18-foot boat which had been abandoned on a mud bank in St John's Harbour. It had been used as a motor-boat for recreational purposes by one of the engineers of the sugar factory some time before that. When this individual had left the island he had simply abandoned it. The engine had been removed and was lying on a scrapheap in the factory and all the other gear and the hull was lying on the bank at St John's.

How we got hold of this craft I cannot remember: whether it belonged to anybody, or whether we paid for it; we couldn't have done that because we didn't have any money. At any rate we took it over, we moved it to one of the wharves in St John's where there was a hand-operated crane. We lifted it out of the water and set to work on it where it was, on the wharf beside the crane. I can't remember which firm the wharf and the crane belonged to, it might even have been McDonalds & Company, or one of the other firms that operated from St John's Harbour. At any rate in Antigua at that time it really didn't matter.

We overhauled the hull and one of the things we had to do was to strip off the copper sheeting on the outside. The boat had been copper-bottomed; this was a technique for keeping the bottom of boats clear of fouling and barnacles which has now gone completely out of fashion, but it was the standard method used in the navy in Nelson's day and it was one of the main functions of the Naval Dockyard at English Harbour on Antigua to provide facilities where the considerable West Indian Fleet, used to protect the Islands from the French, was maintained and it had provision for careening the ships.

In a place where there was practically no rise and fall of tide, the only way of getting at the bottom of a ship was to remove most of the heavy equipment and the guns and haul the boat over sideways until its masts were almost horizontal when one half of the underwater part of the hull was accessible for repair and re-coppering. The ship was then turned round and the other half was done. At the English Harbour Dockyard the copper and lumber store was one of the largest buildings which still exists to this day.

However, all that is by the way. *Isa* had been copper-bottomed but the copper sheets had started to disintegrate, so we took them all off and used anti-fouling paint, which by that time was available. It never occurred to us that the small copper nails or tacks which held the copper on could have penetrated the planking completely, or, if they had done in some cases, that the thick and heavy anti-fouling paint that we used would not seal up the holes. At any rate we got this craft seaworthy, replaced the engine and made it work. The engine was an incredibly crude American single-cylinder two-stroke slow-running petrol engine.

There was no gearbox and no clutch. The engine was directly coupled to the propeller. It was one of the features of the engine, and its very extraordinary ignition system, that it would run with equal facility in either direction. If we started it running clockwise it would continue to do so and if we started it anti-clockwise it would continue to run anti-clockwise, so we had no problem with a reverse gear.

Anyway, having got this boat seaworthy, or so we hoped, we planned our maiden voyage, which was to a weekend party on one of the offshore islands, off the north-east coast, on which there was a house, where some of our friends were going to spend the weekend. We thought we would turn up in style in our own boat having travelled round the coast from St John's, about twelve miles, for the first time that anybody, any white Antiguan, had done it, probably for a generation.

We made all preparations, filled the petrol tank, stocked up with what food we needed and lowered the boat into the water one Saturday morning, prior to starting the trip. As it entered the water and we went aboard we were horrified to see little fountains of water spouting out along the inside of the planking at various places anywhere between the bow and the stern. Some of the holes made by the copper tacks had not been sealed; we hadn't noticed them and water was coming in at a fair rate.

However, everything was ready and we weren't prepared to sacrifice the trip. It seemed we would be able to keep the water under control by constant bailing or pumping. I can't remember if we had a bilge pump, but if not, a bailer would do. We started off on this trip round the south-west corner of the island, bailing at intervals until we reached the destination in the afternoon. We were very proud of ourselves, of our achievement, and we took our friends for an exploratory trip round some of the channels on the north side that afternoon, still bailing at intervals as required.

When night came we had a problem because unless somebody sat up all night and kept bailing at intervals the boat would fill with water, the engine and the ignition system and everything else would be flooded with salt water and would be rendered unserviceable.

So we motored the boat round one side of the island which was fringed with mangrove. In a mangrove swamp the roots of the plants go down into the water and in water two- or three-feet deep the roots start in the mud at the bottom, grow out into the air above and produce seeds which float, so that mangrove growth extends outwards until the water is about three-feet deep. We went along this coast until we found a place where there was a little natural gap between two bunches of mangrove plants. We then drove the boat at full speed so that it went about three quarters of the boat length into the gap, then it jammed, supported on both sides by the mangrove. We then roped the boat to the mangrove so that it could not slide out backwards and stepped ashore, climbing over the mangrove roots and left it. Next morning we came out and found that, although some water had entered, no damage had been done. We were able to use the boat the following day and do quite a bit of exploring of the surrounding area with our friends. Then on the third day we did the same thing and motored back to St John's, back to the wharf where the crane was, craned the boat out and went home.

In the following week or weeks, we tackled the leaks by buying several boxes of matches, searching for the holes and plugging each hole with a safety match pointed at the end with our pocket knives and then sliced off flush with the outer surface and the whole lot painted again with anti-fouling paint.

The *Isa* worked in that condition for the rest of my time in Antigua and we had an enormous amount of enjoyment from exploring the very highly indented north and east coasts of the island. In fact, we were the first white people of our generation who had circumnavigated Antigua by boat of any kind. This despite the fact that we had no charts, none of us had ever seen a nautical chart, and the boat had no compass. We operated by the light of nature and very soon discovered that the way to avoid trouble was to only venture into waters we did not know between the hours of 10.00am and 2.00pm, when the sun is at a considerable angle above the horizon. During that period of the day, coral heads could be seen before we hit them. If we tried to go anywhere that we hadn't been to before, in the early morning or late in the afternoon, we could hit these coral heads before we saw them, even in a boat drawing only two and a half feet.

We had a lot of fun out of *Isa* for the rest of my time in Antigua and when I left for England in September 1923 we still had her. We'd had no offers from a buyer, and I remember going to a farewell drinks party the night before we left and telling everybody that we had this serviceable motor-boat which had circumnavigated Antigua, it was lying in the harbour, and anybody could have it for £5. There were no offers and I left Antigua forever, or more or less forever, the following day and I have no idea what happened to *Isa* after that.

I had no more news or mention of *Isa* for the next sixty years and then by a very strange coincidence, I heard of her while attending the wedding of a nephew in Brighton. It was a West Indian wedding, in the sense that both the bride and bridegroom had been born in the West Indies, and all their families and friends, or many of them, had grown up there. Coming out of the reception I was talking to my nephew about my time in Antigua and I mentioned that we had had a lot of fun out of a motor boat called *Isa* and the woman just in front of me turned round and said, 'I am Isa.' I said, 'What do you mean?'

She said, 'My name is Isa. I was Isa Duncan, my father was the shift engineer at the Antigua Sugar Factory who originally built the *Isa* and used it. It was named after me.' A very strange coincidence.

Chapter 5

Return to England and Entry into the RAF. Flying the Mono Avro 504K, 1923–1925

In about June 1923 I sat back to take stock. I was twenty years old; I had been an apprentice at the sugar factory for three years. The hours had been very long, the work hard and the financial rewards minimal, but the work had been interesting, I had enjoyed it. I had enjoyed exploring every nook and cranny of the island of Antigua on the two-stroke lightweight motorcycle my father had given me, and also exploring all the creeks, lagoons and reef-enclosed waters of the north and east coasts of Antigua in the motor boat *Isa* which other apprentices and I had built. I was living off my parents, who had three younger children to support, and I felt that it was time to consider how I would earn a living.

If I continued with the apprenticeship, I would have to spend another two years at the firm in Glasgow, which was not a very enticing prospect. Two years in a cold damp climate in a country where I knew absolutely no one, and probably living under rather primitive conditions. I came to the conclusion that the prospects in the sugar industry in the eastern Caribbean in the distant future were not very good.

This prophecy of the future proved to be correct because the Antigua Sugar Factory Company continued a steady decline. This had started when the steam engine had come into general use for crushing sugar cane. This broke the monopoly of the east Caribbean islands conferred by their ability to harness the power of the Trade Winds through windmills. The Antigua Sugar Factory Company continued operating for another forty-three years and then, in 1966, while I was actually in Antigua on a holiday from my home in Lymington, to which I had retired after thirty-eight years' service in the RAF, an announcement was made that the company was going into liquidation.

The reaction to this announcement, amongst the local population of Antigua, was quite interesting. The announcement appeared in the local newspaper. On the back page. There were about four lines, without comment, just stating that the company was going into liquidation and would cease trading at the end of the current crop. The first three pages were devoted to many pictures of the annual carnival and discussion of how splendid it had been and what measures could be taken to make it even better on the following year. The fact that the industry on which the whole economy of Antigua had depended for nearly 300 years was finally coming to an end didn't seem to worry anybody.

I think this was because the company had come to be known as a sort of enemy, which held down living standards, worked people for a pittance for long hours and that anything that could be done to diminish that power would be a good thing. What the population was going to live on afterwards was not immediately apparent. I think the general feeling was that the newly independent government would do what British governments did when private companies went bankrupt, that is, nationalise them.

However, they had forgotten one thing, and that is that when British Leyland was nationalised the losses on British Leyland could be paid by taxing private firms like ICI to pay for the losses on the nationalised industries. In Antigua there was no other industry to be taxed and attempts which were made to nationalise the sugar industry failed.

Fortunately, at about that time, in the 1960s, the tourist trade was building up very fast. This has now replaced the sugar industry as the main support of the economy of Antigua and the other sugar islands.

To return to 1923, 1 decided to look around for some other way of earning my living. I was looking at one of the magazines which my parents took out from the local library which obtained copies of *The Illustrated London News*, *The Sketch*, *The Tatler*, *Punch* and other illustrated magazines of that kind. I was looking through *The Tatler*, a very unlikely source of inspiration at first sight, but an article caught my eye. It was an article illustrating a place I'd never heard of: Cranwell, which was described as the Royal Air Force Cadet College.

I had been out of touch with affairs in England for so long. For three years I had not read an English newspaper, I had hardly read a book, I'd hardly written anything at all, and I was absolutely ignorant of what had been happening in the post-war years in England. I did not know that the RAF had a Cadet College.

However, on reading through the article, there was one thing that I found very attractive, and this was a statement that every cadet arriving at Cranwell was presented, free, with a high-powered motorcycle. He was required to strip it down and overhaul it to make him conversant with the workings of the internal combustion engine. He then had the free use of the motorcycle for the rest of his time at Cranwell. This was what really attracted me. The idea of going to a place where one would be presented with a full powered motorcycle, which I in Antigua couldn't possibly afford to buy, I found extremely attractive. The fact that the course also involved learning to fly aeroplanes, on consideration, I thought might be quite interesting, although up until then I had never really considered a career in the air force at all.

I decided, being extremely naive about these things, that if I went to England and presented myself at the Air Ministry and applied for a cadetship at Cranwell, I would almost automatically get one. Surely, they would appreciate having somebody who had had three years' engineering experience, and who had on his discharge report from the factory a statement by the chief engineer, 'McDonald is very good with internal combustion engines.'

Every aviator depended for his life on the correct function of an internal combustion engine all the time he was in the air. I thought that people who joined the service with some knowledge of them would have an advantage on their applications.

My parents were taking a holiday in England and I went with them. I presented myself at the Air Ministry in Kingsway and announced that I wished to apply for a cadetship at the RAF Cadet College at Cranwell. I was ushered into an office. The officer behind the desk said, 'How old are you?' I told him I was twenty in June; by that time it was September. He said, 'Well bad luck, you are just three months too old. The age range for entry into Cranwell is eighteen to twenty. We can't make exceptions, you know, rules are rules. Bad luck.'

I was completely nonplussed at this. I had come all this way. I didn't really have the money to pay my fare back to Antigua. I had nowhere to live in England and no prospects of a job. I started towards the door, looking rather crestfallen, I daresay, and the chap behind the desk said, 'Oh, by the way, I don't suppose this would interest you, because there are no career prospects in it, but we have decided to build up a reserve of trained young pilots for the Royal Air Force. In order to do this we have introduced a five-year short-service scheme. The idea is that you do one year flying training and then four years' squadron experience. Then you go out on to the Reserve. Of course, on the Reserve there is no pay.'

I don't know about other people, but in my case at the age of twenty, five years ahead was further than I could see. Anything which would carry me over for five years was attractive to me. So I said yes, I would be interested in a short-service commission.

Accordingly, in March 1924, 1 reported to No. 5 Flying Training School at Shotwick, but while I was there the name was changed to Sealand. The location was at the mouth of the River Dee, five miles from Chester, just alongside the Queensferry Road Bridge and close to a big steelworks, I think it was called the Shotland Steel Works.

I arrived there knowing nothing about what I was in for. I was told that I would start my flying on an aeroplane known as the Mono Avro, Avro 504K. It was called the Mono Avro because the engine was a very unusual type, designed in France, called the Gnome Rhone Mono-Soupape, which is, apparently, French for single-valve. When I was told this, I couldn't think how any internal combustion engine could possibly operate with a single valve in the cylinder head.

I was very familiar with internal combustion engines. I knew they were of two types, one called two-stroke which is used for lawn mowers and light machinery of that kind, light motorcycles perhaps, which has no valves in the cylinder head. In this type, the charge and the exhaust pass through ports at the bottom of the cylinder which are covered by the pistons at the lowest part of its stroke. The other type, which is in general use for motor vehicles and ship propulsion and all that sort of thing, is the four-stroke which has two valves in the cylinder head, one the inlet valve for letting the charge into the cylinder and the other the exhaust valve which lets it out again after the firing stroke. How an engine could possible work with only one valve, I just could not imagine.

The engine on this aeroplane was, in fact, unique. I never heard of one being used before or since that series of engines which were fitted to the Mono Avro. If the engine on the motorboat *Isa* had been crude, the one in the Avro 504K was even cruder still. For one thing it had no carburettor, it had no throttle; it either ran full power or not at all. The whole engine rotated, it consisted of a crank-case like the hub of a wheel with nine cylinders radiating outwards like spokes of a wheel without a rim.

I was accustomed to handling internal combustion engines that produced power which transmitted through a clutch and a gearbox, but there was neither of these on the Mono Avro. The wooden two-bladed propeller was bolted on to the front of the crank-case and rotated with the engine at the same speed. There was no method of starting the engine, except by seizing hold of the blades of the propeller and pulling it over by hand. There was a set drill for doing this and as the engine fitter would suffer if there was any confusion, he was the one who called the shots in the drill. He would walk up to the aeroplane and call out to the pilot who was in the cockpit, 'Switches off. Petrol on. Sucking in.' The pilot would repeat 'Switches off. Petrol on. Sucking in.' The fitter would then turn the propeller over two or three strokes and, when he thought it was sufficiently primed to start, he would shout, in a loud voice, 'Contact'. This would be repeated back to him by the pilot who would shout 'Contact' as he switched on the ignition. The fitter would then take one mighty swing, standing smartly back at the same time. If he didn't step back smartly enough he was likely to be involved in a nasty accident.

In all my service I only heard of one case where an accident actually occurred. I think this must have been due to the fact that at the station at which the accident happened Mono Avros were not in general use.

This was many years after I left Sealand when a pilot used a Mono Avro on a visit to another station. When he was due to return home, the ground crews came out to start his engine. It may have been that the fitter who did it was not very familiar with Mono Avros. At any rate, when he shouted 'Contact' he didn't step back smartly enough, the engine fired and the propeller blade hit him and broke his wrist. The ambulance and its crew of medics was summoned and the casualty was well looked after.

The pilot, sitting in his cockpit, was of course very sorry for what had happened, but his engine was running and he had to get back to his home station somehow. He thought he would take off and fly back without bothering to stop his engine and examine the blades of the propeller. To have done so would have meant that somebody else would have had to go through the starting drill and the people at that station might have been a bit nervous about that. He assumed there had been no damage to the propeller. Unfortunately, that assumption soon proved to be wrong. He took off in the normal way, climbed and levelled out. When the engine had reached maximum revolutions, it only had one speed and that was full out, the wooden propeller disintegrated. The pilot was faced with a forced landing. The Avro 504K, however, had a very slow landing speed, so forced landings were not usually a problem, and he was unhurt. That was the only occasion I heard of during the whole of my service where this slightly tricky starting operation went wrong.

To return to Sealand, in March 1924, I was introduced to the Mono Avro the morning after I arrived there and taken for my first flight. My instructor took the view that not everybody who started on a flying career was really suited for it. There were a number of people who simply didn't take to piloting air force aeroplanes and they had to be failed. He took the view, if this were the case, the sooner the decision was made the better. Otherwise instructors might waste a lot of time trying to train an unsuitable pilot to fly. In the end he would have to give it up and go out. We were after all only 'acting' pilot officers on probation.

My instructor decided to find out on my first flight if I was going to take to flying or not. He proceeded to throw the aeroplane about in a most violent manner, upside down, loops, rolls, the full works. This made me feel very sick and frightened, but I realised what he was trying to do and, having got into the Royal Air Force, I wasn't going to allow myself to be easily chucked out, so I gave no indication of the real state I was in. When we landed I said, 'That was great, that was great!' I added, 'I thoroughly enjoyed it.' In saying that I was, I suppose, being economical with the truth. In fact, extremely economical with the truth, but the subterfuge worked. The RAF did keep me on; in fact they kept me on for another thirty-six years. This was the most fortunate thing that happened to me in the whole of my life.

After this first, rather daunting, initiation to flying, the rest of the twelve-month course at Sealand was the most enjoyable period of my life. It was like a long holiday at some adventure park and, first of all, I didn't have to pay for it; in fact, I was actually being paid to do it. This was absolutely marvellous.

The first stage consisted of some hours of dual instruction, nine hours in my case. During this period I flew with an instructor who taught me how to take the aeroplane off, fly it round the circuit, do turns right and left, do an approach and landing without actually breaking anything. The most important item in the dual instruction was being taught the technique of 'spin recovery', recovery from a spin.

Most aeroplanes, not all but most, have a tendency, if they get into certain attitudes in the air, to go into a state of auto-rotation and to spin down towards the ground rather like a sycamore seed auto-rotating downwards until it hits the ground. In the early days this used to happen to quite a number of pilots. Although speeds were very low in those days and sometimes the pilot escaped with his life, in many cases he was killed. A spin occurs when one of the main planes of an aircraft stalls. That is to say, it loses forward speed to such an extent that the airflow breaks down, the wing suddenly loses most of its lift and the drag is increased. When this happens to both wings, which is quite a frequent occurrence if an aeroplane is allowed to drop below a certain forward speed in the air, then the whole of the nose of the aircraft drops because of the decrease in lift. The tail does not drop because there is no downward loading on the tail plane, it is purely a stabiliser. The aeroplane goes into a dive which causes it to pick up forward speed, the wings then become unstalled and so control is regained.

However, in some aircraft, it is quite easy for one of the plane's wings to stall and the other to remain unstalled. This happens in turbulent atmosphere or if the pilot incautiously uses the rudder in the wrong way. The aeroplane may yaw to the right, which slows down the speed of the right or starboard wing but increases the speed of the port or left wing. As a result, the port wing remains unstalled while the starboard wing may be stalled. The starboard wing then drops, the aeroplane assumes a lopsided starboard side down attitude, with its nose down, and spirals down towards the ground.

The instinctive reaction to any condition like this was for pilots to pull the control column back to raise the nose again into level flight. In practice this makes the situation worse; it further decreases the forward speed and locks the aircraft into auto-rotation, in a permanent spin. Unless the correct remedial action is taken, the aircraft continues like that until it hits the ground.

Many years ago, in the early days of flying, a scientist who was also a pilot – it may have been Henry Tizard or it may have been Lindemann, who was later Lord Cherwell; I'm not quite sure, but I'm almost sure it was one of them – worked out in theory what causes an aircraft to go into auto-rotation. He worked out a procedure which would stop the auto-rotation and bring the aircraft under control again. He wrote out a drill for doing that and tried it out in the air. He found that it worked and that drill has, ever since, been one of the most important items taught to every pilot before he is ever allowed to fly solo. We were taught this drill on the Mono Avro at Sealand.

The Mono Avro was a good training aircraft from the point of view of training pilots in spin recovery procedure because it was quite easy to induce a spin, start it spinning by handling the controls in a certain way and, having done so, to practise spin recovery and to stop the spinning when required.

However, all aircraft were not like that. Some years after leaving Sealand I was serving in a fighter squadron at Kenley, just south of Croydon, when we were equipped with a new type of single-seater fighter, the Gloster Gamecock. The Gloster Gamecock was at that time the fastest fighter in the RAF and we were very proud of our new aircraft.

Gloster Gamecock Mk I J7896 in 1923, from Arthur's squadron No 23. (*Photo courtesy of 'www.RAF-in-Combat.com'*)

After we had had our Gamecocks for a few weeks I thought I would do a spin-recovery practice on one of them. I discovered that I couldn't because I could not induce it to go into auto-rotation. Whatever I did with the controls it just refused to spin and if I couldn't start a spin there was no way I could work out a spin-recovery procedure. Eventually I gave it up, I decided that, as it was difficult to make the aircraft spin on purpose, it would never ever go into a spin of its own accord inadvertently. I decided, therefore that the best thing to do was simply to leave it alone. A spin is not a manoeuvre which has any combat value. I thought it was better to regard the aircraft as unspinnable and use it in the ordinary way and leave it at that.

However, some weeks later one of our keen young officers decided to investigate this phenomenon more closely. He took a Gamecock up and he did succeed in starting it to auto-rotate and put it into a spin. He came back considerably shaken because, having, after quite a lot of difficulty, induced his Gamecock to spin, he discovered that he couldn't stop it. He was contemplating at what height he should jump out of the aircraft and use his parachute when he thought he would make one last effort. His final effort worked and he managed to stop it, but he landed considerably shaken. He reported all this to me, as I was his flight commander at the time. Having had this report I thought that it would be wise to pass it on to the Experimental Station at Farnborough, the Royal Aircraft Establishment, or whatever it was called at that time. They sent over one of their most experienced pilots, whose name was D'Arcy Greig, who came to Kenley to investigate this curious phenomenon. He took one of the Gamecocks up. We watched him. He did manage to start it spinning and he stopped it. He did that two or three times. He told us afterwards that he was then satisfied that all this story about difficulty and spinning and stopping spins on a Gamecock was simply due to the inexperience of squadron pilots. He decided to do one more. He climbed up to gain altitude and started the attempt to do his final spin. Normally, a pilot starts spin recovery after three or four turns, so we counted the turns and when we got to ten we were beginning to get quite interested because he was still spinning. When he got to thirteen turns there was a puff of white and out came his parachute. D'Arcy Greig had jumped out. He hadn't parted with the aircraft by more than ten or twenty feet when it stopped spinning and went into a straight dive. Of course, if he could have clambered back in again, he could have taken over the controls and brought it home. Clearly that was impossible as the parachute simply yanked him away. He had to watch with horror what we had to watch with horror. The aircraft went into an almost vertical dive, picking up speed the whole way, and was heading straight for the High Street of Caterham, a small town just below the airfield at Kenley. There was nothing any of us could do except watch with horror as this situation developed. The aircraft was quite capable of destroying half a dozen houses and killing quite a number of people. However, the angle of the dive gradually decreased, the aircraft automatically started to pull out of the dive on its own and by the time it reached ground level it was travelling almost horizontal at great speed. It went into the hill on the far side of the valley and exploded in a ball of flames. Fortunately, nobody was injured. There was nobody at the point of impact.

After this incident I cannot remember what remedial action was taken with the Gamecock, or whether any was taken. As far as I was concerned the Gamecock remained an unspinnable aircraft and we continued to use it on the assumption that it would never go into a spin inadvertently. That being so, there was no point in investigating its spin characteristics any further.

To return to Sealand in 1924. After I had completed my dual instruction and had been sent off solo, the rest of the course was pure enjoyment. It was as if we were enjoying all the advantages of the best flying club in the country without having to pay for it. There was a minimum of mental effort involved and a minimum of physical effort also.

Our instructors' attitude to flying training was very light-hearted and casual. I cannot blame them for this because this was the way they themselves had acquired their flying skills. Most of them had learned to fly over the lines in France in the later stages of the First World War. There people learned quickly, showed an aptitude and survived or they didn't. The slow, the careless or the unobservant were picked off by people like von Richthofen and other German aces and simply didn't survive the war. Our instructors were amongst those who had survived.

So our instructors did not so much teach us to fly, as allow us to teach ourselves. I can distinctly remember the only words spoken to me by my instructor in the whole of one training session. He called me over, he pointed to a Bristol Fighter, which was the one we using at that stage of our training, and said, 'You see that Bristol Fighter over there?' I said, 'Yes.' He said, 'Well take it up for half an hour and bring it back all in one piece, will you?' That was all; those were the only words he spoke to me that day. When I came back, after half an hour, with the aeroplane all in one piece he didn't ask me where I'd been or what I'd done. He made no comment at all.

We spent an appreciable part of every working day waiting our turn to fly and while doing so, if the weather was fine, we sat on a grass bank with our backs against the hangar wall, watching our fellow pupils desporting themselves doing various low-flying and aerobatic manoeuvres over the centre of the station. Low flying and aerobatic manoeuvres over the centre of the station were, of course, absolutely prohibited by standing orders, but nobody seemed to take any notice of those. Our instructors seemed to take the view that standing orders only applied to pupils and not to them, or, alternatively, they had never read the standing orders, or, dare I say it, in some cases they couldn't read at all.

Our instructors were survivors from the First World War and they had acquired their flying skills over the Western Front in France where expectation of life in 1915, 1916, 1917 and 1918 was quite short. They were the survivors and in order to survive that they had not necessarily been required to read and write.

In fact, as regards flying discipline, our instructors set us an appalling example. The first thing that happened after breakfast each morning was that we lined up outside the mess, apparently to be marched over the railway bridge into the technical side of the camp just to remind us that we were after all members of a military establishment and not a glorified flying club. While forming up one morning we were watching the instructors doing what they did every morning: that is what was called 'testing the aircraft' before the day's flying. Why aircraft should require testing every day when they had performed perfectly satisfactorily the day before we never quite understood. We gained the impression that our instructors were just enjoying themselves and showing off.

One morning when we were lining up we saw one of the instructors start a spin-recovery procedure over the middle of the station at a remarkably low height, I think he was trying to show off and to demonstrate his very fine judgement as to how much space was required to pull out of a spin. At any rate, he did in fact pull out, very low indeed, over the ground and level with the top of two tall wireless masts. In fact, he passed between the masts having failed to notice, or perhaps not knowing that the masts had been put there to support an aerial wire which stretched from the top of one to the top of the other. As he passed between the masts he carried this large loop of aerial wire away hooked round his tail skid or some other protruding part of his aircraft. He disappeared into the distance trailing a long length of wire with insulators and bits of structure from the masts flapping about behind him. Presumably this was still attached to the aircraft when landed subsequently. We never knew or heard what happened.

When this occurred there was audible muttering in the ranks and one pupil was heard to say, 'That could only have been Crasher Craig.' Crasher Craig was one of the instructors who had the reputation of having destroyed more aircraft in crashes than anyone else in the whole history of aviation.

The periods we spent waiting to fly, watching the antics of our fellow pupils were always entertaining. Two instances are perhaps worth recording.

On the first occasion we were watching the flying one day when we observed a Mono Avro flying across the middle of the station. This was strictly contrary to standing orders, but nobody seemed to take much notice of that. It started, apparently, a spin-recovery procedure. This was normal as we were ordered to practise this from time to time. It consisted of inducing the aircraft to spin by handling the controls in a certain way. We then allowed full auto-rotation mode to establish itself and then pulled the aircraft out of the spin by methods which we had been taught. We watched idly the start of this procedure. Normally a pilot would allow about three turns of the spin before he started recovery procedure. So we counted the turns, one, two, three and then a fourth, a fifth and a sixth, by this time we were becoming quite interested. It went on … seven, eight, nine, ten. By the time it got to ten we were intensely interested and we watched future development with very close attention. In the middle of the thirteenth turn of the spin the aircraft hit the hangar roof. The hangars were old ones, made of wood, and the engine of the Mono Avro punched a hole in the roof and disappeared through it. It carried the rest of the fuselage, including the cockpit with it and stripping off the main biplane assembly and the tail plane assembly which remained balanced on top of the roof in grotesque attitudes.

We, of course, rushed over to the hangar to see what the aftermath of this extraordinary event might be, and when we got there, we found that the hangar was out of use, all the doors were locked and nobody could get in. So the engine, the fuselage and the pilot were inside the hangar. By that time there was quite a crowd outside the hangar without the ability to establish communication. Eventually the keys were produced from the guardroom. By that time there was a crowd of interested spectators, the chief instructor, the ambulance of course with its crew of medics, the fire engine, the adjutant and a crowd of curious pupils as well; in fact Uncle Tom Cobley and all. The door was eventually unlocked and opened, and we all surged through, led by the medics from the ambulance.

The first thing that struck my eye as I went through the door was that the hangar was completely empty, the floors had been swept clean and right in the middle of the floor was the engine of the Mono Avro all by itself looking like a wheel without a rim which had rolled into that position, like a penny.

Before it eventually fell over on its side, this thing had fallen over on the propeller boss with the crankshaft which normally supported it pointing vertically upwards. It looked absolutely ridiculous. In the corner leaning against the wall was a mass of wreckage, splintered bits of wood, torn bits of fabric, ends of wires which had been severed, looking rather like a ball of knitting wool after the cat had finished playing with it. Between this mass of wreckage and the door was the pilot walking towards us, furiously angry and shouting at the medics, 'Where on earth have you been all this time? Don't you realise that it is your job to come and extricate me from that awful mess over there. Look what's happened to me, I've had to push my way out.' He pointed to bleeding scratches or wounds on each side of his face and the backs of his hands dripping blood on to his flying suit. He was extremely angry. The medics took him away. He was taken to the sick quarters. His wounds were only superficial and they were plastered up with sticking plaster. The theory was that the best way of avoiding 'post-traumatic stress', as it is now called, was to get a pilot who had been through that sort of experience back into the air as soon as possible. He was put back into the cockpit of another Mono Avro that afternoon and continued his flying career during the rest of the course without any further interruption.

So this rather spectacular accident resulted in no serious injury to anyone, with one exception. On the following day a civilian in a bowler hat turned up from the Accident Investigation Branch of the Air Ministry in London to try to discover whether there had been any control failure or any failure of the mechanism of the aeroplane to explain why a pilot who normally could have stopped a spin in three turns had been unable, on this occasion, to stop it after thirteen. He probed about in the wreckage for quite a long time but found absolutely nothing abnormal at all. He stood up and scratched his head, preparatory to walking away to prepare his report.

In the meantime a gale had blown up and the panels in the roof, which had been ruptured by the accident the previous day, were rattling and shaking, and a beam which had been loosened fell on the head of this individual and knocked him out. I don't think his injuries amounted to anything more than mild concussion. When we heard the news we thought this was the best laugh of the year, that this little civilian should have been the only one to suffer any serious injury from a very spectacular accident which we had observed the previous day.

I, and one or two others, thought this particularly amusing because we were absolutely convinced that the investigator from the Ministry was looking for something which wasn't there. That is to say, some defect in the aircraft which might have explained the accident. We were pretty certain that we knew what the cause was.

On the night before the accident there had been the monthly dining in, or guest, night. These were always pretty uproarious long-lasting affairs during which some quite serious drinking was done. It is to be remembered that I am now talking about the RAF in 1924. I am not suggesting that this sort of conduct is typical of the RAF today or in recent years. Very late at night, during this guest night party, I can distinctly remember the pilot who had spun into the hangar having an argument with a friend of his about the stability of Mono Avros.

If we call them Pilot A talking to Pilot B, Pilot A was claiming that the Mono Avro was inherently a very stable aircraft. By using the trim tabs he claimed that he would be able to trim one to fly straight and level with hands and feet off the controls for long enough for him to climb out of the cockpit, crawl along the top of the fuselage, lean into the vacant front cockpit and tie his handkerchief round the control column, and get back again before the aircraft assumed any ungainly attitude.

Pilot B bet him that he would not be able to do this and they eventually made a solemn bet of £5, which, in those days, in 1924, was quite a lot of money for acting pilot officers on probation.

The administrative arrangements for carrying out this bet were that Pilot A, before he taxied out the next day would hold his hand up. Pilot B would run out as if he wanted to speak to him, climb up on the side of the cockpit, look into the front cockpit and make sure no handkerchief was tied to the front control column. Pilot A would then taxi out to a short flight, land, taxi in, again hold his hand up and Pilot B would again run out and look into the front cockpit and if he found a handkerchief tied to the front control column he would pay Pilot A £5. If there wasn't one, then Pilot A would pay him £5. They shook hands on it and obviously this was a very serious bet.

The next day Pilot A spun into the hangar roof, so the question remained unanswered. Who won the bet? Could it be that Pilot B had surreptitiously examined the wreckage at a quiet moment, looking for the control column of the front cockpit, to find out whether a handkerchief was tied to it or not. Even if it was, had Pilot A won the bet, because even if he had tied the handkerchief, he had not returned to the rear cockpit in time. We were fairly certain that what had really happened was that he was trying to do this when the aircraft had gone into a spin inadvertently, centrifugal force had tended to throw him off, he had to grip with his fingers on the edge of the cockpit with all his strength because in those days we didn't fly with parachutes. If he had let go, that would have been the end. So the idea in our minds was that he had hung on like grim death until the aircraft had hit the hangar. We couldn't really think of any other possible explanation of the incident.

Another quite spectacular accident, which occurred a few weeks later, is perhaps worth recording. We were as usual sitting on the grass bank with our backs against the hangar wall, watching the flying. On this occasion the wind direction was such that aircraft coming in to land were approaching behind us. They were either passing over the top of the hangar against which we were leaning, in which case they would have to land fairly far out on the airfield and have a long taxi back to the tarmac, or some of them were landing alongside the hangar which we were leaning against, where there was an open space and they could come in over the hedge surrounding the airfield at ten or fifteen feet and land quite short.

We heard an aircraft approaching on our right and in due course a Bristol Fighter appeared. There were two occupants, and whoever was in control had decided to demonstrate the shortest possible landing at the lowest possible speed. Unfortunately, he got the approach very badly wrong, and when his wheels hit the ground very hard, he bounced about fifteen feet into the air, by which time almost all forward speed had been lost, and it was obvious that the next landing would break the undercarriage. Whoever was in charge did the only thing possible. He pushed the throttle wide open and the very powerful Rolls Royce engine immediately opened up to full power. The engine more or less hung on the thrust of the propeller, did a wing-over turn in front of us without quite touching the ground, and started to accelerate past us from right to left, almost at right angles to the original approach track.

In the space of thirty or forty yards it had gathered full flying speed at full throttle about twenty feet above the ground. Unfortunately, it then came face to face with another hangar which was positioned at right angles to the one we were leaning against. If the doors of this hangar had both been open it is conceivable that the aircraft could have flown in one door and flown straight out of the other. Unfortunately, the doors were closed, or at least the one which we could see on our side was closed. The aircraft hit almost the exact centre of the door, about twenty feet up. The engine pierced the wooden door, shedding its propeller blades as it went and the aircraft came to rest with the leading edge of the main blades resting against the outside of the door. The rest of the fuselage was sticking out absolutely straight and level and taking the two cockpits and of course the tail plane. The restraining straps held. The occupants were not thrown forward or out and they were left sitting there, bolt upright.

Immediately they started to undo their straps, preparatory to jumping out. When they looked down, however, and realised that jumping out would involve jumping down almost twenty feet on to hard concrete, they realised that this would be a very painful proceeding, so they sat there shouting, 'Fetch a ladder, fetch a ladder.' By that time, of course, there was a crowd of jeering pupils all around them offering advice. In fact, one individual even quoted Shakespeare at them, 'A ladder, a ladder, my kingdom for a ladder! Ha, ha, ha.' After a time, the humour of this situation, the entertainment value, gradually evaporated and as it was lunchtime we all wandered over to the mess for lunch, leaving the two occupants of the Bristol Fighter still sitting there waiting for a ladder. When or how a ladder was found and brought to them we never discovered. Presumably they were eventually rescued and that was the end of the episode.

These were the two most dramatic incidents which kept us thoroughly well entertained during the quite lengthy periods waiting our turn to fly, but there were many others. The whole of the Sealand course was a very enjoyable and entertaining experience.

We were allowed to teach ourselves to fly, without too much interference from the instructors. There were two things which we should have been taught, and were not. One was the effect of anoxia, shortage of oxygen at altitude, on the performance of a pilot. The other was the only practicable method of navigating a single-seater aircraft from one place to another.

As I have already explained, although we spent quite a long time in the classroom on the principles of navigation, this all applied to the navigation of aircraft which carried a specialist navigator and specialist equipment. None of this could be used in a single seater.

Chapter 6

The Dangers of Anoxia, 1924

The casual attitude to training at Sealand made life very pleasant for us, but it did have some serious disadvantages. It meant that there were some things which we should have been taught which were not taught. This lack of knowledge about these items might have had, and in my case very nearly did have, very serious consequences. In fact one of them almost cost me my life while I was still at Sealand in 1924.

This was the lack of instruction on the effect of oxygen shortage at altitude on a pilot's performance. During the whole of the twelve-month course at Sealand no one once mentioned the word oxygen, or said a single word about what oxygen shortage might do to a pilot. Accordingly, one day I set out to find out for myself. I was flying a Bristol fighter on a fine day, and I set out to find out whether I could go higher than the Bristol Fighter or whether the Bristol Fighter could go higher than I could. I set off climbing.

The Bristol Fighter I was flying was very lightly loaded because all the military equipment had been removed – the guns, the ammunition tanks, the rear mounting for the gun. There was nobody in the rear cockpit. I climbed away from the airfield at quite a fast rate of climb. I went on climbing and by the time I got to 20,000 feet I was thoroughly enjoying myself and very proud of myself. The aeroplane was becoming a little sluggish but I thought we could go higher. I pressed on and I remember seeing 22,000 feet on the altimeter. At that time, I felt no sign of distress at all. I had expected that when I reached the limit I would find myself gasping for breath or in some discomfort of some kind. Actually, I was in a state of euphoria until the engine suddenly cut out, stopped firing altogether. The propeller continued to turn and to turn the engine because of the windmill effect in the rush of the slipstream. There was absolutely no power at all. I lowered the nose instinctively and went into a glide. I was not in the least worried. I thought that from this height one could glide for at least twenty miles and I could glide back to the airfield and make a power-off forced landing, which is something we had been trained to do during our training exercises. When I tried to point the aircraft towards the airfield I found a very strange thing, although it was a brilliantly fine day and I had a map, I could not quite make out in what direction the airfield lay. I thought this was interesting, but I was not in the least worried. My next thought was that I would land in a farmer's field. With the low landing speed in those days this was something that we had been trained to do in case we had engine failure. The prospect of having to do it on this flight did not worry me in the least. However, at the height at which I was the farmers' fields looked about the size of postage stamps so I thought I wouldn't choose one until I was at a lower altitude. I went on descending in slow circles until the altimeter read 10,000 feet. At that height I felt that, perhaps, it was about time for me to try and choose a field. Before doing that, I started to wonder why a Rolls Royce engine should have stopped and for the first time I looked at the engine's instruments. Why I had not done so before I couldn't think, but anyway I did look at them. There were very few in those days and two of them were petrol gauges. There were two petrol tanks, port and starboard and a gauge for each, they were just like the gauges in a modern motor car – a needle travelled over a dial; it started at the top when the tank was full and reached a stop at the bottom when the tank was empty. So normally when the tanks were half full the two needles would be pointing towards each other in a horizontal position. That is what I expected to see but there was something odd about them, the look of them. They were completely asymmetric; one was pointing upwards against the stop and the other was pointing downwards against the stop at the bottom. This indicated that the starboard tank was full to the brim and the port tank was completely empty. Underneath there was a change-over cock which showed that the engine was connected to the port tank which was empty. It didn't require any high degree of intelligence or technical knowledge to realise that a petrol engine which is connected to a tank which is empty will not produce power. There was a change-over cock just under the gauges. So I changed this over and the engine immediately picked up. I flew back to the airfield and landed. I was so ashamed of myself for what

I thought was absolute stupidity that I didn't dare tell my instructor in case he chucked me off the course for being so stupid as to do a thing like that.

I often wondered what my instructor would have said if I had told him. He probably would have concluded that I was really too stupid for RAF training. I wonder if he would have realised, as I did not at that time, that this was the effect which anoxia has on the human brain. The person suffering from anoxia goes into a state of euphoria: he doesn't lose consciousness, but he completely loses the ability to think straight or to remember anything.

I learned all this later on in some detail, but at the time I didn't realise what had happened. So a few weeks later I was flying another aeroplane. It was called a DH.9 day bomber. It was a First World War day bomber, a bit heavier and bigger than a Bristol Fighter. There was a cloud base at about 1,000 feet. The weather wasn't very good, but I had on previous occasions flown through a cloud sheet up into the clear above it. This was a wonderful thing to do because the brilliant light reflected from the white clouds was a marvellous sight to see and I thought I would try and climb through the cloud base that day. I went on climbing in the cloud; it seemed to be quite a thick layer. I realised later that I should have turned back long before I did. In fact I went on up to 15,000 feet and when I reached that height there was a gush of steam from the front of the aeroplane. I looked for the first time at the temperature gauge for the water-cooling system which the aeroplane had and found that it was hard against the stop. My cooling water was boiling hard and I was losing a lot of it. I immediately pulled the throttle back and then remembered that I had forgotten to keep the radiator shutters open; these were like venetian blinds over the radiator. They were under the control of the pilot and he had to keep them open on the climb and closed on the descent so that the radiator wouldn't freeze. I had forgotten to do any of this and I'd lost quite a bit of my cooling water. As soon as I pulled the throttle back the gauge went to the bottom of its range, thus indicating that the sensor was not immersed in water at all but was merely being heated by the steam that came off from lower down in the system. That was bad news and indicated that I might not have enough water to keep the engine running fast enough to keep the aeroplane in the air.

Anyway, there was nothing very much I could do about it except continue down in a glide and, eventually, I broke through the base of the cloud which, at that time, had got a bit lower. The weather was getting worse, and I was horrified to find myself over a large town or city. I knew perfectly well which town it was. It was Liverpool, a very large town. If I had known that I was over the eastern outskirts of Liverpool I would have flown east to get into open country, and so it was that I found myself flying over the city of Liverpool under a low cloud base with a failing engine. I did not know for how long the engine would continue running, having lost so much of its cooling water, and I did not know in which direction the nearest open country might lie in which I could make some attempt at a forced landing without hurting myself or other people. I therefore steered west in the general direction of Sealand and hoped for the best.

The terrain immediately below me was most unattractive from the point of view of putting an aeroplane down without engine power. Streets with tram cars, heavy traffic, church steeples, flat roofs, gabled roofs. I couldn't see any open space anywhere; all I could do was to hope that the engine would keep running. In order to keep it going for as long as possible, I throttled back to the minimum revolutions which kept the aeroplane in the air and went on flying west, hoping that I would come to open country before the engine stopped.

I must, in fact, have been over the eastern outskirts of Liverpool because the streets and traffic and the church steeples seemed to go on for ever. Eventually I came to the river Mersey. That was at least a surface on which I could put down the aeroplane without hurting anybody else. But it was winter and the water in the Mersey looked singularly unattractive as a surface to land on. For one thing, I did not know how an aeroplane with a fixed undercarriage would behave if it was put down in water. It might well have been that the water would have put such a drag on the fixed undercarriage that the aeroplane would flip on to its back and pin me underneath in the water. Even if I managed to push my way out of the cockpit wearing heavy flying clothing, by that time soaked in water, I would have to swim ashore. Swimming ashore in heavy clothing full of water might not be possible.

Anyway there was nothing for it but to continue west. I passed over Birkenhead and eventually heaved a sigh of relief when I came to more or less open country on the west side of Birkenhead. I went on with steam still coming out of the front of the aeroplane, losing height very gradually, but from there on it was downhill all the way and eventually I sighted the hedge on the edge of Sealand airfield. I knew that I was nearly home. I crossed the hedge about twenty feet above the ground, pulled the throttle back, switched off the ignition and put the aircraft down with no engine power at all. The aircraft came to a stop in the middle of the airfield with a stationary propeller, clouds of steam still coming out of the front of the fuselage.

I cannot remember whether I got out of the cockpit and walked to the flight offices and hangars or whether I waited for a vehicle. At any rate I slunk away to the mess and had a couple of stiff drinks to steady my nerves, and once again felt that I had disgraced myself by making an incredibly stupid mistake and that I didn't dare tell my instructor what had happened, in case he came to the conclusion that anyone as stupid as that wasn't really worth training for RAF service.

Neither my instructor, nor any of the other instructors, sent for me or asked what had happened, although they must have seen the aircraft in the middle of the airfield with a stationary propeller and steam coming out of it. It was perhaps surprising that they didn't make any enquiries to ask who the pilot was and what had happened to him. That, I think, was simply the atmosphere at Sealand in 1924.

The accident rate was extremely high. I calculate that the pupils at Sealand destroyed aircraft at about the rate of one a week. Nobody bothered because the RAF, having shrunk to a small fraction of the size that it had been, had inherited an enormous number of aeroplanes in the storage depots and on the production lines which could not be instantly stopped at the end of the First World War. It was obvious to everybody that the vast majority of these aeroplanes would be obsolete before they could ever be used to meet a very small peacetime wastage rate. So there was a general feeling that when a pupil at Sealand destroyed an aeroplane, or rendered it beyond economical repair, that he was really doing the authorities a favour by relieving the pressure on the storage depots which could get rid of another of their surplus of obsolescent aircraft.

So, at the time, I came to the conclusion that these two mistakes that I had made, the mishandling of the fuel control system on the Bristol fighter at 22,000 feet, and the mishandling of the radiator blind system on the DH.9A at 15,000 feet had been simply due to sheer stupidity on my part. But years later I learned that both of these incidents must have had the same cause: anoxia.

Anoxia is the effect on the human brain of the oxygen shortage which occurs at high altitudes. This phenomenon was investigated thoroughly at the School of Aviation Medicine at Farnborough some years after I left Sealand. The equipment used to carry out the investigation was a decompression chamber, large enough for six or eight people to sit round a table, and the investigation took the form that an investigator or instructor wearing an oxygen mask breathing oxygen would sit in the chamber with six or eight 'guinea pigs' not wearing oxygen masks and the instructor could then gradually reduce the pressure in the chamber to simulate the conditions of increasing altitude. At the same time the 'guinea pigs' would each be given a sheet of paper containing columns of figures which they were required to add up, or do other similar simple arithmetical computations. The instructor would then gradually reduce the pressure; there would be an altimeter in the chamber. An altimeter is simply a barometric barometer with an extended scale and it should be noted that at 18,000 feet the atmospheric pressure had dropped to only 50 per cent of what it is at sea level. The 'guinea pigs' would then be required to add the columns of figures up, write down the answers, sign and put down the time at which they completed the operation and then pass on to the next one. It was found that when the altitude had increased beyond 10,000 feet, errors in the arithmetical sums began to appear. Sometimes the individual would doubt the results that he got and would do the arithmetic over again, possibly getting a different answer and getting a bit worried. In other cases, the wrong answer would be written down and the individual would simply carry on to the next addition sum. Eventually a stage would be reached at which nobody could add up a column of figures and get the answer correct. This in spite of the indication that there was anything unusual about their situation. They simply sat back quietly or chatted amongst themselves and you would not have known there was anything abnormal about their mental condition.

Sometimes, just to drive the lesson home afterwards, the instructor would pick out one of the 'guinea pigs' with, perhaps, a slightly unusual wristwatch, Rolex or something of that kind, and would say to that individual, 'What is the time? The individual would read his wristwatch and give the answer probably correctly. The instructor would say, 'That's an interesting watch, would you mind letting me have a look at it?' The individual would unstrap his watch and hand it to the instructor. The instructor would examine it, change the subject, talk about something else, and while doing so he would slip the watch into his side pocket.

Twenty minutes later, when the exercise was over and everything was back to normal, normal pressure, he would say to the same individual, 'What's the time?' The individual would look at his watch, look puzzled and say, 'Well, I must have forgotten it on the bedside table this morning, forgotten to put it on.' The instructor would say, 'Do you often forget to put on your watch?' The individual would say, 'No, I've never forgotten it before'. The instructor would say, 'Well, think carefully, are you absolutely certain that that is what happened?' The individual would say, 'It must have been, because it is not there.' Whereupon the instructor would take the watch out, show it to the assembled people, to demonstrate to them that one of them had unstrapped his watch, handed it to him and was totally incapable of remembering what he had done thirty minutes later. It would be obvious to everybody that an individual whose brain is functioning like that is not fit to be in control of an aircraft and the lesson would be driven home.

After this research had been carried out, a standing order was issued in the RAF that any pilot intending to fly at over 10,000 feet at any time should wear an oxygen mask and turn the oxygen on.

At this point it should be noted that although mountaineers are known to have climbed to nearly 30,000 feet without oxygen, the only reason they are able to do so is the fact that the human system has the most remarkable powers of adaptation. Mountaineers can only climb high mountains provided they acclimatise at high altitudes in base camps for days or weeks before they make the attempt. If anybody flew up in a helicopter to a high base camp and then set straight off from there he wouldn't get very far; he probably wouldn't even start.

So if the facts about anoxia had been known in 1924 and had been passed on to us in our instruction at 5FTS I would not have started out in the Bristol Fighter to find out whether the aircraft or myself could get higher than the other. I would have known that, although the aircraft we were equipped with could perform fairly adequately at 20,000 feet, pilots without oxygen cannot. The attempt would not have been made and the episode of the mishandled fuel supply in the Bristol Fighter and the radiator cooling system in the DH.9A would never have occurred.

Chapter 7

Problems with Navigation, 1925

Another thing which was not taught to us at Sealand, and which caused me trouble later on, was instruction in the correct way to navigate a single-seater aircraft. We were, in fact, given an extensive course of lectures in the classroom on navigation but the lectures were given by the wrong person and in the wrong way.

The instructor who gave us lessons in navigation was a professional navigator, a crew member trained to fly in multi-seater aircraft, such as bombers or Coastal Command aircraft. The total crew would consist of the pilot, a navigator specially to navigate the aircraft, possibly a wireless operator if communication was by Morse code wireless telegraphy, and one or more gunners if the aircraft defensive armament consisted of free-mounted guns firing to the rear.

This individual showed us and taught us how to use all the equipment of his speciality: chart tables, protractors, parallel rulers, drift sights, and so on. At one time, instruction in navigation for bombers even included how to use astro-navigation equipment, that is sextants, chronometers and nautical tables, and astro-navigation was used, or attempts were made to use it in the early stages of the Second World War. However, in a career covering thirty-six years in the RAF, all my flying was done in single-seater aircraft. In a single-seater, none of the equipment we were taught to use in our navigation instruction could possibly be carried or used; there was no room for a chart table, protractors, parallel rulers or anything else in the cockpit of a Hurricane or a Spitfire.

In fact, pilots in Fighter Command in the early stages of the Second World War didn't even carry maps. Any pilot who started to unfold a map on a patrol during the Battle of Britain would have had a very short life. His job was to keep looking around constantly for enemy aircraft and if he failed to spot one when there happened to be some about, the first thing that he would know was that he would be hit by tracer bullets from behind.

This lack of instruction on how to navigate a single-seater plane caught me out on my first posting after I left Sealand. That first posting, in March 1925, was to Number 41 Squadron at Northolt, just north of London. The squadron was equipped with a new type of aircraft. This was the first aircraft to be designed and built after the end of the First World War, in which the main structural members were made of metal, of a light alloy instead of wood. It was called the Armstrong Whitworth Siskin[1], and I found that it handled very well.

Soon after I arrived at the squadron, the squadron commander called me in with another recently arrived pilot who had been on the same course as me at Sealand. He gave us instructions to fly two Siskins up to the aircraft storage depot at Henlow, which is just north of Hitchin, deliver them there and return by train.

This appeared to us to be a very simple matter. The weather was fine, we knew where Henlow was; it was within about less than a mile of the main railway line from Euston to Edinburgh, within a mile, also, of the Great North Road or the road which was described as the Great North Road.

We drew maps and off we went. I doubt if we even bothered to unfold the maps because we thought that the task would be an extremely simple one. We would do what we had done at Sealand whenever we went out of sight of the station. If we did any sort of cross-country flight, we would navigate by Bradshaws as we put it at that time, Bradshaws being the name of a railway timetable. We would find the right railway line and follow it to its destination – as simple as that.

So we set off in close formation. I happened to be leading. We had no communication by radio; there was no radio. We could only make hand signals to each other. I set off to choose a suitable railway line. The first thing that struck me was that there was a remarkable number of railway lines in the northern outskirts of London. There seemed to be railway lines running in, probably, almost every direction. However, I eventually chose one which appeared to be running in the right direction. I assumed it was the line from Euston to Edinburgh and we followed it. My companion seemed to be quite happy with this; he just flew alongside me in formation. We followed this line until it entered a small town or

---

1. We believe this aircraft was known as the Siskin III.

village, passed under a road bridge and we lost sight of it amongst all the houses and buildings in the town. When we looked on the north side of the town for where we expected the line to emerge we couldn't see one. To start with, I thought there must be a tunnel, although there didn't seem to be any reason why there should be a tunnel in flat country. We looked for the exit of a tunnel and couldn't find that either. We realised that that particular railway line had come to an end in that particular town, but which town it was we hadn't the faintest idea.

At this point I suppose we should have unfolded our maps and tried to identify a town where a railway line running in a northern direction came to an end. Had we done so we would have found that the town was, in fact, Buntingford, that there is a branch line which runs to Buntingford and stops there.

However, unfolding a map while flying a single-seater aircraft, finding the right place on it and tracing the run of railway lines is not particularly easy. It was not something we were used to doing, so I decided to take the easy way out. I saw quite a large grass field beneath us with a farmer standing in it. So I landed in the field, which, at the low landing speed of aircraft in those days, was not unduly difficult. Keeping my engine running, I beckoned the farmer over and when he came to the side of the cockpit I said, 'We are looking for Hitchin. Could you tell us in which direction Hitchin lies?' He said, 'Oh, yes. It's over there; it's only about eight or nine miles north-west,' and he pointed in the direction of Hitchin. That was all I wanted to know, I waved him away and taxied to the edge of the field preparing to take off again.

All would have been well except that my companion had got bored circling round while I was talking to the farmer. He thought that landing in farmers' fields was great fun and that he would like to try landing in this strange field. He came in and landed, but, unfortunately, ran into a soft boggy patch of ground; this caught his wheels, tipped him up and the whole aircraft flipped over on its back. He was not hurt; he scrambled out but there we were. His aircraft was upside down in the middle of a field. The propeller was smashed and there was nothing he could do about it, except, in due course, report back to our squadron commander as to what had happened. If he hadn't attempted that landing, we would, of course, have gone on to Henlow, delivered our aircraft gone back to Northolt and said nothing about it. As it was, we had to confess and, as I had to confess that I had been leading the formation, I took the can for an incredibly stupid and inefficient bit of flying.

Shortly after this, the squadron commander of 41 Squadron was asked to provide a pilot to make a contribution to the build-up of a new squadron being formed at Henlow. He was asked to suggest a name from one of his own squadron pilots. He obviously thought this was an admirable opportunity to get rid of this stupid clot, McDonald, and get him out of 41 Squadron. So I was accordingly posted to 23 Squadron, under formation at Henlow. So all the instruction on navigation that I had received at Sealand had been totally useless to me on that occasion.

It was also of no use to me during the whole of my career in the Royal Air Force which lasted for thirty-six years. I did all of the squadron flying, in fact all the flying I ever did, on single-seater aircraft, so none of the theoretical instruction on navigation I received at Flying Training School was ever of the slightest good to me.

In due course I had to teach myself how to navigate a single-seater plane, and this I did. Incidentally, one of the first and simplest things that I thought of was that when flying a single-seater in a southerly direction, one starts by turning the map upside down, so that a line on the map pointing to the west, to the right, would point to the west on the map, getting the map orientated with the ground. This I had not been taught at Flying Training School. There were various other tricks of the trade as it were. One of them was to draw a bold line with a felt-tipped pen on the map on the intended course and to work out what distance would be travelled every ten minutes. I did this by taking account of the intended air speed at the height at which I was about to fly, and the wind speed which would affect it. This gave me both the speed and direction of progress over the ground and I marked the line boldly at every ten minute interval, so that ten minutes after take-off I would know that I should be over the first of one of these cross marks on the chart. I could then compare what I could see with what the map showed to be the situation at that point.

I needn't go into detail, but I managed to work out this system successfully. Many years later I used it when I was on a ground job in India with the Headquarters in Delhi. I was in charge of the organisation and administration of a very large training formation, with training units scattered about at various places on the Indian sub-continent from Quetta in the north to Colombo in the south, a distance of about 2,000 miles, and between Bombay in the west and Calcutta in the east, a distance of about 1,500 miles. I used to travel about, visiting my stations at intervals in a Hurricane or a Spitfire which I was able to borrow from the Communication Flight at Delhi, and I was able to navigate myself.

As a group captain at that time, I would have been entitled to have demanded the use of a cabin transport aircraft, which was a thing called an Anson, with a professional pilot and navigator and have myself ferried about to the various places on the sub-continent by what I might describe as a professional crew. I much preferred to fly myself: for one thing, a Spitfire could travel twice as fast as an Anson, and I would get to my destination in half the time. Anyway, I enjoyed the fresh air and the mental challenge of finding my way around. This I was able to do, and in fact I could and did fly myself to various places in the sub-continent of India in daylight without any trouble.

Editor's note

In fact, we understand that Arthur flew himself to India after he was posted to Rangoon in Burma in February 1942. He travelled from Gibraltar south to West Africa and across to East Africa and then north and east to the Indian sub-continent. Finding his way on this lengthy journey cannot have been easy – more details of this in Chapter 18.

Chapter 8

23 Squadron, Henlow: Night Exercises, 1925

After leaving Sealand I was posted, as already stated, to No. 41 Squadron at Northolt. I very soon got the sack from there for incompetence, and found myself posted to a new squadron being re-formed at Henlow, No. 23 Squadron. On formation, 23 Squadron was equipped with the Sopwith Snipe, the last of the three Sopwith biplanes which were produced in the later stages of the First World War. In chronological order these were the Pup, the Camel and the Snipe. The Pup and the Camel were certainly used in combat to a considerable extent and the fighter aces of the First World War were, in many cases, flying them when they achieved various victories. Whether the Snipe was produced in time to be used in the First World War I am not quite sure.[2] It was the last of the Sopwith biplanes, and the largest with the most powerful engine. The engine was known as a BR2, Bentley Rotary 2, a rotary engine like the others, but bigger and heavier. It was also the last of the aircraft engines produced by the Bentley Company, afterwards well known as the producers of the famous motorcar, the Bentley, which was in production for many years and eventually merged with Rolls Royce. Even up to the present day I think there are models of the Bentley.

The Bentley B2R engine in the Snipe had an orthodox operating cycle. It was not a single-valve like the Mono Soupape in the Avro 504K. The result was that the handling of the of the engine, from the point of view of controlling power by throttle variation, was more or less orthodox, but the combination of a large heavy rotating mass attached to what was really a very small, light aeroplane produced marked gyroscopic effects on the handling of the whole aeroplane.

---

2. The Snipe entered squadron service in the closing weeks of the war and proved to be an effective fighter.

The main characteristic of a spinning gyroscope is that it shows a marked reluctance to change the direction in which its axis is pointing. In this respect, the Sopwith Snipe with its BR2 engine spinning at maximum revolutions showed the same tendency to resist any attempt by the pilot to change the direction in which the nose was pointing, in the sense that he wished it to change. If he wished to raise or lower the nose, the immediate reaction, unless the rudder was used, was that the nose would swing to right or left, and the reverse was also the case.

The practical effect of this on the handling of the Snipe was that on any sharp manoeuvre, such as pulling out of a dive or sharp banked turn one way or the other had to be accompanied by the use of full rudder. A steeply banked left-hand turn required full left rudder, which might have been expected, but a sharply banked right-hand turn also required full left-hand rudder. A loop required full left rudder all the way round; pulling out of a dive required full left rudder; but nosing over into a dive or an outside or inverted loop would have required right-hand rudder.

This peculiar characteristic, added to very sensitive, almost over sensitive, controls made the Snipe quite a tricky aeroplane to fly, particularly near the ground in windy or gusty weather. In fact, on many occasions when pilots were attempting to land in windy weather they finished up upside down. On one occasion, on a very windy day, when I think that most of us would have preferred to stay on the ground, one of our enthusiastic young pilots took a Snipe up and by the time he came in to land the weather had deteriorated still further; the gusts were very strong. He found that he could not get the aircraft to stay on the ground. Even if he managed to get the wheels to touch, invariably the nose bumped up, the aeroplane lifted off, even if he was only moving over the ground at quite a slow speed. It was quite obvious that, even if he managed to get the aeroplane to stay on the ground with its tail up, he would never be able to taxi in a crosswind. So two ground crew had to run out, run alongside of him, as his forward speed was not more than running speed over the ground, and jump up and catch his wing tips and pull him down and keep him down on the ground. When he taxied in, the one on the windward side had to hang on like grim death to prevent the aeroplane being blown over sideways.

However, we got used to these peculiarities of the Snipe and quite enjoyed flying them. The squadron didn't hold on to them for very long because it was due to be re-equipped with the latest fighter designed and built since the end of the war. This was the Gloster Gamecock. We were the first squadron to be equipped with Gamecocks and, at the time when we received them, they were the fastest aircraft in the RAF and also had the fastest rate of climb, so we were very pleased with their performance.

However, it soon became apparent that they had two design weaknesses. These I will mention elsewhere in this narrative, so I will make no further comment on them here. But after we had had them for some time, we discovered there was also a weakness in the armament of the aircraft.

Like all previous single-seater fighters, produced since about the middle of the First World War onwards, they were equipped with two fixed machine guns firing forward on the axis of the aircraft. The pilot aimed the guns by aiming the aircraft, through a sight on the windscreen. These guns were belt-fed Vickers .303-inch machine guns, almost identical with the Maxim guns first used at the Battle of Omdurman in 1898.[3] Even at that time I felt that it was remarkable that the latest RAF fighter should be using a machine gun designed to be used by infantry at the turn of the century. However, the progress in development of aircraft armament seemed to have remained absolutely stationary for all of that length of time.

As I had been appointed the Armaments Officer for 23 Squadron, having done a short armaments course along the way, I thought it would be wise to test out the armament on the Gamecock before we attempted to fire the guns in the air. There was only one place where fighter aircraft guns could be tested in the air in England at that time, and that was on the fire ranges on the salt marshes on the Wash, operating from an airfield called Sutton Bridge.

Apart from that, we could fire the guns against a stop butt with the aircraft on the ground. To do this, the aircraft was wheeled up to face the

---

3. The Vickers machine gun was developed from the Maxim, Vickers having acquired the manufacturing rights of the weapon. Paradoxically, the principal German machine gun of the First World War, the MG08, was also an adaptation of the original (1884) Maxim design.

stop butts in which bullets were fired into a bed of sand. Stout chocks were put in front of the wheels to prevent further forward movement and the tail was raised and supported on a trestle. The engine was run up and the guns were fired. The breech ends of the guns were in the cockpit alongside the pilot, one on each side; the bullets passed through between the cylinders, which were not rotating, so there was no problem about that. They then had to pass between the propeller blades which were rotating. So, for that to be possible without shooting the blades off, there had to be an interrupter gear to make sure the gun didn't fire when the blade was in front of the muzzle. The interrupter gear, known as the Constantinescu, had been developed quite early in the First World War and had been used in British and German single-seater fighters ever since. The Gamecocks were, of course, fitted with this interrupter gear and I thought it would be wise to check the timing of it, because we were the first squadron to have Gamecocks and nobody else would have tested the gun before we took delivery of ours.

Accordingly, I arranged a test on the stop butts and I had the workshops make a disc of plywood with a diameter slightly greater than the distance between the muzzles of the guns. This was bolted on between the wooden propeller and the hub itself so that the bullets would pass through the disc of plywood. When we stopped the engine after a test we would be able to see by how much they had missed the propeller blades. It's just as well that I did this because, although we assumed that the factory had timed the interrupter gear themselves, we discovered that this had not been done. In some of the first tests, we started shooting away the wooden propeller blades. We had to alter the timing to get this right. Having done that, we had solved that particular problem.

However, some weeks after this, the squadron was detached to the armament practice camp at Sutton Bridge, where we were to fire our guns in the air at targets on the salt marshes. The first test of all started on the morning we arrived at Sutton Bridge. Ten targets were set up, ten-feet-square, on the marshes. Ten Gamecocks went out, one to each target. We were loaded with, I think, 500 rounds of ammunition to each gun and we were to fire at these targets at any range we liked. We expected to return from this sortie having torn all the targets to shreds. However, by the time we returned from that sortie, some of us were quite a bit worried about the result. Some pilots hadn't even been able to load their guns. The guns had to be loaded by a loading lever, which had to be pulled over against quite a strong spring to get the first round into the breech. We had done this at the stop butts, but in doing so we hadn't been sitting on our parachutes. Parachutes had been introduced quite a short time before that. When sitting on them the pilot was considerably higher in the cockpit than he was without them. We hadn't bothered to take the parachutes down to the stop butts, so all the tests we had done there had been done without them. When we were sitting on parachutes, some of us could not reach far enough to operate this loading lever. We didn't even get the guns loaded.

In addition to that, the Vickers machine gun was an extremely unreliable weapon. It was subject to stoppages. We had learnt how to deal with these. There were several of them: the number one stoppage, number two, number three and so on. In one of them, the number one stoppage, a lever, which rocked backwards and forwards when the gun was firing, would stick halfway in its travel and the gun would stop. The immediate action for that was to seize a hide-faced hammer out of its holder and strike end of the rocking arm a smart blow to start it off again. In some cases this didn't work and we had to operate the loading lever again. All this meant that some pilots on the first sortie hadn't really fired their guns at all and those that did, seemed a bit unsure of the results they had obtained.

When we got the telephone message from the range officers about the result of all this, those results were absolutely staggering. There wasn't a single bullet hole on any one of the ten ten-feet-square targets.

So the position at that point was that ten pilots in a fighter squadron equipped with the latest fighter aircraft had been unable to hit ten very large stationary targets at all, whereas, our Station Commander, a famous World War I fighter ace, by the name of Raymond Collishaw, had, during the First World War, shot down and destroyed fifty German aircraft, twisting and turning in the course of combat, using an aeroplane and armament designed and built some ten years before. It was absolutely incredible, and we were very worried about it. It was just as well that the nation didn't go to war at that particular time. Gamecock squadrons would have been completely useless.

However, we pressed on with 'do-it-yourself' modifications and by the end of the week or ten days we spent at Sutton Bridge we were making the guns work. We were beginning to hit the targets, not only the stationary ones but occasionally some moving towed targets as well. So progress was being made, but the situation could not be described as satisfactory.

Soon after returning from Sutton Bridge, 23 Squadron moved from Henlow to Kenley which is just south of London. During my time with the squadron at Kenley two incidents stick out in my mind, the first for a very peculiar reason. The first was the total eclipse of the sun which took place in 1926 or early 1927, I think.

The reason that this sticks in my mind is that, because of it, the pilots of 23 Squadron nearly became involved in what would, undoubtedly, have been a very hazardous exercise.

This requires a bit of explanation. The reason is that the total eclipse was only going to be visible in a very small area somewhere in the latitude of Liverpool and the long-distance weather forecast was such that there seemed to be a very good chance that, owing to cloud cover, nobody in England would see it from the ground. As it was not going to be visible in any other country, this meant that nobody in the world would see it in that case. Our squadron commander, Raymond Collishaw, had the idea that he would like to be able to boast and dine out on the story of how he and the pilots of his squadron were the only people in the world to have seen this total solar eclipse from above the clouds.

The Gamecock could fly to very considerable heights, 30,000 feet, and they were fitted with oxygen equipment, so we could have flown to that height, probably above any cloud that was there, and been able to see the eclipse from above the clouds. However, Collishaw was a very unimaginative man. I suppose that one has to be completely lacking in imagination to have been a successful fighter pilot over the Western Front in the First World War I, which he had been, a top-scoring fighter pilot. He could imagine the thrill of being able to climb up through the clouds and see the eclipse but his imagination didn't carry him any further than that. He hadn't bothered to think out how we were going to get back again.

The plan was that we would take off from Kenley, fly on a compass bearing for the Liverpool area, climbing through cloud on the way and arrive there at the appropriate time above the clouds. He didn't seem to have thought out what the position would be when we had viewed the eclipse and were due to return. After that length of time out of sight of the ground he wouldn't possibly be able to know, with any accuracy, where we were, and when we let down we might have quite easily become involved with what we used to describe as 'stuffed clouds', that is clouds stuffed with rocks and trees. This was because there were quite a lot of places in the area in which we would be letting down where the land rose to considerably above 1,000 feet above sea level, such as Snowdonia, the Lake District, the Pennines and so on. If we let down in any of those places, we would become involved with stuffed clouds and that would have been the end of all of us.

Eventually the great day came. We went down to an early breakfast, just as it was getting light. The weather that day was terrible and we were very relieved to start with, because we assumed that when Collishaw turned up he would take one look at the weather and say, 'Well, obviously this weather is no good for this trip today, we'll call it off and you can all go back to bed.' When he did turn up nothing of the kind occurred. He ordered himself a hearty breakfast, sat down to eat it, greeted us amiably and went on chatting affably about this and that while we all tucked into breakfast. As time went on, it became obvious that he hadn't noticed the weather or, if he had noticed it, it hadn't caused him to call off the trip. We got more and more apprehensive as the time went on and the time approached for us to leave the mess and go down to flight for take-off. However, at about that time, a very vicious squall hit the building, sheets of rain pattering against the glass, probably a few hailstones, and squalls of wind. Suddenly Collishaw looked up as if he had noticed the weather for the first time and said, 'Oh dear. Oh dear, I am very, very sorry to disappoint you chaps, but I really do think that this weather isn't suitable for this trip of ours. I am very much afraid we'll have to call it off.' He needn't have been afraid of disappointing us. We were the most relieved bunch of young men that there had ever been.

So it is perhaps not surprising that whenever in subsequent years I heard or read the phrase 'eclipse of the sun' I was irresistibly reminded of that very anxious apprehensive breakfast that we ate at Kenley all those years ago.

The other notable event at Kenley in those days was one aspect of the 1927 Air Exercises. The annual air exercises were designed to test the arrangements made for defending London from air attack. Successive governments in the 1920s and 1930s were very anxious about the vulnerability of London to air attack, because it was believed at that time that any future war would be won or lost in the air by strategic bombing. The British governments were well aware that London was the most vulnerable capital city in the world to air attack because it was so close to the coast and warning of attack would be so short.

I had taken part in the 1925 and 1926 air exercises which lasted for twelve hours, during hours of daylight on one particular day. There had been much resort to standing patrols of fighters in an effort to intercept the approaching raiders, but even so, the percentage of interceptions was really quite small, and it was realised, I suppose, that although standing patrols of some appreciable strength could be maintained during the twelve hours of one annual exercise, in the event of a war which might last for weeks or months it would be logistically quite impossible to maintain standing patrols during daylight every day of the week or of the month.

The feature of the 1927 air exercise which struck me very forcibly was that for the first time there was a night phase to it. The exercise lasted for twenty-four hours and I was sent up for a night patrol. The thing that absolutely astonished me was the fact that I found it very much easier to intercept at night than it had been during the previous exercises when I had patrolled during the day. This was absolutely contrary to what I and, I suppose, everybody else expected. In daylight a fighter on standing patrol can sight a raider from a range of five or six miles. In the dark he would probably nearly have to run into it to be able to see it at all. However, the sky over London was not dark and I was sent to patrol over central London, the West End of London. There was no difficulty in finding my way there: there was no blackout and the street lights were all on. It had been thought unnecessary to put the population of London to the inconvenience of a blackout. The streetlights were left on. The pattern of streets outlined by the lights was clearly visible and I patrolled from about Hyde Park to the City of London and back. The first thing that struck me was the amount of what might be described as ambient light produced by the street lights.

The Gamecock had a petrol system which consisted of two tanks in the upper wings. At the bottom of each tank facing the cockpit, about three feet outside, was a small petrol gauge, about two inches across, with a needle moving round it. Normally at night it would be necessary for a pilot to pull a hand torch out of his pocket and shine the beam on the petrol gauge, but I discovered that at 15,000 feet over London this wasn't necessary. The amount of ambient light was such that by pulling my nose up a bit to get the gauges out of the shadow of the bottom plane I could read the gauges from the amount of ambient light that came up from the streets.

I was satisfied that I saw and intercepted and did dummy attacks on all the heavy bomber raiders who approached London during that exercise, during the time I was on patrol. I could see them from a long way away because of the amount of light there was. A standing patrol in the outer approaches, of course, would have seen nothing, except that the amount of light over the target was adequate for interception.

I believe that there is an important lesson which could have been learned from this but unfortunately was not, and that is that in 1940 and 1941 during the raids on Coventry and London, had day fighters been sent over the targets the results of interceptions would have been very much better and large casualties on the ground would have been prevented.

It is true that there were no street lights on in Coventry and London in 1940 and 1941 but there was plenty of light from the burning fires after the early stages of the raids.

Unfortunately the policy then was to hold the fighters back on the outer approaches to allow the anti-aircraft guns free range over the target. But as the anti aircraft guns, particularly at Coventry, hit nothing,[4] it would have been no disadvantage to shut them down and let the day fighters in.

In fact I happen to know that there was one-day fighter over Coventry. His name was F.P. Stevens and he was a pupil at an operational training unit at Sutton Bridge. He wasn't even in an operational squadron but he was an ex-airline pilot whose wife and family had been killed by a bomb, so

---

4. As the war progressed the anti-aircraft guns became ever more effective. In the V-1 attacks of 1944–45, AA guns shot down more missiles that did the fighters. This information was not released at the time as it would have let the Germans know what their greatest danger was.

he had a particular grudge against the Luftwaffe. Some of the Hurricanes at Sutton Bridge were kept with loaded guns, in case the station was attacked in daylight, when some of the instructors could have taken them up to do something about it. Stevens knew this; he got into one, got the ground crew to start him up, and started off in a north-westerly direction. We had previously heard the raid go over Sutton Bridge in the direction of somewhere in the Midlands but we didn't know where. He hadn't been flying more than five minutes when there it all was: enormous fires, anti-aircraft shells bursting and all the rest of it. When he got close, he saw a line of anti-aircraft shells bursting in the sky and he thought, 'Well that must be the height at which the raiders are operating.' He went in amongst them; he didn't care about himself very much. He came back and reported that he had sighted, identified and engaged two enemy bombers.

Stevens re-learned the lesson that I had learned in the 1927 air exercises. That was that the only way of using single-seater fighters effectively against night raiders was to deploy them over the target. He himself continued to apply the lessons learned on a personal basis in his vendetta against the Luftwaffe, during the winter of 1940 and 1941, but for some extraordinary reason the official historians have never noticed what he did. Some notice must have been taken of it because it is on record that he was awarded the DSO and the DFC. One report credits him with fourteen enemy aircraft shot down, which would put him amongst the top scoring fighter pilots of the Second World War.

I suppose the reason no notice has been taken of Stevens' exploits is that what he did was contrary to official policy. Official policy was that the anti-aircraft guns should have a free hand over the targets and the single-seater fighters, if they were used at all, and very often they were not used, should be held back in the outer approaches, where it was pitch dark and they were unlikely to see anything.

If Stevens had survived the war there is no doubt that he should have written a best-seller which would have formed a worthy chapter in the history of the Second World War. Unfortunately, when the German bombing of British cities ceased, he carried on, freelance with singlehanded operations over the enemy coast as a night intruder, still in a Hurricane, because that was the aircraft in which he had started all his operations. Using a single-engined Hurricane for this sort of operation he was on to a loser and he was shot down and killed.

Chapter 9

Engineering at Henlow: a Smashed Propeller, 1927–1928

During 1927 I was offered a place on the RAF's long engineering course. This was a two-year course at Henlow. I didn't particularly want to leave flying and the other activities of an RAF station for years at a time, but the great advantage of this from my point of view was that it meant a permanent commission for me. Until then I had been on a five-year, short-service, commission, due to terminate in 1929, just at the beginning of the Great Depression. The chance of obtaining a permanent commission was too good to be missed, so I accepted the offer. In September 1927, I reported to Henlow for the long engineering course.

The instruction on the course was almost equally divided between practical experience in the workshops and the classroom. The workshops

Arthur driving his 1925 Frazer Nash chain driven Fast Tourer sports car with Anzani engine, (registration number ES7643) This three seater car had an unpainted polished aluminium chassis which Arthur may have favoured; reduced weight meant increased acceleration. It handled badly though and Arthur eventually sold it on and several weeks later passed it lying in a ditch! (*Thanks to Peter Livesey from frasernasharchives.co.uk for tracking down details about this car*)

came naturally to me because most of it I had done before as an apprentice in the machine shop of the Antigua Sugar Factory. The other part of each day was spent on classroom instruction on theory and higher mathematics. This latter part was not something I was really familiar with and it was a bit of a struggle to get through it.

During this course nothing very dramatic happened. There was one incident, which was fairly dramatic, and I recount it here. One of the things we had to do during the course was to keep up to date in our flying by doing a minimum of four hours a month flying in the aircraft which were available from the Communications Squadron at Henlow.

One day a friend of mine, whom we will call Alan, came up to me and said, 'How are your flying hours? Are they up to date?' I said, 'No, they are not, I must get down to it and put in a few more.' He said, 'Well, I'm in the same boat and I have a suggestion to make and that is that we each take an Avro from the Communication Flight next Saturday afternoon and fly down to Brooklands Flying Club. I know quite a lot of people there and I'm sure they would be glad to see us and give us tea and a pleasant chat. Of course, one advantage of this is that if we are prepared to be a little economical with the truth we can chalk up rather more flying hours than required to fly straight from here to Brooklands and back. We could pretend that we went on by a devious route, or even that we went somewhere else. In an extreme case we could even pretend that we'd been in the air the whole time, but that would be stretching it a bit.' Anyway, the idea seemed attractive and we decided to do this.

On the following Saturday we borrowed these two Avros. They were not Mono Avros. Instead they were the next mark on, the Avro 504N, which had a radial, not a rotating, engine. The starting handle was on the side of the fuselage instead of having to swing the propeller to start the engine, which was an advantage from our point of view. We arrived at Brooklands with no trouble. We had a very pleasant afternoon with Alan's friends there and when we prepared to return there were no RAF ground crew there and we had not taken any of the wooden chocks which were normally placed in front of the wheels when starting the engine of an aircraft. This meant we had to start each other's engines up. There were no wheel brakes on those aircraft, so we had to be a little careful with this. The engines had the normal controls and, provided they were immediately throttled back to idle position as soon as they started, the friction of the tail skid on the grass or tarmac would be sufficient to hold the aircraft stationary. We started each other's engines up and we got into our cockpits, preparing to taxi out when an open car drove up with four young men in it whom Alan knew very well and whom he hadn't seen for some time. We didn't have radio communication so he made hand signals to me, indicating that he'd like to go and just have a word with them and would I mind waiting. I was quite comfortable; I was sitting in my seat, so I put my thumbs up. He got out of the aircraft leaving, it idling at throttle setting. He didn't switch the engine off as that would have involved my having to get out to start him up again. He went over to the open car to talk to his friends. While he was there the engine of his aircraft got warmer, the revolutions gradually increased; perhaps the throttle lever wasn't pulled right back against the stop. After a time the aircraft started to move: very gradually at first, but faster as time went on. I don't know who noticed this first. It might have been me. At any rate there were shouts, Alan came running, chased the aeroplane, jumped up on the side, put his hand on the ignition switch and switched off. Unfortunately, at that very moment, the aircraft had come face to face with a car which had been parked about ten yards in front of it. I don't know if the driver was aboard; he probably wasn't, but there were two old ladies sitting on the back seat. The car had, as many cars did in those days, a cloth top. The propeller of the aeroplane tore the cloth top to shreds and the propeller was shattered. The two old ladies were not physically damaged, but they finished up on the floor of the car and I daresay to use a modern term, they subsequently suffered a certain amount of 'post traumatic shock'. This was a very sad occurrence, but I couldn't help laughing at this extraordinary event; it was nothing to do with me. Alan had to come back in the back seat of my aircraft to Henlow and I left him to go and explain to the authorities why it was that the aircraft he had borrowed from the Communication Flight was on the airfield at Brooklands with a smashed propeller and that in due course solicitors' letters would arrive from the car insurance company and, no doubt, from the old ladies too, claiming quite heavy damages from the Air Ministry for the injuries they had received. That was up to him. I never heard what happened to him, nothing very serious I think, because he went on to have a distinguished career in the service and the matter seemed to pass off reasonably smoothly in the end.

Another event of importance, which took place on that engineering course, important to me at any rate, was the fact that I got married. I married a girl by the name of Mary Gray, whom I had known for several years. We had come to know each other through family connections. Her mother and my mother had been at boarding school together and had kept in touch with each other for the rest of their lives. When my parents came over to England in 1923 they had visited Mrs Gray down at Hindhead in Surrey and I had gone with them and met Mary there. We were attracted to each other but in those days, those long ago days, there was not much we could do about it. It would have been regarded as totally unacceptable if a young girl had co-habited with a young man or started a family outside marriage and I was in no position to offer marriage. In addition to which, Mary's father, being a prudent man, wouldn't even permit her to become formally engaged to an impecunious, short-service RAF officer. It was also the quaint custom in those days to assume that when a man started a family, or got married, he would be responsible for supporting them; this was before the days of the welfare state. In fact, it was the law of the land that any young man who fathered a child was financially responsible for it until it was sixteen years old. In those days the law was enforced.

At any rate, we kept in touch with each other and my selection for the engineering course and the grant of a permanent commission altered the picture considerably, because it meant that I did have a more secure career and that after I retired from the air force I would have an air force pension.

In the meantime, Mary had plenty to occupy her mind. She had spent a year at London University and had gone on from that to take a three-year honours' degree course at Girton College, Cambridge. She was enjoying that, she had many friends at Cambridge of both sexes, but somehow or other she never forgot that I was there somewhere in the background. At any rate in the Christmas term of 1928 she went to the Mistress of Girton and announced that while she intended to complete her degree course, she would like to get married in the next vacation. The Mistress expressed shock and surprise; no one at Girton had suggested such a thing before. She said she would have to look it up in the statutes. When she had looked it up, she announced that there was nothing in the statutes against it, but that Mary's husband could not live in college. Mary replied that she hadn't expected that for a moment. She had discovered that rooms were available on the Grantchester Road not far from Girton where we could live at weekends. As I was stationed at Henlow, only thirty miles away, I could come over for the weekends very easily. In the meantime, she would have dinners in hall at Girton during the week and her life at Cambridge would not be very much interfered with.

It must be remembered that this all happened a very long time ago. Girton is now full of men; in fact they are very proud of the record of their rugby team, which does not include women.

Soon after we got married we went off on a skiing holiday in the Alps. This had been privately arranged by a woman in London; there were no package-tour skiing holidays in those days. In fact, skiing was practically unknown in the Alps.

It seems an extraordinary thing that although the Scandinavians had used skis for moving about on snow-covered country, the villagers in the high alpine valleys, although their villages were snowbound for about three months each year, had never heard of skis. They didn't even use snow-shoes like the North American Indians did; they simply beat a path from hut to hut and stayed home during the period of the snow. They brought their cows down from the high meadows in the autumn. The cows then lived on the ground floor of the buildings to provide central heating for the families who lived above them and who provided enough hay to keep them going, and that is how they passed the winter.

The result of this was that none of the men who were 25 to 30 in the Bernese Oberland, where we arrived for our skiing holiday, knew how to ski. They couldn't run a ski school for us because they didn't know how to do it themselves. They had, however, obtained a supply of skis from Norway, which we were able to hire, and they were the first skis that any of us had ever seen. So our first attempts were amateurish in the extreme. There were, of course, no ski hoists, ski lifts, tow bars or anything of that kind, so we had to earn every foot of downhill running we did by climbing up to start with.

Everything we did was based on Norwegian practice because skiing had been brought to the Alps by the British, some of whom had been to Norway, brought skis back and then taken them to the Alps. That is how the people of the Alps learned about skiing.

The normal day's programme consisted of walking steadily uphill until midday with our lunch in rucksacks, then having lunch, then spending almost as much time coming down the hill as it had taken us to go up. The reason why it took so long to come down was that we had absolutely no idea of how to handle long Norwegian skis, which were, in any case, totally unsuitable for beginners learning to ski on the steep slopes of the Alps. The result of this was that we seldom did more than twenty or thirty yards downhill before we fell down. As soon as anybody fell down everybody would yell at us, 'Gather round!' and we would open a book on skiing written by an Englishman, whose name I remember was Mackintosh. We opened the book to try to find out what had gone wrong. All this took quite a long time, so the whole trip going down the hill took almost as long as going up.

In spite of all these difficulties we found the whole trip to Gsteig most enjoyable. We were in the open air all day taking exercise, we didn't spend hours queuing for ski lifts, as in later years. We were the only people on the slopes. The locals had never had winter visitors before and were delighted to see us. The local men, when they discovered that most of the men in our party were from the RAF, plus some Sandhurst cadets, invited us to have a shooting match against them on their shooting range.

Early skiing picture from Mary and Arthur's honeymoon in Gsteig, Switzerland, 1928. (*With John Cohu, Arthur's best man*)

The Swiss Army was a conscript army and, I think, still is. Every male over, I think, 16 was automatically in the army. After a period of initial training he was issued with a rifle which he kept in his cottage and he was ready to go at a minute's notice, like the Minutemen in the North American colonies in the eighteenth century. So one day we were taken down to the shooting range. We were lent rifles; the rifles were very old, I daresay that in many cases they had been passed from father to son for a generation or two. The alignment of their sights had peculiarities. With one particular rifle, for example, the owner might know that if he wanted to hit the bull's eye he would have to aim the sight at the bottom left-hand corner of the target. That sort of information was not passed on to us and, as a result, the locals won the match by an enormous margin, which delighted them and didn't worry us unduly. We all went off to have a good laugh and a drink afterwards.

We enjoyed the whole trip so much that we decided we would make an annual fortnight's skiing part of our normal programme for the year. We proceeded to do this for the next fifty or sixty years whenever we could. Of course, there were periods when we couldn't, such as three years in Singapore, the war years and so on.

The one snag about that first trip to Gsteig was that the journey out and back was somewhat uncomfortable. We couldn't possibly afford sleepers or couchettes, so we had to sit up all night in a second-class carriage, and the whole thing took about twenty-four hours from Victoria to the railway station at Gsteig, where we got out and got on to a horse-drawn sledge for the last part of the journey. So the second time we went we chose a different place. We chose it from the railway timetable because it was a shorter journey. The place we chose was a place called St Cergue, which is almost on the border between Switzerland and France in the Jura mountains. It wasn't particularly high. There were still no ski lifts or hoists there. There was one advantage which was that the mountain railway that ran from Nyon on the lake of Geneva over into France to a place called Morez went through St Cergue and climbed 500 feet higher. So we could start our day's skiing by gaining 500 feet of altitude on the local railway, which was something. We went to St Cergue for several years. There were still no professional ski schools there, but there was a British ski club called the White Hare Ski Club where we got amateur instruction from the people who ran the club.

Chapter 10

Cambridge University and Imperial College London, 1929–1932

In the summer of 1929 Mary completed her course at Girton, took her final examinations and obtained an Honours' Degree in Natural Science. She therefore came down from Cambridge as a graduate of Cambridge and at the same time we changed roles as it were, because at the same time I became an undergraduate at Cambridge. This was because the RAF had decided to send me and some others from the Henlow course to take an Honours' Degree in Mechanical Engineering, called the Mechanical Sciences Tripos at Cambridge. We were required to do this in two years instead of three in view of the theoretical work we had done at Henlow, so, at the same time that Mary came down from Girton I went up, attached to Peterhouse.

We obtained accommodation in a rented house in the Cherry Hinton Road, Cambridge and Mary became, in the college register, my official landlady. In the men's colleges, quite a number of the students lived out of college as there were not enough rooms in college for all of them. In the women's colleges, of course, this was not so and in Newnham and Girton all the women lived in college.

I cannot say that I was looking forward to my time at Cambridge. The very last thing I felt like doing in the summer of 1929 was to embark on another two years of academic study; it was, after all, nine years since I had left school and I wanted to get back to flying and to ordinary RAF activities. However, I had no choice. I was posted to the Cambridge course and it was an offer which I could not refuse because an Honours' Degree/Cambridge Degree was bound to stand me in good stead in my future career in the RAF and in any employment I took after retiring. It has to be remembered that the career structure in the RAF is a pyramid: for every hundred men who enter on permanent commissions only one reaches the top; the others retire sometimes in their forties or early fifties someway half or three-quarters of the way up the ladder and, naturally, I wanted to go as far as I could. Having a Cambridge degree was bound to help in that respect.

The effect which the Cambridge course had on me can be very well expressed in a quotation from Hazlitt which I came across some years later: 'Much thought on difficult subjects tends after a certain time to kill the natural dancing and gaieties of the spirits, it weighs upon the heart and makes us insensible to the common enjoyment and pursuits of life.' Quite so; that is the effect it had on me.

One of the bright spots during my two years at Cambridge was the long vacation in 1930. There was a very long summer vacation at Cambridge in which the ordinary normal course of lectures was interrupted and students did other things; in some cases they put in a period of foreign travel. In 1930 I persuaded the Air Ministry to allow me to use the long vacation to do some foreign travel back to my home in Antigua. It must be remembered in that, in those days long before there were any passenger services across the Atlantic, arranging a trip to Antigua from England was a lengthy business, not something that could be fitted in to any normal period of RAF summer leave, or winter leave for that matter.

Accordingly, Mary and I embarked on a ship called the *Inanda*, a vessel that carried sugar and had accommodation for quite a number of passengers and we travelled from London to Antigua direct in, I think, ten days and that gave us almost two months in Antigua before we travelled back the same way.

This was the first opportunity that any of my relatives had had to meet my new wife or she them. My parents had met Mary when she was a school girl of sixteen on their visit to England in 1923, but they had not seen her since then and, although I had a considerable number of relatives living in Antigua, uncles, aunts, cousins, first cousins, second cousins and so on, it had been absolutely impossible for any of them to be present at my wedding. But for the fact that my two young sisters were at boarding school in England at the time, there would not have been one single relative of mine at my wedding to Mary at Hindhead in 1928.

So the trip to Antigua came as a very welcome and enjoyable break in the academic work at Cambridge. It was, of course, quite an experience for Mary to visit the tropics for the first time. Everything was novel to her. Antigua 1930 was still quite an undeveloped place, quite different from any experience she had had in England. We stayed in my parents' house in St John's, Antigua; they had plenty of room for us and there was, of course, a round of drinks parties and other social occasions at which we met all the relatives of mine whom I hadn't seen for seven or eight years. It must have been very confusing for Mary because a fair proportion of the white population of Antigua was related to me in some degree or another and she was constantly being introduced to aunt this or uncle that or cousin so and so and it was almost impossible for her to sort out all the relationships. However, that did not matter. We had a wonderful time, we explored the island, managed to get ourselves a drive hire car and even a boat with an outboard engine which enabled us to explore the offshore islands on the north-east coast which I have mentioned previously.

Mary and I even went camping on one of the islands known as Great Bird Island, which I had camped on as an apprentice in the *Isa* all those

Mary's first visit to Antigua in 1931, Mary and Arthur standing with his sisters Melba and Stella, and brother Archie.

years before and which had been offered to me for sale for £5 freehold when I was eighteen years old. It could have been McDonald Island by then but in 1921, when it was offered to me, I didn't accept the offer because of several reasons. I didn't have £5, I wasn't going to live in Antigua and I didn't know what I would do with it. But at any rate when we went back in 1931 there was nobody there except, we were surprised to find, a herd of goats, about twelve or fifteen. There hadn't been any there in the earlier years; how they got there I don't know, and as there wasn't a drop of fresh water on the island. I could only come to the conclusion that goats can live without drinking and get all the moisture they need from the foliage of the plants they eat.

During the few days we spent on Great Bird Island two unusual incidents occurred. On one morning when we went for our morning swim on the bathing beach on the south side of the island, a delightful little half-moon bay with crystal clear water and white coral sand, we had to share the bay with a shark. This had never happened before. In all the years I spent in Antigua we had not bothered very much about sharks; it was the accepted view there at that time that Antiguan sharks didn't eat people or at any rate none of them ever had done so in the past and we didn't think their habits would be likely to change. However, we didn't believe in tempting them too much and whenever we were swimming from the beach or a boat and anybody saw a shark, which one could see in the clear water at quite a distance, the cry would go round, 'Look out for the big fish' and people would watch it or scramble out of the water on to the beach or into the boat.

Anyway, when we went down to this beach on Great Bird Island there was clearly a shark cruising up and down in the bay. Why it should have been there I don't know, but we thought it unwise to go in together because, although anyone standing on the beach can see the dark shadow of a shark at a distance of 100 yards or more, when swimming in the water with one's eyes at water level or in the water, one could easily bump into one without actually seeing it. We thought the risk of this was not worth taking, so we took our swim in turns, one standing on the beach watching the shark and the other swimming and then changing over.

The other unusual incident was, I think, the next morning when we heard a very strange noise in the sky and looked up. I saw the largest aircraft I had ever seen by a considerable margin, a very strange thing to see in Antigua because there were no airstrips or airfields at any of these Caribbean islands, I don't think anyone in Antigua had ever seen an aeroplane of any kind, although a few years later an American company did start a service with flying-boats up and down the island. They used flying-boats because they could land in the harbours and bays and there were no airstrips, but I don't think this had happened in 1930 and I don't think Antiguans had ever seen an aircraft.

At any rate there was this enormous aircraft, a monoplane flying-boat, and I was sufficiently up-to-date in my knowledge of developments in the world of aeronautics to know what it was. It was an experimental aircraft built by the Dornier Company in Germany called the Dornier Do X. With twelve engines on the top of the wing, it was a monoplane and I had heard that it was doing a demonstration trip around central South America, Central America and North America and then back to Germany. The Dornier Do X was never put into production; for some reason or another, it was not a success and the one I saw was the only one ever built – and the fact that I should have seen it from Great Bird Island, Antigua, was a very strange coincidence. Having seen it, we hurried back to St John's thinking it would land there and we could get a close view of it, but it took us some time to get to St John's and by the time we got there the Do. X had gone.

All good things come to an end and eventually we returned to England travelling again on the *Inanda* direct from Antigua to London docks and went back to Cambridge and completed my final work there.

The following year I passed out from Cambridge with an Honours' Degree and, for the record, I was the only one of the six RAF officers who went from Penlothan to Cambridge in 1929 who obtained an Honours' Degree.

At the end of the Cambridge course I was hoping I would return to ordinary RAF duties, but once again I was disappointed. Somebody at the Air Ministry must have gone mad because they posted me to a post-graduate course in advanced aeronautics at the Imperial College of Science at London University for a year. Why they should have spent all this money on my higher education I never understood, but it was something that I felt once again that I couldn't refuse as it was bound to have a beneficial effect on my future career both in the air force and possibly afterwards.

So I spent a year in London. We obtained a flat on the north side of Kensington Gardens, deliberately choosing it in a place where it was quicker for me to get to Imperial College by walking across the park than by any other means and, however late I might have been in finishing my breakfast, there was no quicker way of getting to work than by walking. This meant that every day I walked across the park to work and from work regardless of the weather which I am sure was beneficial to the health during a further year of study in London.

The course in London proved far more congenial then I had expected. There were only six people on it, only one other Englishman; the others were all foreigners, one of whom was an Estonian, a rather older and more mature person than the rest of us, and the six of us got to know each other very well. We normally had lunch together in a pub near the college and we tended to go about together; I introduced the foreigners amongst other things to ice skating. There was an ice rink at Queen's Road, near where we lived, so we spent quite a lot of our spare time together talking politics and world affairs and it was quite interesting to get the views of people from different parts of the world with different backgrounds.

Also the work at Imperial College I found quite interesting. We did quite a bit of wind-tunnel work and also work in an engine laboratory which contained various bits of research equipment which I hadn't come across before. Some of the things I learnt there may have been of use to me in my future career in the air force. One in particular I think probably saved me from presiding over what would have been quite a disastrous event, but I will come to that later on in this narrative.

At the end of the year in London I actually did get back to the RAF again and I was posted to Singapore, but that will be the subject of the next chapter.

Chapter 11

The Singapore Experience, 1933–1935

The three years we spent in Singapore were a new experience in many ways. Singapore was a most extraordinary place at that time, it had something in common with Antigua in as much as it was not a very large island, deeper in the tropics than Antigua was, and Singapore was only one mile north of the Equator.

In Antigua the British had built one of the largest overseas naval bases in their history in the seventeenth/eighteenth century to protect those islands from the French, and in Singapore when we were there they were building a very large naval base to protect Singapore and our trade routes to the east from the Japanese.

In 1666, the Antiguans had learned a strategic lesson about this problem of building naval bases overseas a long way from the parent country and the lesson was this: it is no good building a naval base with half the defences against direct attack from the sea if you leave the back door open and make it possible for an enemy to land on the opposite side of the island, walk across and take the naval base in the rear. This is what had happened in Antigua in 1666. The French had landed on the north side of the island, walked across and taken the naval base at St Erst in English Harbour in the rear. The British regained Antigua under the terms of the Treaty of Breda in 1667 and proceeded to apply the results of that lesson. They proceeded to fortify every possible entry point all around the island and cannon were located on seventeen different locations on the approach places where landing was possible.

One of these forts is still there as far as I know on the north side of the entrance to St John's Harbour. There is Fort James, where the ramparts and the cannon and piles of cannon balls are still to be seen, I believe.

Unfortunately by the 1930s, when the British government built a naval base in Singapore that lesson, which Antiguans had learnt nearly 300 years before, had been forgotten and they made the same mistake as had been made in Antigua originally; they produced a naval base on the north side of Singapore Island, provided very powerful defences against seaborne attack from the east, but did nothing to prevent an enemy from landing unopposed across the beaches on the other side of the island, walking across and taking the naval base in the rear, which is what actually happened and what the Japanese did.

They approached Singapore, not with battleships from the east, but by hordes of little men on bicycles and gym shoes walking across the Strait of Johore on the north side and across the Strait in fishing sampans and landing unopposed on the beaches on the north side of the island with the result that 100,000 Commonwealth troops eventually surrendered to 30,000 Japanese on the island of Singapore.[1]

However, what happened in 1942 was in the future when we arrived there in Singapore in 1933 and nobody took the Japanese threat at all seriously. Life was very hectic, the place was very prosperous, there was a complete contrast with Antigua in that respect. In Antigua in the 1920s the island was coming towards the end of an economic depression caused by the invention of the steam engine and the loss of a monopoly in the mass production of sugar, a depression which lasted for about 100 years. In the 1930s Singapore was booming. After the First World War there had been a rubber boom; the demand for rubber was increasing very rapidly with the increase in the number of road vehicles needing rubber for tyres. Synthetic rubber production had not developed to any great extent, the price of rubber was high and fortunes were being made in Singapore. It was also a centre for trade in that area and whereas in Antigua in the 1920s only about half a dozen ships entered the harbour in the course of a year, Singapore was always crammed with shipping every day, in

---

1. There is a long-established myth that the guns defending Singapore could not fire to the landward side. In fact, all but one gun emplacement had 360-degree traverse and could fire on the mainland. That one exception was due to the topography of the site. Guns did engage the Japanese on the mainland and caused extensive damage and harm. Since the shells were fused to engage naval targets at long ranges, they exploded deep underground, with earthquake-like damage. Moreover, most of the shells were armour-piercing (AP) rather than high-explosive (HE). While AP is effective against ships, it has a much lesser effect against targets such as infantry formations. Here HE is the desired munition.

addition to thousands of Chinese junks which traded down from Hong Kong; they came down in the north-east monsoon and spent six months in Singapore. Each junk was owned by a family who lived aboard and went trading up and down the Malacca Straits and returned to the Hong Kong area in the monsoon at the other time of the year.

Mary and I travelled out to Singapore on a troopship. She was not strictly entitled to a passage because the Air Ministry didn't recognise the state of marriage until an officer reached the age of 30, but she obtained a concessionary passage and, in fact, we had a cabin to ourselves and had a very comfortable journey.

One of the extraordinary things that happened during that journey is perhaps worth recording. It took thirty days from Southampton to Singapore with two stops, one at Port Said and one at Bombay where a number of the troops disembarked and then the remainder went on to Singapore and I think eventually some to Hong Kong on the rest of the voyage.

At any rate, on arrival at Bombay we went ashore for a walk and, of course, some of the troops and officers were disembarking there. As I came down the gangway, within the first five minutes of setting foot on the soil of the Indian sub-continent, a group of local characters approached me thinking I was one of the officers who was disembarking there and offered their services as bearers. It was the custom in the Indian Army for every officer to have a personal bearer who went with him and administered to his needs, arranged his laundry, and looked after his bedroll and travelled with him everywhere and so on. Some of the RAF officers followed the same practice and also had bearers. Anyway these characters were looking for jobs. The people they had served had come to the end of their tour and had gone home and they were out of work and looking for new masters. One of them came up to me and said, 'You want bearer, sahib? Me very good bearer, me got very good reference from Cohu sahib, very good reference.' I thought Good God, Cohu, that's an unusual name; John Mesurio Cohu had been our best man at our wedding and had been stationed in India at Kohat on the frontier. Kohat is about 1,000 miles by train from Bombay, so the fact that this chap was talking about Cohu in Bombay seemed very strange indeed.

Anyway, he flourished a bit of paper in front of my face and I saw John Cohu's signature on the bottom right corner of it. It was in fact a very good reference, but how this chap had got from Kohat to Bombay I never discovered; it is a very long way and it took, I would think, about a couple of days by train travelling day and night. It is just possible, I suppose, that John's bearer had accompanied him down to Bombay on his departure and remained there hoping to pick up a new job off the troopship before returning to Kohat. I never discovered the truth of this, but I thought it was an extremely strange coincidence this meeting of a bearer, who had served my best man in Kohat on the quay in Bombay.

On arrival at Singapore everything was a new experience. The first thing we observed as the ship drew alongside the dock were two very modern factories which looked absolutely splendid and I asked what they were. I was told that one of them was the local Tiger beer brewery. That was good news because we were both quite fond of beer, so it was nice to know that beer was produced in some quantity locally. I asked what the other one was. I was told it was the government opium factory. I said, 'What, opium factory, the British government producing opium?' I was told 'yes'. The population of Singapore is largely Chinese, a lot of whom were addicted to opium; if there wasn't a registration system there would be smuggling, black-market trading and a drugs problem and so the government had decided to register every Chinese who chose to register as an opium addict and issue him with a ration of guaranteed pure opium produced in their opium factory. In fact, we met one of the officials who administered this scheme; he was a member of the yacht club and we raced against him there. When we arrived in Lymington we found that he had retired there and was a fellow member of the yacht club many, many years later.

On arrival in Singapore we were very well looked after by other officers at the base, one of whom was just off on a trip to Japan and lent us his flat while he was away. That's how we started living there. We then got accommodation in a sort of boarding house at a place called Caton, just four miles south of Singapore town, and very quickly became involved in a fairly hectic social programme. We were invited to tennis parties and drinks parties and so on and we became involved in a round of entertainment which consisted of invitations to parties every night for about thirteen consecutive nights. Then one tended to invite the other people back to one's own place to repay hospitality and the round would start again.

This wasn't the way we wanted to spend our three years in Singapore and our determination to break the cycle was fortified when we had a talk with a young army officer about our age with his wife who was just completing his three-year tour of duty in Singapore and was about to return to England. We were asking his advice about places up country which we might visit, such as the old trading town of Malacca, Port Swettenham, Kuala Lumpur, the old station at Fraser's Hill and so on, and were surprised to find that he had no information to offer us. We discovered in the end that in three years' service in Singapore, which

Arthur and Mary's thatched beach bungalow, shown at high tide, Seletar, Singapore.

Arthur and Mary with friends on the veranda of their bungalow at Seletar

was rapidly coming to an end, he had never crossed the causeway, he had never been off Singapore Island. In fact, he had never really been outside Singapore town.

This information fortified our determination to break the cycle of the social round that we had got involved in and we discovered that, next to the air base at Seletar, where I was working on the north side of the island twelve miles from the town, there were two palm-thatched local-style houses on stilts on the beach amongst the rubber trees and the coconut trees, one of which had been rented by an officer who had come to the end of his tour of duty and was returning to England. We arranged to rent this bungalow from the owner who lived in the one next door to us. In due course we moved out to this new bungalow and some of our friends said, 'Well, you know, if you move all that distance from town you won't get invited to parties' and we said, 'that's precisely what we're after, we don't want to be invited to parties night after night!'

The bungalow was in an idyllic situation, on a beach from which there was swimming. It had its own swimming enclosure because, although in Antigua we had taken it for granted that sharks don't eat people, in Singapore that view was not universally held and it was thought prudent to do one's swimming off beaches behind a fence. This bungalow had its own fenced-off area of beach to keep sharks out, and possibly crocodiles because there were stories of crocodiles having been caught and cut up and then wristwatches being discovered in their stomachs, so we thought it wise to do our swimming in behind the fence. Anyway the fence was there; we only had to walk down the steps into the water to have our morning swim.

There was also a little jetty where we kept a canoe. I bought Mary a little small single-handed dugout canoe which she was used to go paddling about on, and which would carry two if necessary. We also invested in a very small auxiliary sailing yacht which was kept moored about thirty or forty yards off so we could go for a sail any time we wanted to.

In many ways this house was very primitive with no running water and no electricity, but we had domestic servants. We had a character called Cabune, who was the gardener, but as we didn't have any garden of any kind, his job was nothing to do with gardening; he brought the water to the house from the village well and also took out the slops and did jobs of that kind.

We also had a most excellent cook-boy who was a Madrassi and worth his weight in gold. He served us extremely well for our time in Singapore, nothing was too much for him, the food was brought to us from the cold storage in Singapore. Their van arrived once a week I think, or maybe twice a week, with cold storage food and a large block of ice and we had an insulated box. The block of ice was put in the bottom of the box and the cold storage food was put on top of it and that kept us going for the rest of the week. We were well supplied with quite a civilised sort of food. The lighting was by pressure lamps, which, provided that you had someone to light them, was perfectly adequate.

The cook-boy, whom we called Cookie, had a remarkable ability to produce fresh hot food, not warmed up at all, at almost any hour of the evening regardless of any different instructions we might have given him earlier in the day. For example if we went to Singapore town to visit the swimming club or the yacht club or wherever and told him that we would be back for supper at 7.30pm and, if on the way we got waylaid by some friend who took us round for a drink and, we actually got home about 9.30, as we walked up the steps on to the veranda there was freshly

'There was no electricity in the house so groceries arrived from Singapore cold storage, weekly with a block of ice.'

prepared hot food appearing on the table. He was able to do this because the last part of our journey to the bungalow was a winding track through the rubber trees and the coconut trees and Cookie, by keeping a keen eye out, would see the lights of our car in the far distance about ten minutes before we actually reached the bungalow. This gave him time to do the final preparations for a hot meal and have it on the table as we came in.

The most impressive demonstration of Cookie's ability to improvise in this way occurred on Christmas Day. I think it must have been 1934. We had planned nothing special for the day, no hot meals, we weren't going out anywhere and we hadn't invited anybody in. We intended to have a cold midday meal – sandwiches, bread and cheese, something like that in case we went out for a sail – and I think some sort of simple hot meal in the evening, but that was all. However, we were sitting on the veranda after breakfast when two of the young bachelors from the mess called in to wish us a Happy Christmas. We stood them a couple of beers of course and they looked over the Straits and there was a very nice sailing breeze and somebody said, 'Nice day for a sail, let's go and sail up towards the new naval base, see how they are getting on with the construction of that.' This was done, the four of us went down to the boat, I hoisted the sails and the anchor and went up towards the naval base and after a time it occurred to us it was getting towards lunchtime, so we turned round and went back towards the house. When we got about half a mile from the house we saw another yacht approaching from the opposite direction, which had obviously sailed round from Singapore town, round the east comer of the island, a distance of about twenty miles. We recognised the yacht and recognised the two people aboard it and the two yachts, ours and the one from Singapore, arrived simultaneously opposite the house. We dropped our anchors, got into our dinghies and rowed ashore and obviously we offered them a drink and, as it was lunchtime, perhaps Cookie might be able to throw up a bit of bread and cheese or an omelette or something of that kind for them, nothing had been arranged at all. So the six of us walked up the steps of the bungalow together, Mary and I, the two young officers from the mess and the two visitors from Singapore. As we got on to the veranda and looked through the bead curtains into the dining room there was a table immaculately laid for six people. Starched tablecloth, starched table napkins made up into fancy shapes and six places laid and, just appearing on the table, six hot meals for six people, a remarkable example of Cookie's initiative and powers of observation. He had realised that the two officers from the mess would be a bit late for lunch in the mess and therefore he was preparing to provide lunch for them; he had seen the other yacht approaching in the distance and had guessed that they would probably be friends of ours and, as it was lunchtime, all of us would be hungry and he'd acted accordingly. It was a very remarkable result.

Sometime later in our stay in Singapore, Cookie approached me one day very diffidently and asked if I would possibly do him a favour. I was only too willing to do that if it was within my power, so I asked him what it is and what it was that he wanted and he said that he hardly liked to ask but wondered if it would be possible for me to lend him $500 (eight to the pound), not a vast sum of money but very considerable for a chap in his position. Naturally I asked, 'Well, what do you want it for?' and he got a bit confused and hesitant and eventually came out with it, he said, 'Well you see I'm getting on a bit and I am not married and I think that it is time that I was and so I want $500 to buy a wife.' I said, 'Buy a wife, what do you mean buy a wife? You can't buy a wife in Singapore.' He said, 'Oh yes you can.' I said, 'Where on earth can you buy a wife in Singapore for $500?' He said, 'It's a fixed price. There are no cheap jobs; they are all exactly the same.' I said, 'Yes, but where?' He said, 'At the convent, the Roman Catholic convent.'

Well I made enquiries and I discovered that he was quite right; the Catholic convent did sell wives at a fixed price of $500. It was an excellent scheme because they picked up waifs and strays off the streets and when they picked up abandoned girls they were saving them. They were children who really had no future at all and they brought them up properly, educated them, taught them to read and write, taught them all the domestic skills of dressmaking, cooking and so on, and produced quite civilised people out of them. They had to provide for their future, they couldn't all become nuns; they didn't all want to become nuns anyway, so they sold them for a fixed price of $500. This was a good deal from the point of view of the girl because a man who paid $500 for a wife was likely to look after her, protect his investment; he was most unlikely to abandon her after three or four months and he would obtain a good wife with all the domestic virtues, educated and so on. It was a good deal from his point of view and from hers. From the man's point of view, of course, he was getting a woman who was educated, domesticated and whose morals were above suspicion.

I lent Cookie the $500 and in due course he produced his new wife. She was coal black, but she was dressed in a white veil and dress and white gloves up to the elbows and seemed very nice. She spoke fluent English and I am sure that they were very happy ever after.

At the end of 1934 we had to engage another member of staff because, in November 1934, Mary produced our first child, a daughter, Ann. Of course, it was appropriate that we should take on what would be called a nanny in England but in Singapore one either took on a Chinese woman who was called an *amah* or a Malay woman who was called an *ayah*.

Living where we were on the edge of a Malay village, it was natural for us to take on a Malay woman as an *ayah*, which we did, and she served us faithfully and well for the rest of our time in Singapore. We would have dearly have liked to have brought her back to England with us when we returned about a year later, but that would not have been practical from any point of view. She herself would never have survived the English climate and the complete separation from people of her own race.

When the *ayah* had been with us for nearly a year she asked of us a special favour: could we give her a day off to attend a Muslim festival in Singapore? We hadn't thought about it but when we came to think about it we realised that she hadn't had a day off, or a half-day off or any time off at all, since she had come to us; she had never mentioned it; nobody seemed to have thought of it. She seemed very happy to live in the house, visit her friends in the village from time to time and left it at that.

So, of course, we agreed and on the day in question a taxi turned up. It must have been quite expensive for a person in her position and off she went to Singapore in the fairly early morning. Not long after midday the taxi turned up and she was back again and Mary asked her what had happened: we thought she was off for the day. She said, 'Yes, that was what I intended, but I became more and more worried, terribly worried, I had to come home to make sure the memsahib could remember how to mix the baby's midday bottle feed.' So, having supervised the mixing of the midday bottle feed, she went off again. It must have cost her quite a lot money in taxi fares to Singapore, and that was it, but it was her attitude; the interest in her charge was at the top of her mind the whole time.

It was in Singapore that we first took up sailing, competitive sailing that is, small-boat racing which has been an abiding interest for both of us ever since. One day we were wandering around Singapore during a day off work and we looked in at a place called the Royal Singapore Yacht Club. It is quite a small club, quite a small building on the general harbour and we went up some stairs on to a balcony in front of the bar, were warmly greeted by a very affable individual whose name would be familiar I think to anybody who lived in Singapore in the 1930s, 1940s or possibly 1950s. He was Henry Worham. He greeted us warmly, stood us a drink and in five minutes had persuaded us that membership of the Royal Singapore Yacht Club was just what the McDonalds needed to make their stay in Singapore enjoyable. In this respect he was absolutely right, and in about fifteen minutes he had us signing application forms for membership.

About a week later we received a letter informing us that we were now fully elected members of the Royal Singapore Yacht Club and we made

Royal Singapore Yacht Club, Henry Worham, Lionel Cox and Arthur and Mary on board 'White Swan'.

considerable use of it for the rest of our time in Singapore. It was a small club in terms of numbers of members, not more than between 100 and 200 I would think, and not a large number of boats, but it was small, friendly, and everybody knew everybody else.

Three classes of boats were raced at the Royal Singapore Yacht Club. First of all there were a small number of 6-metres. The 6-metre is an international class, which at that time was racing in considerable numbers on the Solent, on the Clyde and in other parts of England and Europe, and probably North America. Four of them had found their way to Singapore. They were quite large, over thirty feet in length, very heavy and sophisticated and expensive so that the number of people who could afford them in a place like Singapore was quite small. In addition, secondly, there was a local class, the main class which raced there. It was called the B-class. This was a class of locally designed and locally built centre-board boats, especially designed to suit the conditions in Singapore where the winds were generally very light. The B-class had a very large sail area because of the predominantly light winds and, generally speaking, suited the local conditions very well. There were ten of these. Finally, there were some mixed boats; these were different sized dinghies and small Q boats which raced on a locally arranged handicap.

The first racing we did in Singapore was crewing the Commodore's 6-metre. The Commodore's name was Frank London, I think, and he was one of the four members who owned a 6-metre. They were not a large number, but they raced quite happily amongst themselves. The Commodore took us as new members, very young and inexperienced at that time, under his wing and took us out crewing in his 6-metre. After quite a short time he also invited me to helm the 6-metre in races.

The racing in the Royal Singapore Yacht Club continued throughout the year and there were many challenge trophies to be won, arranged in a way so that each consecutive race in a series of three counted for points for one of the trophies; every three races there was another trophy to be won and London invited me to helm his 6-metre in one of these series which in fact I won. I still have the little silver replica of the challenge trophy with the name *Kathleen* on it. That was the name of his 6-metre.

The 6-metre was a beautifully balanced boat, delightful to handle, light as a feather on the helm and one of the pleasantest and easiest boats to helm that I have ever sailed, then or since.

While we were starting off by gaining experience in the 6-metres I set about getting a share in one of the B-class boats. This was the main racing class, there were ten of them and they raced with normally three owners up in the crew, plus a Malay for fore deckhand or boat boy. A fore deckhand was an essential part of the organisation because, in an enervating and hot climate like Singapore, the *tuins* (meaning big chief or the boss or whatever) who owned boats would not think of sweating away hoisting their own sails or cleaning off the bottom of the boat or doing anything like that. It was all done by the boat-boy, one in each boat. The boat-boy also came racing in the B-class, so normally a boat raced with four people up, three owners and the boat boy.

I acquired two shares in a B10 named *Merlin*, a third share was owned by a young army officer by the name of Scrase and Mary and I and Scrase took it in turn to helm a series of three races for a trophy, so when a trophy was won it was won definitely by one of we three individuals. We have a considerable number of mementoes of these races in the form of small miniature replicas of the challenge trophies with the name of the trophy and the club and some of which were won by Mary and some were won by me, but we have completely forgotten which are which.

The boat-boy in *Merlin* was named Bulat. He was an essential member of the racing crew because he completely took charge of the spinnaker and, in a big boat, handling the spinnaker was a bit of a trick. The whole sail area of the boat was very large; the spinnaker pole was fifteen feet long, a long spindly pole, and the inner end was mounted not on the mast like the inner end of spinnaker poles on modern racing yachts, but on the middle of the fore deck. This meant that there was no way in which you could fit a downhaul to the spinnaker boom to keep the outer end rising into the air under the pull of the spinnaker when it was full of wind. This is done on a modern racing yacht because the inner end of the spinnaker poles, which are in any case much shorter in relation to the length of the boat, are fixed to the mast four, five or six feet above the deck and there is a downhaul from the middle of the spinnaker pole to the foot of the mast, a very powerful downhaul to prevent the outer end rising, the upward pull on it being very considerable. In the case of the B-boat being mounted on the middle of the fore deck there was no possibility of fitting a downhaul and the only way of preventing the outer end being pulled vertically upwards when the spinnaker was pulling under a brisk wind was Bulat. He, in his bare feet and wearing a sarong, climbed along the pole like a monkey and, as the wind got stronger, went further out so that his weight acted as a counterpoise to the upward pull of the sail and kept the spinnaker pole at its correct angle, which was almost horizontal, certainly above the horizontal. In a brisk wind this meant that Bulat was perched on the outer end of the pole hanging over the water several feet outside the outer edge of the boat and if any of us had suddenly let go of the guy rope or sheet attached to the spinnaker, the pole would have dropped into the water, Bulat would have been washed off or shaken off into shark-infested water. A slight exaggeration to say shark-infested, but there were sharks in Singapore harbour and, unlike those in Antigua, they had been known to eat people. The circumstances in which this happened were rather bizarre and perhaps worth recording.

When we arrived in Singapore on the troopship, as the ship was being tied up to the quay on one side we heard some shouting on the outer side and went across the deck to see what was going on and found a number of Malays manoeuvring about in incredibly narrow and unstable looking dugout canoes offering to dive for coins if we threw coins into the water. They said they would dive after them and catch them before they reached the bottom or sank out of sight. So we threw the coins and they did this, incredibly skilfully because they then had to get back into these very narrow, very unstable canoes. As an alternative demonstration of their skill, one of them picked up a tennis ball, threw it into the air and hit it with the flat of his paddle like a tennis player serving at Wimbledon. He hit it with the side of his paddle against the side of the ship, it bounced back and was hit by somebody else and kept going bouncing back and forth like a ball in a squash court. This was incredibly skilful itself because these chaps were in these very unstable canoes. But the climax of this demonstration, the high point as it were, was provided by one individual who was obviously much older than the others who was the whole time puffing away at the stub of a cigar, clouds of cigar smoke the whole time, and when a coin was thrown anywhere near his canoe he would drop his paddle, stand up, dive headfirst into the water and, as he dived, his right hand would make a movement towards his face as if he was about to hit himself in the mouth. He would disappear from sight under water for ten or fifteen seconds and then emerge waving the coin in his left hand and making the same sort of motion. As he emerged from the water, his right hand towards his face and back again, I couldn't see exactly what he was doing. He would then climb into the canoe still puffing away at a lighted cigar. Absolute magic. I mean, what had happened to the cigar when he was under water. Well we were never actually able to see what he was doing but it was quite obviously that there was only one way in which he could have achieved this result. He must have very quickly and skilfully turned the cigar inside out, end for end, so that the lighted end was in his mouth and he kept it going by inserting pressure from his lungs, pushing air out through the cigar from the burning end to prevent the water coming in at the other. When he emerged from the water again, he quickly reversed the thing and went back to normal with the burning thing outwards. He kept it going in that way. This was really quite a trick.

 Anyway, we hadn't been in Singapore very long when we heard or saw in the newspaper that this man who used to do the cigar trick had been taken by a shark. Singapore sharks apparently did eat people or at least parts of a person and at any rate the old man had been killed. We thought when we heard the report that the others would take the warning and cease this sort of activity altogether, but we were quite wrong and next day all the others were back there again still diving for coins, although none of them had acquired the skills to do it while smoking a cigar!

Apparently there were three arguments for not resisting this apparently rather dangerous performance. Firstly, they said they were Muslims; they were fatalists, they believed that a man died when Allah decided and anything the individual did didn't really matter very much. If Allah had decided the old man had reached the end of his days that was it. The other reason they put forward was that the old man was getting on a bit and wasn't as alert and quick as the youngsters; they all did this performance with sheath knives in their belts and reckoned that if a shark approached they would see it and fight it off with their knives and everything would be alright. The third reason they gave for assuming that what had happened to the old man wouldn't happen to them, was that they thought that perhaps this trick of keeping a lighted cigar in one's mouth while you were swimming under water rather took his attention off what was going on alongside him and they didn't do that, and so they thought that provided none of them took up that particular trick everything would be alright.

This is a digression, so to get back to Bulat. In our three years at Singapore, Bulat never did fall into the water and so the theory of whether or not sharks would have eaten him if he had was never solved.

We obviously paid Bulat too much because, in the three years we had him, on two occasions he asked permission to get married. As a Muslim, he had the legal right to have four wives if he could afford four wives, but of course a fore deckhand on a small boat at the yacht club isn't the sort of person who could be expected to afford more than one, so the fact that he got married a second time in the three years might indicate that we had overpaid him. As we weren't paying him an awful lot anyway this didn't worry us unduly.

One day when we had owned Merlin for some time – I think it was a Bank Holiday or something of that kind and there was no racing – Mary and I decided to go cruising in the boat by ourselves, to go to foreign parts. Foreign parts? Yes the Dutch Islands on the far side of Singapore

Strait were all within sight only about fifteen miles away, so we thought it would fun to be able to claim that we had been to a foreign country or dependency of a foreign country in our B-boat and we would sail to the nearest Dutch island on the other side of the strait and back. Hindsight suggests this was a rather foolhardy idea, but anyway we did it, just Mary and me. We didn't take Bulat or anybody else, and set out very early in the morning. It was fifteen miles to the nearest Dutch island and I suppose going more or less windward it would probably take us two or three hours to get there, but we enjoyed the experience. The beaches there were much cleaner, the water was much clearer, the whole situation was different because the amount of mud and sludge forced down by the big rivers in Malaya made the water on the Singapore side of the strait rather cloudy and muddy the whole time, but around these Dutch islands it was clear and transparent like the water in Antigua.

We wandered around the island a bit, but we didn't meet anybody. I don't know how we would have explained our presence as foreigners in that part, but anyway it didn't matter and, at about four o'clock in the afternoon, we set off back to Singapore. At that distance the buildings of Singapore and all the ships in the harbour were well over the horizon; all we could see was the outline of the land and we didn't have a chart but we knew near enough where we had to go; so off we went and although the wind had increased a bit we didn't take a reef in. We put up full sail, and as the wind was aft, from behind, of course the B-boat travelled very swiftly under those conditions and we had a very exhilarating if rather tense ride back to Singapore. As we got away from the land the waves got bigger, we found ourselves surfing down the front of a wave having to cling on to the tiller and wrestle with it quite hard to keep the boat straight and realising, that if we let go only for moment it would slip from our grasp, the boat would probably broach round and roll over and if that happened it didn't think bearing about what our situation would be. The boat would not sink, so, we would be able to sit on it, but we would be quite incapable of getting up again and getting moving again and we would be absolutely stuck there until somebody found us.

In that climate there was no risk of dying of hypothermia or exposure or anything of that kind; you might have suffered from sunburn but not much else, but I suppose in the end we would have probably died of thirst because we hadn't taken any reserve of drinking water. We hadn't taken any distress flares; we'd never heard of a distress flare at that time in our sailing careers and so we had no way of attracting attention. Although quite a lot of shipping went through the Singapore Strait it might have been some time before anybody saw us and even if a Chinese fisherman had picked us up we'd have had to abandon the boat and it might have been very difficult to hire a launch to come out and find it again, shifted back and forth in the quite strong tides in the Singapore Straits. Pity we hadn't thought about all this before, but anyway there we were. All we could do was hang on, enjoy the ride, which was very exhilarating, and all was well. We found our way back to the yacht harbour and tied up and went home. I can't remember whether we had taken the precaution of telling anybody where we were going, I hope we had, but I'm not sure that we had so we got away with that one; but I decided then and there that we would not do it a second time.

Apart from the weekly races on Sunday morning in Singapore, there was an annual round-the-island race on the August bank holiday weekend. We couldn't race right round Singapore Island because there was a causeway between the mainland and the boats could be locked through that, through a swing bridge which carried road and railway. In any case, it would have been rather a long day for an open boat, to sail over sixty miles. So the arrangement was that we raced from Singapore to the causeway round the west end of Singapore island on the Saturday and left the boats there. The boat-boys would manoeuvre them through the locks to the other side and we'd go back on Sunday morning and start the second half of the race from the causeway round the eastern end of Singapore Island back to Singapore itself. I did two of these races and I think I won both of them. I'm not sure; at any rate I do know I did win one and I do know that I have amongst the numerous pewter beer mugs and other trophies that I brought home, or have, that there are two beer mugs marked Round the Island Race, but in one case, the island is Singapore and in the other it was Wight because many years later I took part in the Island Sailing Club's annual Round the Island Race. Not that I won anything in that: it was quite a long race with mixed crews of over a thousand boats of all shapes and sizes, so to finish it at all was a victory in itself. They used some of the entrance money to buy a tankard for every

Arthur receiving one of a number of trophies which he won at the Royal Singapore Yacht Club.

finisher, so one of my Round the Island Race tankards is simply for finishing the 'Island Sailing Club Round the Island Race', round the Isle of Wight.

Once the Royal Singapore Yacht Club sent a team of 6-metres, three of them to Batavia in Java to team race against the Dutch. The Dutch also had 6-metres; in fact they had more of them than Singapore did and they invited us to do this and a Dutch shipping firm shipped three of our boats out from Singapore to Batavia as deck cargo free of charge. It was a nice gesture and we thoroughly enjoyed these parties, they lasted a week, and I was asked to crew the Commodore on two occasions. The first occasion Mary didn't come because she wasn't required as crew and she used the time to make a trip up the east coast of Malaya in a coastal steamer.

Up the east coast of the Malay peninsula there were, at that time, fishing villages and small towns which had no communication with the rest of the world except by sea. There were no roads across the central spine of jungle-covered mountains except for two places; so those communities were in the same sort of situation as a lot of the communities in the small islands off the Norwegian coast all the way up from Bergen to the North Cape. Those Norwegian communities depend now entirely on the coastal steamer service, one steamer in each direction each day, each day of the year, an absolute Godsend to them. But that's a diversion. The villages on the east coast of Malaya depended in the same way on the steamer service

– not as often as once a day but once a week or once a fortnight – which travelled the length of the peninsula, and, in the south-west monsoon they anchored off and communication was by motor boat or rowing boat with the village. During the period of the north-east monsoon, which is not a long period – about two months January time, the sea was too heavy for this and the steamer service had to stop and all these villages were then completely cut off, but as they knew it was coming they would lay in stocks and everything else and this didn't worry them.

On the second occasion a year later, when I was invited to crew again, Mary came to Batavia as a supporter and we were accommodated by one of the yacht club members in Batavia, the Royal Batavia Yacht Club, Konickle Yacht club. The member we stayed with had an interesting history; he had been an officer in the German Navy in 1914 and was stationed at that time on a gunboat on the Pearl River between Hong Kong and Canton. They were there on 4 August when the UK declared war on Germany.

They realised there was nothing they could do in that situation so they scuttled the ship and then made their way overland into Hong Kong. The officer who was our host booked into a hotel in Hong Kong and, while he was there, someone I guess noticed his German accent and called the police. The police came in and asked him for his passport. He spoke really good English so he said, 'Yes, no problem. It's up in my room, I'll just go up and get it.' He went up in the lift and must have gone down the outside fire-escape staircase on to the street, mingled with the crowd and got away. He then made his way to the harbour, booked a sampan and got the fellow to take him off to a Dutch ship anchored in the harbour. He walked up the gangplank and asked the captain for asylum. He was on neutral territory as the Dutch were neutral. The captain accepted him and eventually took him to Batavia in Java. On arrival in Batavia he made his number with the German consul there who gave him a job appropriated to a naval officer which was to arrange a collier of coal to refuel a German commerce raider called the SMS *Emden*. When war broke out in 1914, the *Emden* was loose in the South Atlantic and Indian Oceans and was sinking British oceangoing ships whenever she could find them. It was thought that she might need to refuel and if this officer could have a collier of coal it might prove a way of doing this. The *Emden* never came his way. His coal was never used by *Emden* and was eventually sold off to somebody else, but he stayed in Batavia for the rest of the war and eventually married a local woman. She was mixed race – half Chinese, half Malay. She was our hostess, a charming lady. She spoke perfect English and, of course, Dutch and they had some delightful children who went off to school on their bicycles every morning and we had a very pleasant week's stay with them.

Before continuing with this narrative, the final story in the account of *Emden*'s exploits must not be missed. She made her way to Malaya and entered Penang harbour early one morning. Penang harbour is sheltered behind a large island with quite a tall hill on it so that ships approaching from the sea cannot be seen from the town until they round the point at the end of the island. It so happened that there was a Russian cruiser at anchor in Penang harbour. The captain and crew on this cruiser imagined they were a very long way from the war and they could afford to relax a bit. It was Sunday morning and they'd had a tremendous party on the previous Saturday evening and a lot of them were sleeping it off. There were still quite a number of women aboard and, suddenly, round the point at a range of not much more than 1,000 yards appeared the *Emden* with, of course, the crew all at action stations. So the *Emden* just brought her guns to bear, fired one salvo at point-blank range and blew up the Russian cruiser.

The *Emden* then went south and, according to all accounts I heard, passed through the strait between Singapore Island and Johore, which at that time did not have a causeway. Then, according to the account given to me, the causeway was built after this, to prevent any future incidents of this kind. At the time *Emden* arrived there was no causeway and she passed through the strait possibly at night and just to the east of Singapore Island there was the estuary of a very big river running down from the Malay Peninsula. I can't remember the name of it. Anyway *Emden* was in need of certain repairs and renovations and went up this winding river with tall trees all round it where she was totally invisible to anyone except the local Malays. She dropped anchor there and stayed there for some time while she did a bit of refitting. The local Malays saw this extraordinary craft. They didn't know what it was; I doubt if they even knew there was a war on. She eventually moved off to the east and was finally, I think, destroyed by ships from the Royal Australian Navy.[2] I am not quite sure of her final fate but at any rate she didn't last very much longer after that.

We very much enjoyed our stay in Java. We were struck by the extraordinary differences in the lifestyles, both of the Europeans and local native population between Java and Malaya. For one thing there was a density of population difference. The Malay Peninsula and Java have about the same land area, I suppose, but the population of Java was at least ten times as great as that of Malaya. There were indications of this everywhere one went. In Java we drove inland quite a bit, and on all the hills there were terraces for rice, growing food for the population. The hills in the central part of Malaya were all virgin jungle except for the areas which had been cultivated for rubber or for oil palms for export.

The lifestyle of the Europeans in Batavia was also very different from the lifestyle of the Europeans, or the British anyway, in Singapore. The British in Singapore regarded themselves as being there only for a short time as they were on contract. Their homes were in England and their children were sent to school in England, to boarding school, and not very many British children went to school in Singapore. The Dutch on the other hand in Batavia had gone there for life. They didn't reckon to retire home to Holland and their children were educated locally. They went off on bicycles to school as they did in Holland. I don't think the whole time we were in Singapore we ever saw a European child on a bicycle.

We tried to think of why there should have been these differences and the only thing that ever occurred to me as regards the lifestyle of the Europeans, the Dutch and British, in these respective places was the topography. The Dutch in Batavia could escape the humid heat of the tropics by going up the hill behind the town and having weekend houses there so that they could get away from the heat at weekends and possibly to some extent even daily. In Singapore, however, there was no escape from the constant humid heat, long before the days of air conditioning. The hill station at Fraser's Hill near Kuala Lumpur was the nearest place where one could get up into the cool and that was a very long day's drive

---

2. Emden was damaged badly by the Australian cruiser HMAS *Sydney* on 9 November 1914 and was then run aground on the Cocos Islands. The wreck was broken up for scrap in the 1950s.

away so that people wouldn't go to Fraser's Hill for a weekend, but only for periods of a week or fortnight's leave. It was recognised in Singapore that this constant exposure to humid unvarying heat had a debilitating effect on Europeans after a certain time and it was the custom of the big firms to let their executives have lengthy periods of leave in England at quite frequent intervals. In those days the journey took three weeks by P & O liner and it was no good giving a chap three or four weeks if it took him three weeks to get home. The normal period of leave was something like six months and the juniors had to stick it out for three years, or perhaps four, before they got a leave period, but as they got more senior, the intervals between leave periods became shorter and the commercial firms in Singapore seemed to think that this arrangement led to efficiency rather than anything else.

As far as we were concerned we noticed this difference quite strongly because during the first six months in Singapore we felt very fit and energetic. We enjoyed all the various activities, tennis, sailing all the rest of it and we decided that all this moaning and groaning about the climate was entirely due to the fact the locals drank too much gin. It never occurred to us that perhaps they drank a lot of gin because of the climate; I don't know, but at any rate we decided in the first six months that, at the end of our three-year stint, we would apply for the extension of one year if this was possible and do a fourth year. That was our firm intention for some time. But, as time went on, our opinion entirely changed, we got more and more lethargic, our health deteriorated. We started getting boils and sores and that sort of thing and we realised that this constant exposure to humid heat wasn't really doing us any good. So, at the end of our three-year stint, we thankfully got on the P & O liner to return to England.

I can't help feeling that this effect of the climate was the basic explanation of the extraordinary failure of the British forces in Singapore to put up a show against the Japanese. The fact was, I think, entirely my own idea, that the senior officers there had been there too long. They had been there on the outbreak of war and because of the war they had not been rotated round as frequently as in peacetime. This debilitating effect had had its effect on them. In contrast, the Japanese came down from the north fresh and fit and used to jungle warfare and all that, and so the Commonwealth forces didn't put up much of a show in Malaya. Churchill sent signals saying that senior officers in Singapore should stand and die with their troops, but the fact is they didn't: they surrendered.

Chapter 12

Water Sports at RAF Base Seletar and Return to England

When I arrived in Singapore, the facilities for recreation for the non-commissioned ranks at the RAF base of Seletar, on the north side of the island on the Johore Strait, were very limited. They had rather a dull life. There was, of course, the usual NAAFI canteen but that was about all. Games of football and cricket were arranged from time to time, but the climate wasn't very conducive to games like football and the men in their spare time were really pretty much at a loose end.

The officers were much better off in that respect because they nearly all had their own cars. They could drive to Singapore, twelve miles away, and go to places like the Singapore Swimming Club, which was a very large club with 6,000 members. It had an Olympic-size pool filled with saltwater, high diving boards and all that. Games of water polo were organised, competitive swimming, and so on. There was also a cricket club and a social club called the Tanglin Club, which had its own swimming pool.

The other ranks at Seletar couldn't even swim although the station was on the beach on the edge of the water. Because of the risk of sharks and crocodiles in the rather cloudy water of the Johore Strait, swimming wasn't allowed. There was no boating because there weren't any boats there. However, all this changed after the arrival of a new station commander. His name was Bill Burling. He was not married and he lived in the mess. He'd been a yachtsman all his life and it appeared that his pride and joy was a large 8-metre yacht which he had left at his home base in the Isles of Scilly. So, as soon as he arrived, he set about providing water-sports facilities for the other ranks at RAF Seletar.

First of all he acquired a club house for a sailing club. When the base was first started there, the headquarters building was improvised by the production of a thatch-roofed bungalow of considerable size. This was soon replaced by permanent brick buildings and so the original thatched-roof building was available. Burling got hold of it, and converted it into a club house for a sailing club. He furnished it very nicely and even provided a piano so that evening sing-songs and that sort of thing could happen there. I think there were bar facilities.

He designed a sailing dinghy to be used there, specially designed for the purpose. It was a 12-foot pram dinghy; that is a dinghy with flat ends at either end. He persuaded the local firm of Thorneycroft in Singapore to build these things on a production basis, a considerable number of them equipped with bamboo masts and cotton sails. In other words, sailing dinghies which could be raced or cruised by two or three people. All this he persuaded Thorneycroft to produce for £12 each. This meant that three airmen could put down £3 each and become boat owners. This was a tremendous thing for them because not only would they have the pastime of sailing and racing but the ownership of a wooden boat is a hobby in itself because the maintenance, repainting and scrubbing the bottom for barnacles and weed, is a constant chore and an interesting one that keeps a chap occupied, as I well know.

So Burling built the sailing club up and I was only too willing to help him in doing this when he asked me to and took quite an appreciable part in building up the sailing club. My contribution was to give lectures on the racing rules. These were very important if they were going to take racing seriously.

Mary and I had taken the trouble, when we started racing in the Royal Singapore Yacht Club, to learn the rules from a book pretty thoroughly. We thought that was the sensible thing to do. In fact, not long after we went there, we became involved in a protest at the Royal Singapore Yacht Club in which our boat, called *Merlin*, collided with another one when rounding a turning mark. One of the rules lays it down that if two boats come into contact at any stage during a race and neither of them takes any action to protest or retire, then both shall be disqualified. We knew this so, when this collision occurred, we didn't think that we had done anything wrong, so we put in a protest. It was upheld by the Protest Committee of the Royal Singapore Yacht Club who disqualified the helmsman of the other boat. This would have been alright, except that the helmsman of the other boat happened to be very experienced and was, in fact, the Vice Commodore of the Club. He really couldn't take it that these complete newcomers, which is what we were, with Mary, a little chit of a girl, at the helm, had put him out of a race. He said he would appeal to the Royal Yachting Association, or the Yacht Racing Association, as it was called in those days, I think. To do this, one sent the case up to them for final adjudication and in due course the reply came back. The reply was that *Merlin* had been correct and that the Vice Commodore had infringed the rule and must be disqualified. These cases are published every year and this result must be on the record. I think that it was in 1934 between *Merlin* which was our boat and *Punei* which was the other one, *punei* being the Malay for pigeon.

But to get back to Seletar, we built up this yacht club and encouraged racing. We insisted that the racing was done strictly according to the rules. In due course, Burling was able to field team racing and challenge other clubs and take teams from Seletar abroad. I think he took a team to Hong Kong and to other places, but this was after I left. Anyway, it was high standard racing and when this had been going for some time he set about providing facilities for swimming. After all, we were on a beach and, but for the threat of sharks and crocodiles, the water was right there. The way that the McDonalds swam at their bungalow farther up the coast was that they had a little swimming *pagar* – simply a protective fence to keep out sharks and crocodiles. That, however, was outside the base. Burling arranged for the building of a swimming *pagar* of considerable size at Seletar, just outside the Yacht Club Headquarters. Having done this, the men could not only get swimming, they could develop competitive swimming, enter teams against the army and other teams in Singapore, and play water polo. All these activities were a tremendous boon to people who had previously found their spare time in some cases hanging heavily on their hands.

I haven't said anything about what my job was in Singapore: I was in charge of the aircraft repair section. During the three years I was there we faced a continuous problem which I had never expected to encounter. This was the problem of severe corrosion of light alloy structures forming the framework of the latest products of the aircraft industry.

The aircraft industry was just changing over from a wooden framework braced by wire and covered with fabric for both the fuselage and the wing covering, to using light alloy tubes for the framework although they were still using, for the most part, a fabric covering over the light alloy frame. The alloy used in the early days was very subject to corrosion in the Singapore climate. Whether aircraft in the United Kingdom and other places suffered so severely I don't know. I never heard that they did. Certainly, in Singapore there was constant humidity and I suppose a fairly high salt content in the air, being right on the coast and spray being thrown up by sudden squalls and that sort of thing. Corrosion was severe the whole time. Most of our repair work was repairing the ravages of the corroded framework of aeroplanes. In one particular case, I had to tell the group commander, the OC of the group, that he couldn't go on a trip that he had been looking forward to because of this trouble.

What happened was that a new type of aircraft was supplied to the flying-boat squadron there. It was, I think, the largest aircraft in the RAF at that time. It was a four-engined flying boat built by Short Brothers and called, as far as I can remember, the Short Singapore.

Three of these aircraft had been flown out from England, and in those days a flight from England to Singapore was often a very leisurely proceeding, because the range of intermediate stages was quite short. In any case, the trip was used to demonstrate the aircraft at various places en route, so that by the time they reached Singapore they'd been en route for, probably, some weeks.

The OC was impatiently awaiting their arrival because he intended to travel in one of these splendid new enormous flying boats to other places in his area of interest, such as Hong Kong, Brunei and Borneo and certain other places. These aircraft eventually arrived in Singapore on a Friday evening and the OC planned to depart on the Monday morning. He was very impatient to go and he'd made all the arrangements. I had to tell him he couldn't go. He was absolutely furious. I said, 'Well, it's up to you, you make the decision, but before you go I want to show you something.' We went into the hangar; the flying boats had been hauled out on the landing gear which was attached to them especially for hauling them up the slipway. Standing in the hangar, the bottom surface of the underneath of the planes was about six feet from the floor. All along the trailing edge of the bottom plane there was a series of little drain holes. These had been placed there because there were openings on the top surface of the lower plane, where control rods and that sort of thing came through. It was obvious that in a rain squall rain might enter the inside of the wing and these drain holes had been designed to drain out any moisture that had got in. This was a very bad design on Shorts' part because they hadn't thought of one thing, and that was that when a flying boat is in the air, or when it is taking off, there is a fairly high negative pressure on the top surface of the plane and that in fact is what produces three-quarters of the lift and the positive pressure on the underside so that a jet of air is sucked through these drain holes during the course of the take-offs. During take-off the bottom surface of the plane is drenched in spray thrown up from the hull, sucked in through each of these holes and sprayed out inside. I took a pocketknife out of my pocket and cut a triangular slot out of the fabric of the plane and shone a light inside. The OC could see that all the framework near the drain hole was covered with a white powder. In fact, I put my hand in and pulled one of the bits of the rim structure with my finger and broke it off and showed it to him. The whole thing was being corroded at an enormous rate and it wouldn't have been very long before some of the structure would have collapsed.

Short Singapore Mk. III K3592, no 205 Sqn based at Seletar, Singapore. This is the actual plane that Arthur tested, modified and took up on a test flight. (*Photo courtesy of 'www.RAF-in-Combat.com'*)

I said 'Well, I have to advise you, if we go on using these aeroplanes in that condition this is what might happen.' He had to agree, and we had to set about all three boats, repairing and replacing the corroded parts. We pasted patches over the drain holes because they were doing far more harm than good.

That's all I need say about my work in Singapore; I think. I did get some flying because I went up on a test flight of every aircraft which we overhauled. I usually took the rigger who had been working on it up with me, so that if the wings fell off, or anything like that happened, he would suffer as much as I would!

Return to England

At the end of the three-year stint Mary and I were only too glad to get on board a P & O ship for the return to England. By this time our daughter Ann was one-year-old and she, of course, came with us. So we had to say a fond farewell to Aya who had looked after Ann, to Cookie who had looked after us, to the Kabun who had looked after us also and to Bulat who had looked after *Merlin* and us.

We travelled home very comfortably on the *Rawalpindi*. Our departure was very comfortable. I had acquired, during my time in Singapore, a quite commodious six-cylinder American car. It was very old but it worked alright. I sold it to someone who had just arrived out for almost what I'd given for it. We made an arrangement that I would retain possession of it until I reached the quayside to go onboard the ship. So, when we left the bungalow at Seletar we all piled into this large motor car with our luggage, drove down to the ship and had our luggage taken aboard. The new owner took over at that point. Nothing could have been more convenient.

The voyage home was uneventful. We spent part of a day in Penang and came to realise what might have happened there when the *Emden* came in because we went up the hill in the entrance to the harbour. It was quite a high hill and there was a cable car up and a hotel at the top which was sufficiently greater in altitude than Penang itself to make an appreciable difference in temperature. I think it is one degree for every 300 feet so if this thing was 600 or 900 feet it would be 3 degrees cooler, which was worth something. Anyway that was interesting; we saw that.

As I said the ship we sailed in was the *Rawalpindi*. She was sunk in the early part of the Second World War, when acting as an armed merchant cruiser under the command of Ludovic Kennedy's father. Ludovic Kennedy has told the story in his autobiography. He describes how his father had been in the navy, retired but had come back for the Second World War and was in charge of the *Rawalpindi*. The ship was patrolling when it was sighted by two German battle-cruisers and Kennedy, the skipper, didn't have a hope in hell. He was out-gunned enormously and the ship was sunk. Coverley Kennedy received a posthumous Mention in Despatches.

Chapter 13

Return to Competitive Sailing, 1936

When Mary and I returned from Singapore we had become very keen on competitive sailing. We hoped very much that we would be able to carry on with it on our return to England. Biggin Hill, however, was not located anywhere near rivers, lakes or coastal waters where small boats could be sailed or raced, so there were certain difficulties of organisation to overcome.

The first conclusion we came to was that we would have to do our racing in our own racing dinghy which could be kept at home and carried by trailer behind the car to the nearest place where racing would be available. We hoped to do our racing in a fairly sophisticated sort of racing boat. There was only one class up to the end of 1935 which provided these facilities. This was the 14-foot International Club which was not only a national class in Britain, but also an international class, used in many other countries, including North America.

The great snag about the 14-foot International was that it was a beautifully built wooden double-skin mahogany hull with very complicated fittings. It was a craftsman's job and the whole thing cost £300. This may not sound like very much today, but in 1936 it represented about twice the showroom price of a family car. The McDonalds in 1936 couldn't even afford the showroom price of a family car, they had to do with a secondhand car. So, the price of the 14 put it out of the count and we had to think of something else. This was just as well, because later on we discovered that the 14-foot International would not have suited us at all because it required more weight and strength in combined crew weight than we possessed. However, that's another story.

Fortunately, at the end of the winter of 1935/36 the Yacht Racing Association, YRA as it was called at that time, decided that there must be a lot of people like the McDonalds who would like to race a sophisticated modern racing dinghy but who couldn't afford the price of a 14-foot International. So, with the help of a character by the name of Uffa Fox, they drew up the rules for a sophisticated modern racing dinghy to be constructed of a clinker-built hull of overlapping wooden planks, and everything was kept simple, with the whole idea of keeping the price down. This was, in fact, achieved successfully and the National 12-foot Dinghy Class was formed in the winter of 1935 to 1936.

To start with, the National 12s cost one-sixth of the cost of a 14-foot International; that is to say that the total price was limited by rule to £50. The owner and the builder of the National 12 had to sign a declaration that not more than £50 had been spent on it.

This was within the McDonalds' means and, in due course, I placed an order for one to be built for me. I placed the order with a man by the name of Jack Holt who, afterwards, became very well known as the founder of quite a large business organisation, Holt Allen Combine. I went to see Jack Holt in his workshop and found him working singlehanded in a small shed, almost under one end of Hammersmith Bridge, knee deep in shavings, building 12-foot dinghies. These were his very early first steps in a career which ended in his being the head of a very large organisation.

I knew nothing about racing dinghies at that time. I knew that the rules of the National 12 had been drawn up and I simply asked Jack Holt to build me one. I didn't specify who the designer should be and, because there was a wide scope in choosing the shape of the hull, the only thing that was definitely limited about it was its total length and its minimum weight. I don't know what he did about that; he probably had his own idea. At any rate he produced for me a fairly normal-looking 12-foot racing dinghy. I had stupidly used one of the options in the rules to say that I would have a dinghy without a deck. Why I did this I cannot now imagine, but I think my reasoning must have been that the model of what a racing dinghy should be was the target to aim at, something like the International-14. The International-14 didn't have a deck and the reason for that, I eventually realised, was that it had been developed from the pulling dinghies which the officers used to use to commute from their moorings to the jetties. The rules of the class had developed in such a way that the 14-foot Internationals were not permitted to have a deck. I believe that is still part of the rule of that class. At any rate I asked for a National 12 without a deck and got one. I very soon found that combination didn't work at all. In fact the first dinghy I had was not really competitive.

On deciding where to do our racing, we were introduced to the Ranelagh Club just above Putney Bridge, who raced on the Thames between Putney and Hammersmith bridges. This was a club which raced throughout the winter, one of the few places in England at that time which did this. In fact, there was more competition in the winter than in the summer because some of the first-class helmsmen who raced at Cowes and other places, when racing packed up there at the summer, brought their boats to Ranelagh and raced them throughout the winter; so the competition throughout the winter was very good.

We did a bit of racing at Ranelagh in our new National which I called *Chobaj*, the Malay word for endeavour. Mary became heavily pregnant with our second child and had to give up for a while. During this period in August or early September 1936, the first championship meeting for the new National 12-foot Class took place at Poole Harbour, based on the Parkstone Yacht Club. I decided to have a go at this and departed for Parkstone with the National on a trailer. I had a National 12 with no deck and no crew, hoping for the best.

If light winds had prevailed during the week of the championship racing, this might not have mattered very much. In fact, however, it blew hard the whole week and, within ten minutes of starting the first race, I realised I was absolutely on to a loser, I couldn't possibly do anything worthwhile with this dinghy because water came in over the bow so fast that, single handed, I had to heave to and bail out every now and again which made for extremely slow progress. I was tempted at this stage to pack up and go home, but having come all that way, I thought I would press on regardless and see what could be done. At the end of the first race I went ashore and into the town and bought a roll of canvas, a packet of tin tacks, a hammer and a pair of scissors. With this equipment I cut out a canvas screen or foredeck to fill the gap between the bow of the boat and the mast. I tacked it on to the gunnel of the boat and the mast and had a rough sort of canvas dodger to keep some of the water out. This improved things a lot, but I still didn't have any crew. On the second or third day of the meeting, I was just launching off from the beach; there quite a number of people were standing around and I somewhat rashly said, 'Nice day for a sail. Anybody like to come with me. No previous experience required?' By that I meant, no previous experience of dinghy racing was required. A charming girl said, 'Yes, I'll come.' She stepped into the boat and I pushed off. I hadn't gone ten or fifteen yards when I discovered that she had taken me at my word; she had never been in a boat at all before. The idea of her crewing a National 12, which was a very unstable sort of craft, and getting the weight in the right place at the right time was really quite beyond her. The combination wasn't very good. However, we pressed on and had a race. I don't know where I finished, but I did finish. The girl stayed with me for the rest of the week and improved in skill, of course, as she got experience. At the end of the week I thanked her very much and started to pack up to go home to see how things were there. I didn't even bother to look at the score board to see how many points I had scored in the week's racing. I knew I hadn't won any races. I assumed that I was right at the back of the fleet as far as total points were concerned. It was only some years later, when I was looking at a book written by Uffa Fox, one of the classics of boat racing at that time that I read a detailed description of that week's racing including, at the end, a summary of the points scored by the first ten boats out of the forty-seven. I certainly didn't expect to find my name amongst them, but I came across an extraordinary statement, I found it difficult to believe, that tied for sixth place out of forty-seven over all was Charles Nicholson's *Can Can*, the name of his boat, and Flight Lieutenant McDonald's *Chobaj*. This was almost unbelievable. What I think must have happened, and I hadn't really noticed it during the course of the week, was that the class was new, people didn't know how to rig their masts properly, there were a lot of broken masts, a lot of capsizes and I was one of the few boats that finished in every race.

By the following year, 1937, as the championship week for the National-12s approached, I disposed of *Choba* because I had come to the conclusion that she would never be really competitive. I looked out for a replacement. About four or five weeks before the championship week came round, I had the opportunity to buy secondhand, one of the very early Nationals to be built, number N23 with the name of *Farandole*, which I believe is a French country dance. The owner of *Farandole* had decided, for some reason, that he hadn't done very well with her, and he was going to have another boat. She had been designed by Uffa Fox, she was what was known as an Uffa King.

Uffa Fox had been a great benefactor to the National 12-foot 30 Class. He had given the class a flying start by designing a boat to the rules, which he said wouldn't be outclassed for at least ten years. This claim had to be believed because Uffa had made his name in the previous years as the chap who had designed an International 14-foot dinghy by the name of *Avenger* in which he had won fifty of the first fifty-three races in which he had competed. He was, obviously, one of the best small boat designers in the country. I took the view his claim was justified, that the boat designed by him could probably be made competitive for a considerable period.

I bought this boat *Farandole* and took it back to Biggin Hill and then looked carefully through the rule book. There was nothing I could do about the shape of the hull, of course; that was fixed, but Uffa had not designed the rig, he had left that to individual owners to decide what kind of rig they wanted to put on their boats, particularly because in the National 12-foot Class, when it started, it was thought that many owners would wish to race them singlehanded. If they did that, they might prefer to put the whole of the sail area into one single sail for ease of handling. The rules of the class were that the only restriction on sail area was the measurement of the actual sail or sails themselves, a total area of 90 square feet. This could be arranged in two sails or in one, in any proportion distributed between mainsail and foresail. This meant, of course, that the rig could be very different in each case.

At this point I must make it clear that the National 12-foot Class and the International 14-foot Class were not one-design boats. They were not intended to be all the same, they were what was called restricted class: certain rules were laid down and you could build any boat you liked, provided you didn't exceed any of the limits imposed by the rule book. As far as the hull was concerned, about the only limits were the maximum lengths: fourteen feet in one case and twelve feet in the other, and minimum weight. I remember the minimum weight of the National-12 was 190 pounds. The limitations on the rig were fairly simple: the maximum height of the mast was twenty feet, the minimum weight of the mast was laid down at 16 pounds; I can remember that figure, and only one pair of cross-trees or spreaders was allowed in the rig. This was a very simple arrangement, compared with the 14-foot Internationals which had three or four pairs of spreaders. Within these limits an owner could use any combination he liked. I got hold of the rule book and went through it clause by clause. I took the mast out to see how I could exploit the limitations of the rules to the maximum advantage. When I came to do this, my previous training in engineering, stressing and all that sort of thing came in useful. The first thing I did was to weigh the mast, because an excessive weight above the minimum prescribed was obviously a handicap. I found, in fact, that it was about 25 per cent heavier than the minimum allowed. I took a wood plane, planed off the outside and brought the weight of the mast down to the minimum allowed by the rule. In doing this, I had to make sure that the height of the centre of gravity of the mast was not lower than a certain percentage of its length. That I did; the mast was perfectly legal, but it was 25 per cent lighter. I then examined other rules and ended up with three variations which might be described as *Farandole*'s secret weapons. These were perfectly obvious to anyone who looked at the boat. Some of my competitors noted them and copied all three or copied some of them. Others noted them and took no notice. They thought that they were just gimmicks, not worth copying.

One of the modifications was a development rig in the small-boat racing world which has continued to this day, that is to say, instead of the spread of the cross-trees being at 90 degrees to the axis of the boat, straight across, I arranged mine swept back about 30 degrees, with top shrouds above them and the lower shrouds from the root of the cross-tree to the hull at a point well aft of the position of the mast. This gave the mast extra strength in the fore and aft plane and increased the strength about ten times, I would think. It also enabled the curve to be rigged in the mast either straight or curved back at the top by altering the relative tension of the two pairs of shrouds. That was one of my three major modifications. Another one was that I increased the height of the fore triangle, which is the height from the interception of the forestay to the deck, by two feet. This was a lot in a 12-foot dinghy. I was able to do this because the rule limiting the height of the forestay simply prescribed that the pin or the axis of the pulley block which took the halyard of the foresail must not be more than fourteen feet above the deck. Most of the boats had been designed with the pulley block in the mast. This meant that the whole intersection height of the fore triangle was limited to fourteen feet. The rule didn't prevent me from putting the pulley block on a 2-foot length of wire and attaching it two feet higher up the mast as the pin of the block was still only fourteen feet above the deck. In

124   Helping Stop Hitler's Luftwaffe

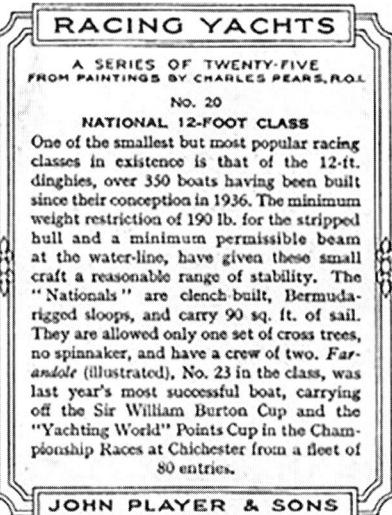

John Player Cigarette Card No.20 from the series 'Famous Racing Yachts' N23, Farandole, Arthur and Mary are visible crewing the yacht. (*Painting by Charles Pears*)

Reverse of Cigarette Card No.20 showing information about N23, Farandole.

order to do that, of course, I had to arrange a different way of bringing the downhaul back to the boat and that I did by taking it down parallel to the forestay, yanking the jib on to the downhaul of the halyard as well as the forestay, through a sleeve in the stem, and the halyard then ran under the deck into the hull where I arranged a tackle for tensioning it. All this sounds very technical, but it was a major difference in rig, and it's one of the reasons, I think, that *Farandole* became, in the next twenty years, the best known, the most famous or the most notorious; I don't know what the right expression is, but she certainly was well known throughout the dinghy racing world. A photograph of her appears on the dust cover of one book on dinghy racing, and a picture of her, '*N23*', appears on a cigarette card, for those who can remember what cigarette cards were. There was a series of cigarette cards called 'Famous Racing Yachts' which started with the King's racing yacht *Britannia*. This was the racing cutter *Britannia* which belonged to Edward VII and George V, which was scuttled when George V died. As Mary and I had just won the National Championship for 1937, *N23* featured on the cigarette card depicting the National-12 Class.

The Burton Cup Championship for National 12 ft Dinghies, Arthur with his crew Mary by their dinghy Farandole, N23.

I made other modifications which I needn't go into now, but altogether there were four differences in rig between *Farandole* and any other National-12 of which I ever heard. This must have given her an edge in improved performance over all the others, because Mary and I went down to the second championship meeting at Hayling Island at Chichester Harbour in early 1937 completely unknown in the dinghy racing world. We'd hardly ever raced *Farandole* before in open water and we were up against small-boat racers with an international reputation. One of these was the famous Stuart Morris, once described as the greatest small-boat helmsman of his generation. He'd won the Prince of Wales Cup for the International-14 Annual Championships, even then I think, something like nine times. There were others like Colin Ratsey from the great firm of Ratsey and Lapthorne, sailmakers, and one of the Nicholsons from Gosport, and so on, all people with international reputations. Mary and I were absolute beginners; no one had ever heard of us and we won not only the Championship race, but also the Yachting World Trophy for the best points score for the whole week.

Winning the Burton Championship race really was a bit of a fluke because I made an appalling start and, to cut a long story short, coming up to the first windward mark, beating against the tide, I was well back in twentieth or twenty-fifth place or something like that, and Stuart Morris, as was perhaps to be expected, was leading the fleet. Then something happened which had a very dramatic effect on the results of the race. The first windward mark was in the main channel running into Chichester Harbour, in which there was a very strong contrary tide, so strong in fact that a National-12 beating to windward couldn't make any progress against it. The only way of making progress towards the mark was to do short tacks in the slack water near the shore line until well past it and then make a judgement as to when it was safe to make one long tack out and get round it. Well, Stuart was the first one to make the long tack and I watched him. He missed getting round the mark by about half a boat's length. He couldn't round it. What he should have done then was to have tacked back in to the shore line, gone further up on short tacks and made another try from there, but he might have lost two or three places if he had done that. So he decided to try and do short tacks out in the middle channel to get round the mark. This was a mistake. He couldn't make any progress at all. I was far enough back, in the slack water, to observe what had happened and noted the point at which he had made the decision to tack out, so I went about two boat lengths beyond that point, and got round the mark which put me up to first place. By the time Stuart eventually decided to come in to the shore line to tack further up and try again, he had lost thirteen places. Being Stuart, he picked up seven places during the rest of the race, but couldn't do better than that and finished sixth overall.

Close behind me as I got round the mark was Charles Curry, who afterwards, in 1952, was a silver medallist in the Olympics. He was a well-known dinghy sailor, and he and I proceeded to have a very close race for the next four rounds of the course. It was a long course, five rounds altogether. Sometimes he was ahead, sometimes I was. On the last leg into the finish we had to round a moored dinghy which was the last turning mark and by then I had achieved a lead of about twenty yards over Charles. We rounded the mark, Charles came round afterwards and, as he rounded the mark, his crew dived overboard to lighten the boat. She pulled herself into the moored dinghy, and he came after us, singlehanded in a light wind without his crew. As a result, his boat was considerably lighter in overall weight and this, of course, gave him an advantage. He could possibly have caught us because of that. There was no rule against doing this at that time; it was perfectly legal but the Yacht

Winning the Burton Cup 1937, Arthur holding the cup which is only kept for a year, Mary holding the replica kept by the winners.

Racing Association, or YRA, passed a rule a fortnight later to the effect that nobody must leave the crew of a racing boat in the course of a race. This could not be made retrospective, so Charles kept his second place.

Looking at some of Uffa Fox's books on sailing that described this race in great detail, there is a photograph showing the last turning mark with *N23* leading. About twenty yards beyond it, is Charles' boat, which was *275*, I think, rounding the mark. With a magnifying glass one could see that the crew in Charles' boat was standing crouched at the side of the boat, as if she was being sick. That was not the case: she was actually in the act of diving overboard to lighten the boat. Neither the photographer, nor Uffa himself, noticed the significance of the photograph. It was described without comment as simply depicting the last mark and the first two boats rounding it.

After winning the 1937 Burton, Mary and I continued to race *Farandole* with much enjoyment for the next nineteen years or so, with the exception of the war years of course, until 1955 when I was posted to Pakistan. We were based during the whole of this time at the Ranelagh Sailing Club just above Putney Bridge. We did a lot of racing on the Thames in the winter. In the summer we trailed *Farandole* all over the country for open meetings. At the Burton Cup in 1938, which was at Felixstowe near Harwich, we got a second. Even in 1948, after the war, we again raced her in the Burton Championship Race and got a second. So *Farandole* was in winning form, top of the class as it were, in the first leaders in the class, from 1937 until 1948 – that is, for eleven years. Uffa King's prophecy that the Uffa King would not be outclassed in ten years proved to be true. Of course, the war had quite a lot to do with that, because for five years or so there was no serious dinghy racing and no development in the class, which there otherwise would have been.

In the run up to the 1939 Burton Cup Race, which was at Torquay, we had made all preparations to compete. We had taken *Farandole* down on a trailer and done pretty well in the preliminary races. The day before the Burton Race itself, I think it must have been 1 or 2 September 1939, I got a telegram to report back to duty at once, because unfortunately a chap called Hitler had organised a war. So I had to go.

I said to Mary, 'This boat has won the 1937 Burton and came second in the '38. She really must go out tomorrow, you must take her out, although I won't be there.' So I went off. Mary discussed this with a friend of ours and he said, 'Oh yes, my sister will crew with you. She's had twelve years' sailing experience.' Mary accepted the offer. A rather large and slightly ungainly woman turned up and they went afloat. It was a windy day unfortunately. It soon became obvious that the lady in question had done all her racing in a fifteen-ton cruiser. It bears no comparison to a 12-foot National dinghy, where the positioning of the weight in the boat is of vital importance; this lady didn't know how to do that. They were in serious trouble, so they had to retire, but they did at least start. I discovered recently a photograph, which is a press photograph from a firm in Torquay. It's not dated but I'm almost positive that it is actually a photograph of the start of the 1939 Burton Cup Race. It shows *N23* rather at the back of the fleet, which if I had been handling her would have been unlikely. There is a figure in the stern which must have been Mary. So, that is quite a historic photograph. How we came to have it after all these years I don't know.

So that was the last sailing that *Farandole* did, prior to the Second World War. She spent the war in a boathouse at the Ranelagh Club. The boathouse there was a wooden building, crammed from floor to ceiling with wooden boats, stacked three deep, one slung up under the rafters, another below that and a third resting on the floor below the other two, with hardly room to walk between the rows of stacked boats. Anyhow, we took *Farandole* there and slung her up under the ceiling and left her there for four or five years. I never expected to see her again. That was a wooden building absolutely full of wooden boats and if one 4-pound incendiary bomb had gone through the roof the whole lot would have gone up in smoke. At that stage in 1939 the general opinion, held by everybody from the prime minister downwards, was that London would be damaged from one end to the other, very seriously damaged, burnt or shattered. This fortunately didn't happen, although it did happen to the German cities and if London had been in the shape that Hamburg, Berlin, Dresden or Cologne was at the end of the Second World War, *Farandole* and a lot of other things would have gone with it. Anyhow, when we went back after four or five years there she was exactly as we'd left her, sails inside; nothing had been touched at all. The Ranelagh Club had been racing during the war, as some people who lived there hadn't been away.

The first time we visited Ranelagh after the war and after I came back from overseas, was on a Sunday, a day when there was a race laid on. We found *Farandole* where we had left her and lowered her down, took her out on to the towpath, put the mast in and discovered that the wire shrouds had become rather rusty. I had anticipated this and provided myself with a roll of piano wire from a music shop, which was what we used for the shrouds. We proceeded to cut the worst one, the one that was most badly corroded. We cut it out and replaced it with new wire. We no sooner finished doing this when the ten-minute warning signal went for that day's race. I looked at the other shroud and it was rusty, but it didn't look too bad so we decided to go racing with one new shroud and one old rusty one. We put the boat upright, put the sails on and went afloat.

When wooden boats are out of the water for a long time, the moisture content decreases as they dry out. As time goes by, they lose quite a bit of weight in the process which gives them a racing advantage but, of course, it doesn't last very long when they go back in the water again. At any rate, *Farandole*, having been out of the water for four or five years, was light as a feather and went like the wind. We won that first race, and the people who had been racing at Ranelagh throughout the war were a bit disconcerted that we had been away for all that length of time and had

Arthur and son John preparing Farandole for the National 12 ft dingy championship.

come back and on our first ever race had beaten them all. The reason was not only superior skill in sailing, but the fact that *Farandole* was certainly the lightest boat afloat that day. This advantage, of course, didn't last very long and our competitive edge soon settled down to what it had been before the war.

We continued to enjoy racing for the next ten years. During the whole of this time *Farandole* was based at Ranelagh, but we trailed her behind the car to open meetings and races as far apart as Harwich and Falmouth for the Burton Cup and other open meetings. Even when I was stationed at Andover Staff College, during the winter, when there wasn't very much to do, we used to drive up from Andover to Putney in London in

Photo of Mary and Arthur that appeared in the Tatler 1954.

order to have a race in *Farandole*. The roads were quite empty the way we were going because thousands of Londoners driving out to the country on a fine Sunday to enjoy the fresh air, at the time when we were going in to London to enjoy racing in *Farandole*. This went on for most of the time that I was at the Staff College at Andover.

Farandole remained competitive for quite a considerable time. We got a second in the Burton Cup Race in 1948.

N23 in the lead on the Thames at the Ranelagh Yacht Club.

After that, in the early 1950s, the newer designs gained the advantage. The newer Nationals were developing with a much greater breadth of beam, as much as two feet greater. *Farandole* was 4-foot-6-inches in beam and some of the boats by the 1950s were 2-foot more than that, 6-foot-6-inches, a tremendous difference. This gave them a distinct advantage in planing away off the wind, in strong winds. So gradually *Farandole* began to become uncompetitive, at any rate in strong winds. We continued to race her, off and on, until 1955 when I was posted to Pakistan. We sold her at that point and never expected to see her again. In fact we did come face to face with her nineteen years later in 1974. The Secretary of the National 12-foot Class Association wrote to me and asked me to present the prizes at the Burton Cup Week for the National 12s which was being held at Weymouth. So Mary and I went down there for the whole week to see what was going on. By that time the number of starters had increased to something like 170 or 180 and an enormous number of Nationals were lined up on the beach. The first morning we arrived, we walked down the line and came face to face with *Farandole* again. I expressed surprise to the owner that he was racing such an old boat, and he said, 'Of course I don't expect to be anywhere in the first half of the fleet, but I come about 130 out of 170. There are always other old boats to race against and I like doing it.' I said, 'Well if you are not really interested in the points score,' which he obviously wasn't, 'perhaps you would lend it to Mary and me for one of the preliminary races this week.' He said, 'Yes'. So Mary and I went afloat again in *Farandole* round the Burton Cup course, in the same boat in which we had won the Burton Cup thirty-seven years earlier and almost twenty years since we'd last sailed in her. We didn't do much good, of course, but we did finish and when we came down to the gybe mark the wind was strong, some of the youngsters ahead of us were fluffing their gybes and capsizing and I said to Mary, 'We haven't gybed this boat for twenty years, do you think we can do it?' She said, 'Well, we can try.' So we did try and we did it and, of course, we passed the boats which had capsized and whose crews were floundering about in the water and about twenty or thirty others. We finished about 130th out of 170. It was quite a thrill to race the same boat again thirty-seven years after we had won that particular championship in her. So that was the last we saw of her, the end of the *Farandole* story. I don't know what has happened to her since then.

Chapter 14

Biggin Hill, 1936–1937

I was posted to RAF Biggin Hill in 1936. This was my first return to regular flying for some time. I had been off regular flying for eight years, two years at the engineering course at Henlow, two years at Cambridge University, one year at Imperial College, London University, and three years doing a ground engineering job in Singapore. So, I suppose I was a bit out of practice, but anyway I was the flight commander of one of the flights there and it was an interesting re-introduction to regular squadron flying.

When I arrived at Biggin Hill we had Bristol Bulldogs, the latest single-seater fighters to be introduced to the RAF. Soon after I started at Biggin Hill, No. 32 Squadron was re-equipped with Gloster Gauntlets. These

Biggin Hill, 1937. The 'Hucks Starter' used by the RAF for starting piston-engined aircraft in the 1920s and 1930s. Built on a Model T Ford chassis, a chain driven from the gearbox power take-off rotates a telescopic shaft which fits into a 'claw' clutch at the front end of the propeller boss. Arthur is seated facing the camera.

were the last open-cockpit biplane fighters used in the RAF. This meant that the general concept of single-seater fighters had not changed at all since quite an early stage in the First World War. That is to say they were all biplanes, with fixed undercarriages, no wing flaps, no wheel brakes, open cockpits and two Omdurman-type machine guns in the cockpit. I call them Omdurman-type guns because they were virtually the same as those used by the infantry in the battle of Omdurman in 1898. The pilot had to fire through the blades of the propeller with an interrupter gear to prevent the rounds from hitting the propeller.

Only one biplane fighter was produced after the Gauntlet. That was the Gloster Gladiator which did not vary very much from the Gauntlet but did have a closed cockpit. It had two machine guns in the wings, so that they could operate without interrupter gear. I only flew a Gladiator once or twice, so I am not quite sure, but I think it is highly probable that the guns in the wings were Browning machine guns, an American design which succeeded the Omdurman-type Vickers/Maxim guns which had been used by the RAF ever since the middle of the First World War.[1]

I commanded A Flight at Biggin Hill. In 1936 my flight was chosen for what became known as the Biggin Hill Experiment. – to find out whether ground controllers could direct RAF fighters by radio to intercept enemy aircraft. I can only think that Biggin Hill was chosen because we had obtained much better than usual results from our radio communications and the whole system, which the experiment was designed to produce, depended on good radio communication. At Biggin Hill for the first time in my flying career we had radios in our planes. This made a tremendous difference to the way in which fighters were operated in a defensive role, but the original radio set was not a terribly efficient one. It had a single channel and the pilot had to tune the receiver to get the tuning right and to get good reception from the ground transmitters. The frequency seemed to drift at times and not everybody was very good at this.

However the squadron commander of 32 Squadron when I arrived, a man by the name of Richardson, had made a determined drive to

---

1. Initially the Gladiator had two Vickers MGs in the fuselage sides and two Lewis guns, one under each wing. Later Gladiators had four Browning .303-inch MGs, two in the fuselage and two mounted under-wing.

produce the best possible results from this radio set, known as the TR9. He'd instituted a scheme by which if any pilot called base and didn't get a response, or the other way round, if base called the pilot and didn't get a response from him, the failure had to be logged in the radio section, investigated and the cause determined. This put everybody on their toes and Richardson was very strict about it.

One day, when he was flying himself, he called base and couldn't get an answer. When he landed and could get through at a shorter range, he stopped his aeroplane in the middle of the aerodrome with the engine running and called out on the radio to the radio section, 'I want to speak Flight Sergeant So and So [the man in charge of the maintenance of the radio sets] in my cockpit here on the aerodrome, and at the double!' So the fat old flight sergeant had to waddle across the aerodrome as fast as he could, and jump up on the side of the Bulldog, with its engine still running. As he did so, Richardson gave a burst of throttle and blew the flight sergeant's cap off, and gave him a tremendous raspberry for his failure. Anything like that, of course, made people quite keen. The result of this was that 32 Squadron had the reputation of getting much better reception from their radio sets than any other squadron in Fighter Command. In fact our effective range was about double what it was in the other squadrons, I think.

According to the book, the effective range for a TR9 was fifteen miles from base, but we got to the stage where we could test a new aircraft by flying it to a place fifty miles away, at low altitude, which reduced the range anyway, and call from there. If we didn't get through from there that would be regarded as a failure.

Before I write about this experiment in ground-controlled aircraft interception in more detail let me tell you why it was needed. In the mid-1930s the British government became increasingly worried about the prospect of German air raids on London, in the event of war with Germany. In the First World War, German day raids on London had been intercepted and it had been proved that it was possible to intercept them given the right ground organisation, but the introduction of German monoplane bombers in the 1930s had made the interception problem much more difficult – so difficult, in fact, that it was regarded as being insoluble. Standing patrols were out of the question as the number of aircraft and pilots required could never have been made available. Hence Stanley Baldwin's statement that 'the bomber will always get through'.

The reason why the interception problem had become more difficult was that the German monoplane bombers were about three times as fast as the biplanes used in the First World War. This meant that the time which elapsed between when a raid was detected and it reaching its target was reduced by about two-thirds. Unfortunately, on the other side of the equation, one factor had remained practically unchanged: the time taken by pilots and aircraft kept at readiness on the ground to take off, after the alarm had been given. This reaction time was about five minutes in the First World War, but still about five minutes in the 1930s, and, as far as I know, it is about five minutes today. In the First World War this reaction time represented only about 8 per cent of the time interval between raid detection and bomb release. With the new monoplane bombers, this reaction time would represent over 30 per cent of the time between detection and bomb release, assuming the same range of detection outside of the coast. Also, although Second World War fighters would be three times as fast as the First World War fighters in level flight, their rate of climb would not be three times as great. It had thus become apparent by the mid-1930s that unless the range at which raids could be detected could be increased over the range which was possible with sound locators and visual observation, then interception by aircraft kept at readiness on the ground would be impossible.

To tackle this problem, the Committee for Scientific Survey of Air Defence was formed in 1935 with Professor Sir Henry Tizard as its chairman. During 1935, an experiment at Daventry persuaded Tizard that radar, as it subsequently became known, was possible (and further work at Bawdsey achieved a range of seventy to eighty miles beyond the coast). Tizard realised that radar by itself, so far as the defence of Britain was concerned, was a solution to only half of the problem, and that radar could only be exploited to the full if some completely new technique of interception were devised, and it would, Tizard knew, be unrealistic to hope that this could happen amid the confusions of war. A peacetime experiment was therefore necessary.

Tizard proposed a series of experiments to discover two things:

1) The percentage of occasions on which fighter interceptions could be expected by day, if the position of the raiding aircraft could be known at regular intervals with increasing accuracy, as it approached the coast.
2) How close to a bomber, whose position and track had been found from the ground, it was possible to direct the fighter by use of radio instructions from the ground.

To many senior officers the proposals were novel, if not revolutionary. To others they seemed a waste of time. In spite of the somewhat casual reception of the idea, Tizard succeeded in convincing the authorities that experiments should be carried out. It was agreed that they should start on 4 August 1936, and last for two months. A flight of Gloster Gauntlets of No. 32 Squadron was to be used for interception while three Hawker Hinds were to simulate the raiding bombers.

A team was assembled at Biggin Hill to carry out the trials, consisting of Dr B. G. Dickens, a scientific officer from Farnborough; Squadron Leader R.L. Ragg, an experienced navigation specialist and former experimental pilot, also from Farnborough; Flight Lieutenant W.B.G. Pretty, the stations signals officer; Wing Commander E.O. Grenfell, the station commander, and me.

We seem to have been on to this very quickly because I believe the first of the Biggin Hill experiments took place on 5 August 1936 and my log book shows that I made the first 'Wind finding' flight on the 29th, only three weeks later.

The basic method was as follows: target plots were placed on the operations-room map as soon as received, and the order to take off was then given to the fighters. Assuming a standard reaction time of five minutes between order to go and take-off, this gave controllers five minutes to do two things. Firstly, to work out course and speed of the target from the plots, as they appeared on the table, and secondly to work out the course to intercept for the fighters which would lead to an interception without further correction.

This proved to be very difficult in practice. If three minutes were allowed for working out the course and speed of the target, that would only leave two minutes to work out the course to intercept, but the course and speed of the target might not be very accurate. If four minutes were allowed to work out the course and speed of the target, these would be more accurate, but only one minute would be left to work out the course to intercept.

For several weeks attempts were made to find the best compromise. All kinds of strange instruments were devised to speed up the computation and the RAE at Farnborough even put in hand a computer to help with the job. Then one day, E.O. Grenfell, the station commander, after watching all this feverish activity in the operations room, suddenly announced that he thought he would make a better job of it by eye. He was given the chance to do so and immediately proved the point. He brought off a perfect interception, judging the fighter course by eye and altering course as necessary, to bring about an interception.

All the instruments were then thrown away, and from then on during the rest of the Biggin Hill experiments, and right through the Battle of Britain, this was the method used to give interception courses to the fighters. It had the advantage that if the target altered course, alteration of the fighters' course to intercept could be made instantly.[2]

It now seems incredible that it took so long for anyone to realise that judging the interception by eye was the solution to the problem, but then hindsight is always easier than foresight.

I would suggest that it was Grenfell's experience as a yacht racing helmsman which led him to the conclusion that he could judge interception angles by eye with sufficient accuracy and much more quickly than they could be worked out with instruments. As he sat on the dais watching the bomber and fighter tracks converging on each other, he must have been reminded of the thousands of times when he had been in an interception situation when yacht racing.

When boats in a race are beating to windward, boats on opposite tacks will converge and cross each other's tracks many times in each race. Whenever boats are converging, the helmsman of the boat on port tack is required by rule to keep clear of all boats on starboard and must decide, at as early a stage as possible, whether he is heading for a perfect interception,

---

2. To do this they used the 'Principle of Equal Angles', a line was drawn from the bombers to the fighters, making this the base of an isosceles triangle, the two formations would meet at the apex of the triangle. Colloquially known as the 'Tizzy Angle' after Tizzard.

i.e. a collision, with a converging boat or whether he will cross clear ahead or astern. In the small open-cockpit boats, which Grenfell had raced for many years, the use of charts and instruments to measure converging angles was not practicable and the angles had to be judged by eye. At any rate, Grenfell's intervention solved a problem which had been worrying Ragg, the navigation specialist, and Dr Dickens, the scientist, for weeks.

During the whole of the experiment, experience showed that what really mattered was the speed and accuracy with which target and fighter plots could be put on the table. Provided that plots could be tabled quickly and accurately, interception courses for fighters could be judged by eye and subsequently altered as necessary to bring about an almost prefect interception. When interceptions failed, it was almost invariably due to plots being late or inaccurate.

But the plots of the target (Hind day bombers) could be provided by the crews of the Hinds themselves and reported by radio. A crew member in the bomb aimer's position, looking down through the bombsight, could not only determine the aircraft's position with great accuracy, but could also work out, using the bombsight, the aircraft's ground speed and track, which might be different from its heading. With this information the navigator could maintain a minute-to-minute plot of the aircraft's position, relying on DR (dead reckoning) when the ground was obscured by cloud. So, from the beginning of the experiment, there was no difficulty in obtaining accurate plots of the target.

The main problem that had to be overcome was to obtain accurate plots of the fighters' positions. The methods used for the Hinds could not be used for the Gauntlets, for two reasons:

1. A single-seat fighter pilot cannot see the ground immediately below him, particularly on the climb.
2. The fighters had no chart tables on which a DR plot could be made.

For both reasons it was impossible for the fighter pilots to plot their own positions.

This left only two alternatives for providing fighter plots, either HF/DF (High Frequency/Direction Finding)[3] radio fixes, obtained from the fighter's radio transmissions, or dead reckoning plots, from take-off to

---
3. HF/DF was also known as 'Huff-duff'.

interception. Radar plots for the fighters were out of the question, as the first generation of coastal radars were not designed to plot inside of the coastline.

Although HF direction finders had been used in Fighter Command before 1936 they were found to be too slow and inaccurate to meet the needs of a ground-controlled interception system. The HF/DF System, which was developed at Biggin Hill during the first part of the trials, was the first which could produce plots with sufficient speed and accuracy for use in plotting interception tracks. The HF/DF system also included a timing device which could be fitted in each of four formation leaders' aircraft. Each of these transmitted automatically in sequence, for fourteen seconds in each minute so that four separate formations could be plotted simultaneously. This combination of fast fixers and automatic timers became known as 'Pip Squeak'[4] and was used after May 1937 during the Biggin Hill Experiment and subsequently during the Battle of Britain, because no radar plotting was available, inside of the coastline, until after 1940.

It took Flight Lieutenant Pretty and his team of signallers seven or eight months of hard and dedicated work to develop the Pip-Squeak system. In the meantime, the rest of the Biggin Hill Experiment team had to produce results, i.e. a fairly high percentage of successful interceptions. Tizard had been promised the use of 32 Squadron for interception trials for only two months. If, at the end of that time, the team had not been achieving a reasonably high percentage of successful ground-controlled interceptions it is highly probable that the whole of the Biggin Hill Experiment would have been terminated, including the work on Pip Squeak. The team, therefore, had to resort to dead reckoning to provide plots for the fighters for the first seven or eight months of the trials until radar plots were available.

The DR calculations had to be done on the ground, by the plotters in the Operations Room and, in order that the plots produced in the Operations Room should accurately represent the fighters' position in the air, several problems had to be overcome.

---

4. Pip-squeak, named after a contemporary comic strip character, emitted a 1 kHz radio single from fighter planes at regular intervals. This was used by 3 ground stations to triangulate the aircraft's position.

The formation leader had to learn new techniques in flying. He had to learn to concentrate his attention continuously on two cockpit instruments: the air speed indicator and the compass, instead of continuously scanning the sky for other aircraft, as is the normal practice in fighter operations.

The plotters had to make allowance for the fact that, although the fighters would be climbed at the fixed indicated air speed required to maintain optimum rate of climb, the true air speed would increase with altitude, since the reading of the ASI, (Air Speed Indicator) only represents true air speed at sea level. Furthermore, in order to correct the air speed for altitude the plotter had to know the expected altitude of the aircraft during each minute of the climb. This information he could obtain from a graph on which true air speed was plotted on one axis against time from take-off on the other. This graph had to be constructed from the results of climbing tests with Gauntlets at Biggin Hill and, even after this procedure had been worked out, it took time for the plotters to learn how to carry it out quickly and accurately. Even then the team was only halfway towards achieving the ability to put accurate plots of the fighters on the operations room table.

The second piece of unusual equipment around was a sound locator. This was used when low cloud prevented the smoke puff being seen by the camera obscura operator. The procedure was for the pilot to fly over the sound locator at the prescribed height. The sound-locator operator would track the aircraft. The pilot would then fire a smoke puff and call on his radio 'Firing smoke puff now!' On hearing the sound the sound-locator operator would make an X on the fighter's track and start a stopwatch. The fighter would then fly an ellipse and approach the smoke puff from the same direction as before and call out 'Passing under smoke puff now!' The sound-locator operator would them make another X on the fighter's latest track and stop the stopwatch. The line adjoining the two crosses would indicate wind direction and the distance between them divided by the time interval would give the wind speed! The sound-locator method of wind finding was less accurate than the camera obscura method but had to be used when low cloud blanketed the camera obscura.

The DR methods of plotting the fighters used in the Biggin Hill Experiment were replaced by HF/DF plotting, otherwise known as Pip Squeak, in spring 1937.

142   Helping Stop Hitler's Luftwaffe

Almost every reference to the Biggin Hill Experiment contains the statement that the first interception of a non-co-operating target plotted by radar, i.e. a civil airliner, was made of a formation of aircraft from 32 Squadron, but there is complete confusion as to when the first radar-controlled interception took place and what aircraft were used. One report gives three Hurricanes of 32 Squadron in 1938 and another gives three Gauntlets, serial numbers K7797, K7799 and K7800.

Both these reports must be wrong.

I led the formation which made, I believe, the first successful interception of a non-co-operating target. It was of a KLM airliner, flying above cloud at 6,000 feet over the Thames estuary on its way to Croydon. The aircraft we flew were Gauntlets and the serial numbers were K5320, K5319, etc. The date was certainly in 1937 and, as my flying log book shows, I am almost certain that the actual date was 14 June. An interception by three Hurricanes of a civil airliner may have been made in

Extract from Arthur's flying logbook detailing the probable date of the first ground controlled interception of a non-co-operating target, a Dutch Airliner, underlined by Arthur. It is only labelled 'Interception above clouds' in the logbook because of the top secrecy surrounding the experiment.

Gloster Gauntlet Mk II, K5317 of No. 46 Squadron in 1936. This is just 2 serial numbers away from the actual Gauntlet which Arthur flew during the interception. (K5319) (*Photo courtesy of 'www.RAF-in-Combat.com'*)

1938 but, if so, it was not the first. Gauntlets with serial numbers starting 77 could not have been used as these aircraft were never in 32 Squadron. They were in 79 Squadron.

I think that the confusion over the circumstances of the first radar-controlled interception arise from the fact that this interception was arranged on the phone on the spur of the moment, entirely unofficially, by Wing Commander Raymond Hart, who was attached to Bawdsey, and me. I don't think that anyone at 11 Group in Fighter Command knew anything about it and there may not have been any written record of it anywhere, at the time.

But in June 1937 I was on my way to the flights one morning when I looked in at the Operations Room at Biggin Hill. I was called to the telephone. It was a call from a friend of mine, Wing Commander Raymond Hart who had been attached to the Experimental Station at Bawdsey as a liaison officer. He told me that the device they were working on was functioning and they were picking up Dutch airliners flying from Amsterdam into Croydon which was then the airport for London. Would I like to have a go for real? I said, 'Of course, I will be at readiness in about ten minutes.' He said, 'Right then, the first one we pick up after that time I will pass the position plots through to Biggin Hill Operations Room on this tie line which can be scrambled so as to make it secure against eavesdropping – and you can have a go for real.' I went to readiness and about fifteen minutes later the buzzer went and we went through the normal procedure.

The weather was perfect for such a trial because there was ten-tenths cloud from about 2,000 to 4,000 feet so that we lost sight of the ground about two minutes after take-off and from then until just before landing we never sighted the ground again. The system worked perfectly: we were given various alterations of course. When we broke out into the clear it was brilliantly clear and bright above the clouds. We were told to go to 6,000 feet and, after some time, I received the message, 'Target dead ahead on reciprocal course, five miles.' I looked up and there it was, a monoplane, a Dutch DC-3 flying on a reciprocal course to ours and due to pass about half a mile north of our course and about 500 feet below. We were in a perfect position to do a turn into a dummy attack, but in view of the fact that the whole development had been given a very high security grading, I thought it better to carry straight on so that any German passengers in the aircraft would not come to the conclusion that we had worked out a way of intercepting aircraft approaching Britain above cloud. We therefore went straight past so that occupants of the Dutch airliner would conclude that this was a purely chance encounter between their aircraft.

This interception was very accurate, and I have always assumed that this was because at the point where the interception took place the target was flying west and was almost due south of Bawdsey. As Chain Home (CH) stations gave accurate range, even if bearings were unreliable, the 'latitude' of the target would have been accurate even if the 'longitude' was much in error. Therefore, all that the Biggin Hill controller had to do was to put us in the same latitude, flying from west to east, and there was bound to be an interception sooner or later. There was and it was a very good one. This accuracy was only possible because the target was flying beam on to the Bawdsey station at the time of interception because the early radars only provided the range of target accurately, direction was not accurate. Therefore accurate position plots could only be obtained when two or more stations were plotting the same target. The range obtained was read into a 'filter room' where range information from two or more stations was translated into accurate position plots, which were then passed on to the fighter operations room.

This was the only attempt to intercept an airliner which I remember being made during my time at Biggin Hill. I left in January 1938.

For the first seven or eight months of the interception trials at Biggin Hill, a dead reckoning method of producing the fighter plots had to be used and, before such a system could be used, one had to be invented, or devised, because no method of plotting fighters on the climb by dead reckoning had previously been used in Fighter Command, or ever was used anywhere except at Biggin Hill. It was because the development of an accurate method of plotting fighters on the climb by dead reckoning took so much time that trials planned to take two months actually lasted for over a year.

The dead reckoning method of plotting fighters could never have been used in wartime conditions, but the effort devoted to its development was well worthwhile because it enabled Tizard to convince sceptics in the Air Ministry that ground-controlled interceptions were possible many months before he would otherwise have been able to do so.

It was also worthwhile because it enabled operation room procedures for controlling interceptions, as described in paragraphs above, to be developed and put in place by the time the first HF/DF equipment for fixing fighters became available. It also enabled plans to be made in advance for the HF/DF fixing equipment to be installed throughout Fighter Command as quickly as possible in the certain knowledge that, as soon as this equipment was available, ground control-interception would be the norm throughout the command.

When AV said the system was ready by Good Friday 1939, he presumably meant that a chain of coastal stations, filter rooms and fighter operation rooms were all linked up, ready to go. But this system had its limitations; it did not plot inside the coastline. It did not plot our own fighters. That is what the Biggin Hill Experiment had been all about. We had developed a system for providing position plots for our own fighters which did not depend on radar, and which was quicker and more accurate than the radar station/filter room combination. It was only much later that we had radar stations which provided cover inside the coastline and which provided accurate position plots of both fighter and bomber targets on the same cathode ray tube instantaneously.

All of the accounts of the Biggin Hill Experiment published so far leave unanswered two important questions:

1. How would Fighter Command's fighter-control system have developed between 1936 and 1939 or 1940 if the Biggin Hill Experiment had never taken place? or
2. Worse still, if it had started, as planned, in August 1936 and had failed to produce results by the time it was planned to terminate after two or three months, would CH stations and the HF/DF fixing stations in each Fighter Command sector have been ordered, built and put into operation by 1939 or 1940?

Many of those who have written with hindsight after the war about the development of our fighter defences during the period 1936–1939 seem to have jumped to the conclusion that once radar had been invented the problem of defending London against daylight raids by unescorted German bombers from bases in Germany was solved. This was definitely not the generally held opinion at the time, as the following remarks by Lord Swinton, the Secretary of State for Air at the time, illustrate.

Lord Swinton visited Biggin Hill a few weeks after the trial started, to find out what progress had been made. While there he made the following remark to the leader of the fighter formation involved in the trials – me: 'I hope you young men realise that the whole future of this country depends on the results of what you are doing here at Biggin Hill.' This was a clear indication that, at the time, neither the Secretary of State for Air or anyone else in authority regarded the problem of intercepting daylight raids on London as having been solved; until results at Biggin Hill demonstrated that a very high percentage of daylight raids could be intercepted before they reached their target, and that night raids could also be intercepted, as soon as airborne radar, with a range of four–five miles, became available.

Winston Churchill, out of office at the time, visited the project. He drove up from Chartwell and spent half an hour in the operations room watching a trial interception with interest. Dowding also drove down from Bentley Priory to see the experiment in action. At the time of his visit we were using basic English instructions to the pilots. He was the one who suggested we adopt codewords to make our interactions clearly, shorter and more secure.

The day after Dowding's visit, as there was no flying due to bad weather, I asked one of the flight commanders to get a group of pilots together to devise a code. The result of this was words such as, 'scramble' which have now found their way into the English language.

Without the Biggin Hill Experiment there would have been no Pip Squeak and without Pip Squeak and the Biggin Hill Experiment there would have been no effective system of ground-controlled interception in 1940. Adolph Galland, the German fighter leader, would not have had to write in his memoirs:

> From the very beginning the British had an extraordinary advantage which we could never overcome through the whole war: radar and fighter control … the British fighter was guided all the way from take-off to his correct position for attack on the German formations.[5]

Neither would Ronald Clark, Tizard's biographer, have been able to claim that the Biggin Hill Experiment had been 'The greatest achievement of Tizard's life' (p. 149) or 'Thus there grew up, between the summer of 1936 and that of 1937 the basic techniques of operational control without which the Battle of Britain would not have been won and could hardly have been fought.' (p. 155).

---

5. Quoted in *Britain Alone*, by Herbert Agar, p.124.

Chapter 15

Andover Staff College and The Dowding Experiment, 1938

At the beginning of 1938, I was posted to The Royal Air Force Staff College at Andover as a pupil for a twelve-month course. I wasn't particularly looking forward to it but, from a career point of view, it was something which couldn't be missed: it was an offer I couldn't possibly refuse. So off I went. In fact, in my farewell speech at Biggin Hill I was rude enough about Andover to say that I was rather regretting having to leave the fresh air of Biggin Hill for the hot air of Andover. That was a slur on Andover which I afterwards very much regretted, because when I got there I found that the Staff College was intensely interesting and useful. I wouldn't have missed it for the world.

1938 Andover Staff College, annotated by Arthur, 2nd from back row, far left.

To start with, the course took a form which was totally unexpected, by me at any rate. I had thought that we would spend all our time discussing air tactics and strategy and new aircraft and weapons that were being developed or had been developed in recent years. On the contrary, for the first three weeks of the course the directing staff gave us a crash course on the use of English, our own language. Considering that we, the pupils, were educated young men in our late twenties and early thirties, I found this very surprising; on the other hand, when it came to the point, it became obvious that things that we thought we should have learnt at school we'd either never learned properly at all or we had forgotten them. It was demonstrated to us that we could improve our skills in communicating in speech or writing when dealing with complex subjects.

The next phase of the course dealt with methods of solving complex problems by going through a methodical and logical series of steps, which at Andover we called 'The Appreciation of the Situation', or methodical thinking. Here again we imagined that this was the sort of thing that every educated person automatically does. Study of the history books showed that this is not the case: the majority of human beings tend to jump to conclusions, to trust their intuition, and to miss out some of the steps which are necessary to get the right answer. An important example of this is what happened at the beginning of the last war: Hitler not only trusted his intuition on very important matters, but he boasted of it. He said his intuition was always right. He and Göring between them so messed up the things from the German point of view, that when they had entire British Expeditionary Force at their mercy at Dunkirk, they let them go.

Göring jumped to the conclusion that his air force could prevent the British army from being evacuated. He wanted his air force to have the credit for that and he managed to persuade Hitler of this. Hitler disregarded the advice of his generals and held his troops back. Had he not done so the British army would have been completely destroyed at Dunkirk and goodness knows what would have happened during the rest of the war. Could we have carried on? The history of Western Europe for the last fifty years might have been very different. So it was very fortunate that neither Hitler nor Göring had ever been to a staff college, at any rate not one that operated like the one at Andover.

Later in the course we received a number of lectures from outside lecturers, the air staff at the Air Ministry, and technical experts from various places on tactics and strategy, which is what we had expected the whole course to be about. It was very interesting that we were given a lot of theories about this. This was in 1938 and, within two years, the theories which we were given at the Staff College were put to the test. We were involved in a very desperate war. When they were put to the test it was found that every single one of them was completely wrong.

I don't want to go into a lot of detail in this account, but, basically, what we were told about any future war with Germany was that it would be won by strategic bombing: it would be won in the air. The army operations would hardly come into it at all. There would be no repetition of trench warfare as there had been in the First World War. The French line of fortification, the Maginot Line, would keep the Germans out of France. We wouldn't have to send an army to France. Everything would depend on the bomber campaign. For that reason, it was important for the British to build up a stronger bomber force than the Germans. They would operate in daylight and bomb precisely with sophisticated modern equipment, like gyro bombsights from high altitude. They would defend themselves by rear guns in hydraulic turrets: the British air force were the only ones going in for hydraulic turrets. It was supposed that they would have the same effect on effective gunnery as they had had at sea. When the navy changed over from fixed guns, which only fired sideways out of their battleships, the *Victory* and all that lot, and went into turret-mounted guns on the deck, the efficiency and range increased enormously. It was assumed that the same thing would happen in the air. This was all very theoretical. We were told that the new monoplane fighters, the Spitfire and the Hurricane, which were coming along, would go too fast to be used for dive-bombing; they wouldn't be able to pull out of the dive, so they wouldn't be fitted with bomb racks and all bombing would be done from high altitude.

One of the pupils, a well-known character by the name of Harry Broadhurst who made a tremendous name for himself later on in the Second World War, stood up in a discussion and challenged this assumption. He said, 'I don't believe it, you give a fighter squadron, any fighter squadron that I know about, give them Hurricanes and put bomb racks on them. You'll find that they can dive-bomb from the air and hit the targets and get away with it.' Experience later on showed that he was right. Later the US Navy and Marine Corps found them very effective in the Pacific campaign.

Another example was that we never mentioned photo reconnaissance at all in the whole of the Staff Course. It was known that in the First World War photo reconnaissance had been used, but it had been under the control of the army commanders. Each army commander had a certain number of squadrons which he used for tactical reconnaissance on his own front, on the front-line positions of the enemy and so on. All the fighting over the Western Front was devoted to ensuring that our reconnaissance could get through and the German reconnaissance aircraft couldn't; very bitter fighting it was, too. But as there wasn't going to be any trench warfare there wasn't going to be any of that. The idea that it might be possible to carry out strategic reconnaissance over the whole of enemy territory from the air was never mentioned at all at Andover.

In fact, by the end of the war, the British had a very effective system of obtaining strategic photo-reconnaissance from every part of enemy-occupied territory in Europe. We were the only country that did it. Even the Americans, when they came in, had to be shown the way and all this was no part of pre-war planning and never mentioned at Andover (see Chapter 20).

One of the most interesting events which occurred at the 1938 staff course when I was a pupil at Andover was that we pupils were taken to witness the closing stages of a piece of operational research, known at the time as the Dowding Experiment. This took place on Salisbury Plain and we went to witness the last part of it. I have described how many of the theories put forward and discussed in the 1938 staff course, when put to the test in war two years later, proved to be wrong, and how one student, Harry Broadhurst, challenged one of them and said he didn't believe what we had been told about using single-seat dive-bombers, and how events proved that the pupil was right and the lecturer on the platform wrong. There was another individual who doubted some of these theories which were flying about all over the place. He was Air Chief Marshal Sir Hugh Dowding, Commander in Chief of Fighter Command.

Dowding was always a non-conformist, and a lot of the controversy about how he was treated at the time of the Battle of Britain arises from that fact. He did not go along with some of the other big chiefs in the air force on some of the theories they were putting forward. One thing which he challenged was the assumption that the best way of defending our cities, and London in particular, from destruction by the German bomber force, was to build up a more powerful bomber force than the Germans had, and to attack their bombers on the ground before they started – in other words the theory that 'offence is the best defence'. This was the continuation of Douhet's theory that a future war would be decided by strategic bombing and nothing else. Dowding pointed out that a lot of these other theories cannot be tested in peacetime because you can't fire live ammunition at aircraft containing live people. He said, 'There is one of these theories which you can test. I suggest that it should be tested.' Well, to start with, he didn't get much response from this but he made a nuisance of himself for a whole year until the Air Staff gave him his way and he was allowed to do what he wanted.

What he wanted to do was to lay out eighteen aircraft on a dummy airfield on Salisbury Plain. He pointed out that in war, of course, you should not keep your aircraft closely packed together in hangars, which would probably be the targets of enemy bombers and might be set on fire, but you would disperse them around the airfield. If you had time you might make blast-proof pens for them, big banks of earth all round in a U-shape with the aeroplane in the middle. This would stop splinters from bombs dropped near the aircraft from hitting them. If you hadn't got time to do that, if you spread them well out around the perimeter the chance of individual aircraft being hit would be quite small. Well, nobody believed this. At any rate, he was eventually given eighteen obsolete aircraft. Those were laid out on a dummy airfield on Salisbury Plain and Bomber Command, a bomber force which we were developing at that time, was given two days to destroy them. The weather was fine, beautiful; there was, of course, no defence of any kind, nothing to distract the bomb-aimers, no anti-aircraft guns or anything of that kind. So, it was assumed that the destruction of these aircraft wouldn't take very long. We went there from Andover on the afternoon of the second day. The weather had been excellent the whole time. Most of the aircraft were still serviceable; we couldn't believe it. The bombers had done what they had always planned to do: they bombed from altitude from a giro-stabilised bombsight. With big bombs and little bombs, and every kind of bomb, but they hadn't hit the aircraft. They had made a lot of holes in the area, but the aircraft were still there.

When we arrived on the second day, they were trying 4lb incendiary bombs. The bomber formation took thousands, or tens of thousands of these things up; they were made of aluminium. Watching from the sidelines it looked like a shower of rain coming down. We thought, 'Well, this is absolutely bound to do it, because if one of these things hits an aeroplane it will set it on fire.' But it didn't happen. The grass in the area had not been mowed as there was no flying to be done, and it was a dry summer. The incendiary bombs set the grass off. It burned. For obvious reasons, there was no groundcrew near the aircraft, so that by the time anybody got down there to deal with the fires some of the fire from burning grass had crept along and burnt one or two of the aeroplanes, but not many. Some of them were still serviceable.

This was the most astonishing result of all this. At the end of two days the bomber force that we were developing could not destroy aircraft dispersed around an airfield. In other words, to rely on our bomber force to destroy German bombers before they started was an absolutely hopeless way of looking at it. This had all happened without any enemy opposition at all, no enemy anti-aircraft gunfire to distract our bombers and no defending fighters to shoot them down. Nevertheless, they had not been able to do it.

As a result of this trial a report must have been written, of course. A report must have gone to the Air Ministry, but the result was so unwelcome to all the other big chiefs that that report has never been published. It was pushed under the carpet in 1938 and has remained there ever since. I have never seen a written report of it. I have never met a retired officer who had ever heard of the Dowding Experiment. In a long symposium at the RAF Staff College, in 1993 I think it was, it was never mentioned. It did have one effect which is recorded and which must have been one of the decisive factors in the winning of the Battle of Britain. From about 1922 onwards, because of this theory that superiority in bombers is what mattered, bomber production was given higher priority than fighter production in this country. The aim, I think, was two bombers to each fighter. That was what we were told during the first half of the 1938 Staff Course. In the last few weeks or months the emphasis seemed to have changed. There was no more talk of priority to bombers. There was talk of building up fighter production. It is on record that, in the autumn of 1938, priority was given to fighter production rather than bomber production. This was the only thing that gave Dowding enough fighters to win the Battle of Britain two years later. It was a very near run thing as it was, and if this policy decision had not been made almost certainly we would have lost the Battle of Britain, and lost the war. So, it was a very important event. But it was so unwelcome to the theorists who had worked out all these theories that it was never published. It was a most extraordinary thing.

The fact that during the Battle of Britain, German attacks on British airfields did destroy a considerable number of RAF aircraft on the ground might seem to disprove what I have just said. The fact is that the German tactics for attacking airfields were entirely different from the tactics which Bomber Command used, and which they had been trained to use, and were much more effective. The Germans used dive-bombers at low altitude. This was one of things we had been told that modern monoplane fighters couldn't do. Later in the war, Allied fighter-bombers had a decisive effect in Normandy and Africa and other places. In 1938 and 1940 our bomber crews were not trained to do that; they were trained to fly in close formation at high altitude, to use a gyro bombsight, relying on their rear guns to protect them. The result of all this was that the results achieved were entirely different to the results achieved by the Luftwaffe when they attacked Allied and British aircraft on the ground in the early stages of the Second World War.

At the end of 1938 I was posted from the Staff Course to a technical job in the Air Ministry, but before leaving the 1938 Staff Course at Andover it is perhaps worth recording a rather dramatic and unusual incident which occurred quite early on in the course. It concerned an individual whom I have mentioned before in this narrative. In the previous occasion I described him as Alan, and I described the earlier incident when I was describing an engineering course at Henlow in 1927, which was eleven years before the Andover course. I described how Alan and I did a flight to

Brooklands Flying Club to practise our flying. On that occasion, he was in charge of an aeroplane which savagely attacked a parked car and did a lot of damage to it, frightening two old ladies in the back seat almost to death. He wasn't in the aeroplane at the time, but had started the engine and got out and left the engine running. Anyhow, we met this same Alan again at Andover: he was one of the students who arrived there for the 1938 course. Soon after the course started he invited some of us to a housewarming party. 'Housewarming': that's what he called it, but it got a bit too hot to handle.

He had rented, for the duration of the course, a delightful very old thatch-roofed cottage in the village of Abbots Ann, not far from Andover. When we arrived he said, 'I've got a treat for you people. We're going to have one or two drinks and then there is a competition. There is a prize for the competition, whoever wins the prize there it is,' and he pointed to something, I don't know what it was; I can't remember, a bottle of Champagne or something of that kind. Then he went on to describe the competition. He had been to Brocks, the people who make fireworks, and had bought a model fire balloon. This was an object of about six feet in diameter made of thin paper with a little wire opening at the bottom, and little wire frame. You put a pad of cotton wool soaked in methylated spirits at the bottom, lit it and the heat from the burning methylated spirits went up into the balloon. As the warm air filled the balloon it would develop lift and when it had done so you let it go. The duration of the flight could be regulated by the amount of methylated spirits used and the size of the pad of cotton wool. The more there was the longer it stayed in the air. Alan had done some experiments on this and had worked out a combination which would cause the balloon to fly for about twenty minutes. The idea was, we would go out into the garden, launch this fire balloon and then track it with motor cars wherever the wind took it and, when it eventually landed after twenty minutes, the first individual who reached it would win the prize. It might, of course, finish up anywhere – somebody's garden, a farmer's field, the top of a tree, in a wood or whatever. If it was in a tree it was agreed in the rules of the competition that the individual who reached the tree first and touched the tree in which the balloon was stuck would be the winner. Every detail was worked out, all the rules. So we had one or two drinks and went out into the garden and went through the procedure of putting the methylated spirits on the cotton wool and the balloon duly developed lift and was released and took off. Unfortunately, the wind was upwind of the house. So, when it got above the level of the surrounding trees, the wind carried it away across the top of the cottage; the bottom of the balloon touched the chimney and that shook off one, just one, drop of methylated spirits which fell on the thatch. One strand of the thatch, about the size of a little fingernail, caught fire, a little tiny flame. We all thought that was an immensely amusing thing to have happened. And all we had to do, we thought, was to get a ladder and go up and just pat this little flame out with the flat of the hand, make sure it was out and then we could go after the balloon – very simple. There was a ladder there, so somebody went up and did this and the flame went out. He started to come down the ladder but, when he got about six feet down, he looked back and there was a little, rather unpleasant wisp of smoke coming out from the inside the thatch. He hurriedly went back up the ladder and put his hand in and opened up the thatch to see what was going on inside. There was a whoosh as the air got in and the thatch was alight inside, on the underside, out of sight. He thought water was required and gave a shout for water. 'Water! Water! Water!' The wives in the party, including Mary, went down to provide water in buckets. The cottage was a very old one, the plumbing was all very primitive and the only water supply was a well in the kitchen and you got the water up from this well with a semi-rotary hand-pump; you pumped it up into a bucket and then distributed from there around the house. So this was done and a bucket of water was sent up the ladder and poured on the thatch. There was a lot of sizzling and steam and so on. Then everything seemed to be alright, but when somebody just put their hands in and opened the thatch again, as soon as the air got in came another whoosh. It was obvious that the water had just run off the outside of the thatch and the fire was still alight inside. This was a bit of a problem, but we thought it would be alright. We had another go, we had two people up there, one of them opened up a hole in the thatch and the other one would throw the water upwards into the gaping gap in the thatch and put the fire out that way. Anyway, this was tried once or twice. Each time it seemed to work for a while but when a final test was made it was found that it was not: the fire was still there.

Just at this point, when we thought we were getting the answer, there was a cry from the kitchen, 'The well is empty! The well is empty, what shall we do? There's no water in the well!' The men on the roof got irritated with these stupid women downstairs and said, 'Well of course go to the goldfish pond, there's plenty of water there!' A bucket chain from the goldfish pond was organised and in a very short time there were half-cooked goldfish slithering down the thatch. Plenty of water was available. As time went on it became obvious that none of this procedure was going to work.

Quite a long time had elapsed by then. We then decided that after all we would have to send for the fire brigade. So the fire brigade was telephoned and they came charging up from Andover. They then discovered that the goldfish pond was getting a bit dry and there was no water within reach of their hoses, anywhere within reach of the cottage. They had to send back to Andover for more hose before they could get to work. This was done, but by that time the whole thing was completely out of control. The end of the operation was that they had to take large hooks and hook all the thatch off the roof and soak the whole thing in water. Of course, all the furniture inside had to be taken out. The whole house was in a bit of a mess.

This was a very sad occurrence and, although Alan's previous accident with the aeroplane in 1927 must have been fairly expensive for somebody, this business with the house was probably more expensive. We thought, being young and irresponsible, it was rather a joke that the owners of the house, elderly people, had some quite valuable antique furniture in it. They had instructed the house agent not to let it to any wild young RAF officer on the Staff Course who might have small children who might scratch or damage this very valuable furniture. Alan was able to persuade the house agent that the only child he had was an infant, and this infant was not capable of doing anything more than lying flat on its back on a blanket and saying 'Glug, glug.' It couldn't possibly do any damage to furniture. The house agent was reassured by this and let the house to Alan. If they had known a bit more about Alan's character, I think they might have realised that they had let it to the wrong chap. Anyway, Alan of course had to move out of the house and get other accommodation. What the final bill came to, and who paid it I really don't know. It was quite a dramatic incident at the time.

Chapter 16

Outbreak of War, 1939

At the beginning of 1939 I was posted from the Andover Staff College, to my next appointment, which was a technical planning appointment in the Air Ministry in London. As an engineer specialist, from time to time I had these jobs to do on the technical side of air force operations. So, I proceeded there. We rented a house somewhere near Hammersmith and I went to work in the Air Ministry which, at that time, was housed in an eight-storey building in Berkeley Square. While I was there, as I have described in the story of *Farandole*, we took *Farandole* down to Torquay and I have described how I left Mary there with *Farandole* to compete in the 1939 Burton Cup race while I returned to duty at the Air Ministry in London.

I was called back two or three days before the war started. The atmosphere was quite extraordinary; I don't think the younger generation can ever understand what people were thinking at that time. I can tell you that the head of the department I was working in got us all together and said, 'This war that we have been so terrified of is about to happen, we think. I have no doubt that the Germans will start with a pre-emptive strike and destroy large parts of London. As they undoubtedly know that this building houses the Air Ministry staff they are bound to target it, and no doubt they'll blow it up. It would be unwise for us to be in here when they do that.' It was arranged that if the outbreak of war occurred during the night, or when we were at home, we were not to make any attempt to return to the Air Ministry building. Somebody had organised a number of pick-up points in various parts of London, according to where one lived. I lived in the West Hammersmith district. We would go to these designated places where we would be told what to do. The idea was that we would all be evacuated to Harrogate in Yorkshire, the whole Air Ministry Staff. This was all taken very, very seriously. We went off with those instructions; the war hadn't actually started.

The following Sunday, 3 September, I went up to the Air Ministry. We were still at peace, and during peace the Air Ministry didn't open on Sunday, so I wandered round the West End. Shortly after 11 o'clock I was walking down Horse Guards Parade. There was a crowd of people there and somebody had a car radio going. We all gathered round and we heard the voice of Prime Minister Chamberlain saying, in very solemn tones:

> This morning the British Ambassador in Berlin handed the German Government a final note stating that unless we heard by 11 o'clock that they were prepared at once to withdraw their troops from Poland, a state of war would exist between us. I have to tell you that no such undertaking has been received , and that consequently this country is at war with Germany.

The broadcast was made at 11.15am and Chamberlain finished with the words:

> Now may God bless you all. May he defend the right. It is the evil things that we shall be fighting against – brute force, bad faith injustice, oppression and persecution – and against them I am certain that the right will prevail.

So the war had started and we wondered what the outcome would be.

Within ten minutes the air raid sirens went. I thought to myself, 'My goodness, the German Luftwaffe were quick off the mark.' A very efficient force, we had been told they were capable of doing anything, and they were apparently capable of attacking London ten minutes after the declaration of war. Anyway, this was not a very encouraging thought, but in the meantime, in the last week or two before that, people had been digging air-raid shelters all over the place like mad. There was one just at the edge of Hyde Park, and those of us who were around solemnly trooped down the stairs into an underground shelter. Absolutely nothing happened. I can't remember whether an 'all clear' went on the sirens or not, but eventually we decided that nothing was going to happen after all. Nothing actually happened for nine months. No bombs were dropped on

London for at least nine months after that. I can't remember the sequence of events, but I do know that we went back to work on Monday at the Air Ministry in London and nothing happened. No sign of air raids, but the plan for evacuation went ahead.

We all, and our filing cabinets and enormous amounts of gear, were transported by train to Harrogate. On the journey there, of course, rumours went around that this character, known as Lord Haw Haw the chap who used to broadcast from Berlin, had broadcast a message to say that 'We know that the Air Ministry is going to Harrogate and we shall be after them there.' This was a rumour. I don't know if there was the slightest truth in it as many of the so-called Haw Haw broadcasts were figments of overactive imaginations.

We arrived in Harrogate. Harrogate is a small spa town, and we were accommodated in one of the hotels, a very old but quite large hotel. All our gear was being moved in there when somebody on the ground floor looked up at the ceiling and discovered that the ceiling hadn't been designed to bear the weight of hundreds of filing cabinets filled with documents of all kinds. The ceiling was bulging visibly. Plans had to be changed. At any rate we settled more or less into this place. Then I enquired about accommodation, what we were to do, where we were to live. I was allocated one of the cubicles in one of the spa baths, the swimming baths. It was extremely uncomfortable. This cubicle had been designed as a changing cubicle for people going into the water.

This was the place I had to sleep in. We had to feed wherever we could find food in the town. That's how we started. In the meantime, Mary and the family had driven in the car to her sister who had a country home down in Cornwall, and she was sharing that with her. After a time, several weeks, nothing seemed to be happening. I was living in this uncomfortable cubicle in Harrogate. I managed to get hold of a rented furnished house and wrote to Mary. She got into the car with the family and drove them all the way from Cornwall to Harrogate and we settled in this rented house. There we stayed for some months. After a time, with no bombs being dropped on England, it was decided that the Air Ministry might as well go back to London. So the move was made. I can't remember whether we went back into the Berkeley Square building, but I rather think we went back to the original Air Ministry building at the bottom of

Kingsway, at Adastral House. Anyway we went back to London. By the way, five years later, when we'd had a pretty desperate war and we'd won it and the Germans had surrendered, I happened to go back to Berkeley Square on business to see a friend of mine who was a motor agent, he worked in the RAF during the war. I went to see him in his office which was in the same building, which had been the Air Ministry in 1939, and none of the building had had a scratch. The whole five years of the war, no indication that even a window had been broken, nothing at all. It is quite astonishing how terrified people can become of quite imaginary dangers.

When the Air Ministry staff returned to London I did not immediately return to the house at Hammersmith, because we didn't know what was going to happen from day to day. We didn't know how long this lull was going to last. Mary stayed at Harrogate in the rented house. In the department in which I worked in the Air Ministry there were two Canadian officers and it so happened that one of them had got quite a large flat at a place called Dolphin Square, a well-known block of flats by the river. The other Canadian had quite a large rented house at Wendover near RAF Halton, where he had been posted before he came to the Air Ministry. They had formed a syndicate and one of these officers had two children and as they didn't know what was going to happen they thought a good idea would be that the officers would live at Dolphin Square during the week and one of the wives would run the flat, cook food and so on. The other would run the house at Wendover; the children would stay at Wendover so that if any bombing started they would be well out of the way. At the weekends the officers would all go to the Wendover house, and the wives would then change over. There was spare accommodation for Mary and me and our two children, so we joined the syndicate and Mary moved down to London. Sometimes she spent one week in three in Dolphin Square running the flat, and two weeks in every three at the house at Wendover. The children all stayed at Wendover. That system worked for some time but eventually friction developed. All those women changing over from one place to another didn't get on very well with each other. They had different ideas about different things. So Mary and I wandered around London looking for separate accommodation for the McDonalds.

By this time the lull in the war, with nothing happening at all, became known as 'The Phoney War'. It might go on for a very long time. Anyway, we stumbled on a place in Twickenham. First of all, we got hold of a railway timetable and chose an area where there was quick access to the Air Ministry; I'm pretty sure that the Air Ministry was back at Adastral House in Kingsway. We discovered that Southern Railway ran a train from Richmond, Surrey, to Waterloo station in fifteen minutes. I could cycle from East Twickenham across Richmond Bridge to the station. I then caught the train to Waterloo and walked across Waterloo Bridge to the Air Ministry.

Chapter 17

The Duxford Invisible Flight Path, 1941

While I was at Biggin Hill there was another development, in connection with flying techniques, which started me off on the creation of a new night-landing system. This only came to full fruition some years later, in 1941, at Duxford when I was station commander there, and it could have had some quite important effects. This was the use of a sector light as an element in the lighting system for landing aircraft at night.

The standard layout for landing aircraft at night remained unchanged from the earliest days of flying until 1936 and it was what we used at Biggin Hill. It was a very simple, straight line of paraffin flares set out on the grass airfield, in line with the wind, a hundred yards apart, six or seven of them in a straight line, then a cross-piece at the end forming an inverted L or a T, and that was all. This pattern of lights served two purposes: firstly, it was a distinctive pattern which approaching pilots could pick out from all the other odd lights which, in peacetime, were scattered about the country – streetlights, house lights and so on. They could see this pattern in the middle of the dark area of the airfield on which there were no other lights and go into a circuit round it. So that was one function it fulfilled.

Then, when they were given permission to land, by signal lamp or whatever, they turned in from the circuit and landed alongside the straight line of lights, fairly close to them. That gave them the horizontal line which they had to maintain and also the vertical line as an indication of the level of the ground on which they had to level off and land. It wasn't necessary for them to actually see the surface of the grass at all. Points of light were quite sufficient.

Anyway, we were flying one night, using this system, and a not very experienced pilot was going round the circuit. His navigational lights were on, so we could see him. We didn't have any radio communication with him. He was unusually low all the way round the circuit; we couldn't warn him as there was no radio communication. Unfortunately, on the way the flare was laid out that evening there was a belt of trees on the approach path, about half a mile outside the airfield. As the pilot came round to do his final turn in to a straight landing his navigation lights disappeared. We realised what had happened, he'd got below the level of the tops of the trees. We hoped that he would realise the same thing. Unfortunately, he didn't. We couldn't do anything about it. We just listened intently. Eventually there was a rather expensive crunching noise from the trees. He had flown into them.

Trees, if you hit the ground at an acute angle, make a very good shock absorber. So, the pilot himself was not very seriously damaged but the plane was written off. When we asked him why he had made such a low approach all the way around the circuit, he was indignant. He said he hadn't made anything of the kind; he had made a perfectly normal approach angle and we had turned the lights off, which was ridiculous because they were paraffin lights and we couldn't have done it. But that was the impression he had. We pointed out that this was not what had occurred at all. As a result of all this, it occurred to me that this was a pretty stupid way of destroying an expensive airplane. It would be desirable to give approaching pilots a more definite indication of what the minimum glidepath angle was.

Amongst the people standing round at the time was an officer who had served in the Fleet Air Arm. The Fleet Air Arm had had the same problem with judging the angle of approach for landing on their carriers, for a different reason. They didn't have belts of trees on their approaches, but the line of lights along the side of the deck by which the pilots had to land was continually altering its angle. If the carrier was pitching into an Atlantic swell, this line of lights would be pitching up and down by quite a number of degrees. This made judgement of the correct approach path very difficult. The navy had adapted a device which had been used at sea for generations. This was called a sector light. A sector light gives a different colour or appearance according to the angle from which you approach it. It had been used on lighthouses for many years. Many of the lighthouses around the coast are sector lights, such as the Needles lighthouse. The principle is very simple. If a ship is approaching the light on a course which is going to lead it into danger, reefs or shallows or anything, the light appears red; if he moves into the green sector he knows he is alright. From the user's point of view nothing could be simpler – for safety's sake, stay in the green sector and quite simply keep out of the red. In the case of lighthouses, of course, the sectors are related to each other horizontally, the green sector to the right or the left of the red sector and so on.

It did occur to me that the same principle could be used for landing aircraft if we turned the sector through 90 degrees so that the red sector was the lowest sector and the green sector would be above the red sector. Then we put in an amber sector above that.

To produce this sector light was very simple. We simply used an ordinary photographic slide projector, such as used for projecting photographic slides on screens. We made up a slide of gelatine filters, three multi-coloured strips, arranging red at the bottom, then green, then amber at the top, so that a pilot approaching on the correct angle would be in the green sector. To make the adjustments minor, we used two of these devices, alongside each other, and set them at slightly different angles. An approaching pilot who was in the correct angle of approach would see two green lights close together; if he got a little bit too low one of them would turn red which was a warning. If both turned red, it was time to take action to increase his altitude. So, we started using these things at Biggin Hill; we adopted them purely as a safety device, for no other reason at all.

I hadn't been using them very long when I realised they had another quality. That was that most of the way around the circuit when you were outside the beam of the light, you could see absolutely nothing at all. As you entered the beam, which could be quite narrow, the lights suddenly appeared as if they had been quite bright. There was no mistaking them, but it looked to the observer in the approaching aircraft, as if they had just been switched on. If he continued round the circuit without turning in on to them, as he moved out of the beam they suddenly went out again. It did occur to me that we might make use of this quality in time of war to conceal our landing systems and pattern of landing lights from enemy night fighter intruders. This idea came to me in 1936, before the war had even started. In fact, I wrote a paper on it before the war started.

A complete landing system for night landings, which gave absolute protection against intruder attack, contained other elements and was developed gradually. It came to full fruition only at Duxford in 1941 when there was a war on and intruders were attacking all round Duxford causing many casualties.

Second World War aircraft night landing system
System invented by me and initiated at Duxford RAF Station.

(A) The Pre-existing System
The normal system for night landing was the same as that by day, and was very simple. Aircraft approached the airfield by normal navigational means, and then sighted it. The approach circuit was usually anti-clockwise. Each plane landed in turn from this circuit. Permission to land came from the landing control point by radio. During the war the airfields were totally blacked out at night, except for the landing lights. These were usually laid out in an inverted L, as illustrated.

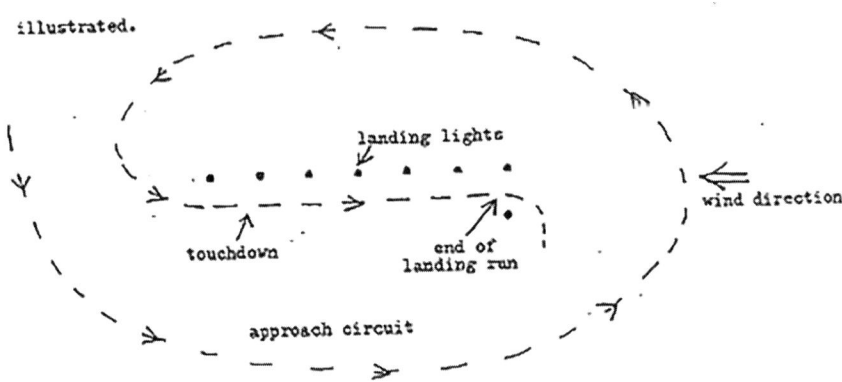

Arthur's sketch of the pre-existing flight path system.

The landing lights were quite bright and visible from all quarters. They had to be left on all the time night-flying was in progress, since they were the sole means by which pilots could recognise their airfield and by which the landing circuit could be maintained. This system indeed made it very easy for RAF pilots to locate their home airfield at night, but it was also all too easy for Luftwaffe night-fighters to locate the airfields and landing circuits. These intruding fighters then had a rather easy task.

They habitually crossed our coast intermingled with returning RAF bombers, and were consequently difficult to detect by the contemporary radar system, by the Royal Observer Corps, or by any other means. They were then able to select one of the airfield flarepaths, which were visible for miles, join the associated landing circuit, shoot down one of the aircraft in the circuit from behind and escape into the darkness.

As far as I know, the only Luftwaffe intruder who came to grief in this type of action was one who joined the Bassingboume circuit in the usual left-handed sense. The Luftwaffe pilot was unaware that this circuit was operated right-handed. The reason for this unusual arrangement was that this airfield was so close to Duxford that the landing circuits virtually overlapped. It would have been unacceptably dangerous for night-flying to have both landing circuits operating in the usual sense, so that aircraft would have been travelling in opposite directions in the region of near-overlap. The result of this mistake by the Luftwaffe pilot was a head-on collision with an RAF Wellington bomber, resulting in the deaths of all crewmembers of both aircraft.

(B) The Duxford Invisible Flare Path

The Duxford System greatly reduced the risk from intruders because there were no naked airfield lights and so nothing to home on to from all

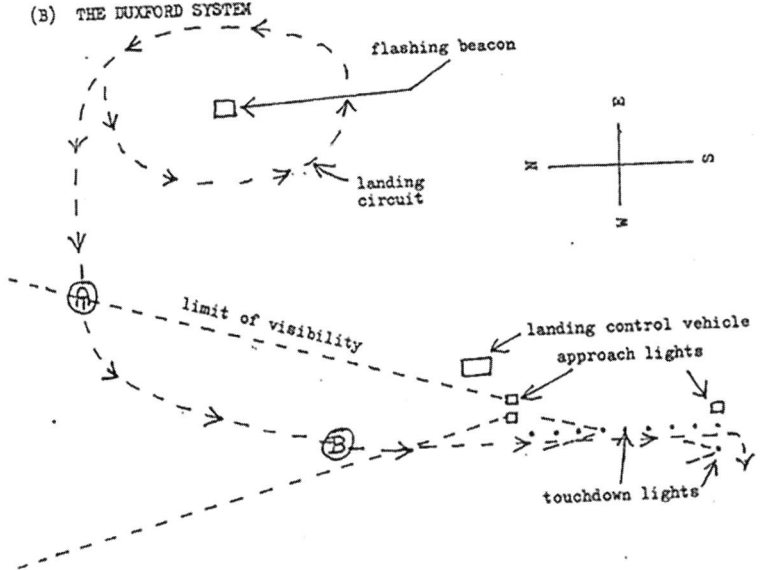

Arthur's sketch of the Duxford invisble flight path.

compass points. No losses due to night intruders were experienced with this system, which worked as follows.

The first consequence of installation of my landing system was that several hundred men in three anti-aircraft batteries and a battery of searchlights[1] were put out of a job because it soon became obvious that although stations all round Duxford such as Bassingboume, were being attacked by intruders at fairly regular intervals. Duxford could never be attacked as long as the invisible flarepath was being used.

I therefore set about developing a trap for intruders which would be deployed on the dummy airfield and would be designed to attract intruders to that location where they could be engaged by the search lights and anti-aircraft batteries which would be moved there from Duxford.

The dummy decoy airfield at Horseheath did not receive any attention from the intruders because it was dead, there was no activity there and they were much more likely to be attracted to stations like Bassingboume which was a Training Station with a very active night-flying programme. It was therefore necessary to produce some activity at Horseheath which would attract the intruders and, to do this, a live bait was required. This took the form of a 3-ton lorry with arms out on either side carrying port and starboard navigation lights, and one arm out at the back carrying a stem light, so that when it was driven round the Q site it would have the appearance from above of a taxiing aircraft. It was necessary to get a volunteer to drive this vehicle, who would be the 'cheese in the trap' as it were. By the time this stage was reached there was no difficulty in getting volunteers during development trials at Duxford; the searchlights had already killed a pilot. Unfortunately, the pilot who was killed was not a German intruder pilot but a pilot of an RAF Hurricane who had wandered into Duxford air space without prior announcement.

While the truck was being modified to represent a taxiing aircraft on the Q site, development of the trap itself continued at Duxford. The searchlights, nine of them, were arranged in a large ring around the perimeter of the station, each operated by an individual who could train the light around in the horizontal plane and the vertical plane; each

---

1. The figure would have been close to 1,000. It would have been still higher had heavy AA batteries been deployed.

operator wore a headset connected to the commander of the unit. The system was that when the CO of the unit heard the noise of approaching engines or aircraft he would order 'aircraft approaching from the east' (or whatever other direction), 'train on', and the operators would turn their searchlights on and point them roughly in the direction of the approaching sound. Up to then the lights were completely covered and nothing was visible, but on the order 'expose', nine searchlight beams would spring out and the approaching aircraft would invariably be brightly illuminated from four different directions. This would enable instant recognition. In the meantime, the anti-aircraft guns would also have been training round to face in the same direction and within two or three seconds they would be able to open fire on an identified aircraft if it proved to be hostile.

I was flying target for this arrangement on the night of 14 June. I had just done one run on which I had been illuminated by the searchlights. I then decided to go a considerable distance away from the station out of earshot before circling around and making another approach from an entirely different direction. While I was doing this, I saw a bright flame from the direction of Duxford that caught my eye. I called the duty control on the radio and said, 'What is going on at base? There seems to be a large fire there.' My controller's reply was, 'I am very glad to hear your voice because what has happened is that a single engine aircraft approached the station. Everybody thought it was yourself making your next run in, it was illuminated by the searchlights, it immediately rolled over, the pilot must have been dazzled, plunged to the ground and is now burning on the side of the airfield. Everybody at Duxford thought you were in the middle of it.'

This was a very unfortunate incident, but after it had occurred there was no difficulty in persuading a volunteer driver of the decoy, mock-up of an aeroplane that the defence would get the intruder before the intruder got him. He was already aware that the searchlights alone without any help from the guns had destroyed an aircraft which had ventured into the area.

The intruder trap was eventually deployed at Horseheath, but not very long after that intruder operations ceased altogether for the time being. (German intruders re-appeared in considerable numbers later in the war, in 1944, and caused many casualties at that time.)

The intruder trap at Horseheath failed to attract any attention from the intruders except for a stick of bombs aimed at it from high altitude on one occasion. The aircraft which aimed them was too high to be engaged. The counter-attractions of Bassingbourne, Coltishall and Wittering were too great and intruders found their way to those other stations whenever they crossed the coast.

There was a case of intruder action at Duxford on 5 May 1941. No Duxford aircraft were involved, but it was a very dramatic demonstration of the extraordinary contrast between the absolute security provided by the Duxford landing system and the high risks involved in landing at other stations with open flarepaths.

Simon Parry mentions this incident in his book *Luftwaffe Night Fighter Intruders over Britain* and simply states that an aircraft from Coltishall was shot down in the Duxford circuit. It was, however, not the normal Duxford circuit that was the cause of the trouble. On 5 May, the night in question, night flying was in progress at Duxford and I visited the landing control post. This was an open vehicle about fifty yards from the touchdown point, with a radio set from which the landing control officer could control the last stage of the approach and landing, all the way from the rendezvous beacon right down on to the runway. While I was at the control post a message came through by landline from the operations room to the effect that a Coltishall Hurricane had been diverted to Duxford because Coltishall had been bombed by intruders and the landing area had been cratered.

Not long afterwards an aircraft was seen approaching from the east with navigation lights on. The pilot of this identified himself on the radio as the Coltishall Hurricane and, first of all, I advised him to switch his lights off, pointing out that at Duxford navigation lights were never used. I then asked the pilot what lighting system he was used to; obviously he had to be given whatever lighting system he was accustomed to using at his home station. The pilot asked for an open flarepath which was what was expected but then went on to ask for a floodlight in addition. I was absolutely appalled at this because floodlights had not been used at Duxford at any time, nor at any station that I had ever served on. I had never understood why they had been issued to the RAF because they were never used by any other air force or by any civil airport as far as I knew.

Even in peacetime I took the view that they made landing more difficult instead of easier. However, the pilot had asked for a floodlight and had to be given what he asked for. Floodlights were standard equipment and, in standing orders dating back to peacetime days, it was laid down that they had to be deployed whenever there was night flying so that visitors from other airfields could use them if they so wished. As soon as the floodlight was switched on I became conscious of the fact that the brilliant light which it emitted in a blacked-out countryside would catch the eye of any intruder pilot within a range of about forty miles and in May 1941 the chance that there might be an intruder pilot within that range of Duxford was quite high; so I hoped that the Coltishall pilot would make as short an approach as possible and get his wheels on to the ground in the shortest possible time, after which all lights could be turned off. Instead of this the Coltishall pilot did a very wide circuit, took his time about it, made a long approach in and then, when he was within ten or fifteen seconds of touchdown, he put his engine on, overshot and called out on his radio in a very slow and deliberate tone, 'I am perfectly alright but as this is a strange airfield I think I will just go round again to make sure.' The only thing that he made sure of was his own death within the next thirty seconds. I could do nothing but watch and wait.

One of the disadvantages of the floodlight was that it was driven by an engine, the sound of which made it impossible for the landing control officer to hear the movements of aircraft in the vicinity of the airfield by listening for the sound of their engines. With the engine running this was no longer possible. When the Hurricane was about three-quarters of the way around its second circuit a look-out on a watch tower in the centre of the station, who was out of earshot of the floodlight engine, came through on a land-line with the very hurried message, 'There is a twin-engine aircraft following the Hurricane around the circuit.' (The Luftwaffe intruders were usually twin-engine Junkers 88s.) I at once seized the microphone and shouted to the Hurricane pilot, 'Intruder on your tail, evasive action, lights off,' but before I had finished speaking there was a stab of bright red tracer fire from 200 yards behind the Hurricane whose navigation lights could still be seen. The taillight of the Hurricane acted as a bulls-eye to aim at, so the intruder pilot could not miss. There were eight or ten bright red tracer cannon shells, none of which missed the

Hurricane. All struck home; the Hurricane blew up in a ball of flame and fell to the ground, half-a mile from the Duxford married quarters. The pilot must have been dead before the aircraft hit the ground.

I was extremely angry. An entirely avoidable incident, a young life wasted for nothing, and what particularly saddened me was the thought that if one pilot at Coltishall was in the habit of using floodlights to land with then it seemed probable that there might be others and perhaps others at other stations as well. With the number of intruders operating quite regularly in the skies of East Anglia, this seemed to me to be suicidal lunacy. This incident was very salutary for the Duxford pilots and no one was tempted to ask for the open flare path afterwards.

Soon after this incident I visited Wittering, flying up in the evening in a Hurricane in order to persuade the station commander there and the squadron commanders at least to come and have a look at the Duxford system. It seemed to me to be extraordinary that, in spite of writing reports on it and, in one or two cases, giving demonstrations at other stations, no station commander or staff officer at group or command had ever seen the system in operation, except for one of my contemporaries by the name of Edward Jones, always known as E.J., (who became an air marshal with a knighthood) who tried the system for himself at Sutton Bridge when I was developing it there. He had immediately been convinced of its merits in a wartime situation and had used it for the rest of the war at East Fortune in Scotland, but that was the only station, as far as I knew, where it was used.

However, on setting course for Wittering, I had no difficulty in finding my way to the station. Wittering used an elaborate and expensive system known as the DREM system for landing aircraft at night, which consisted not only of bright runway lights on the airfield but of lines of lights outside the airfield as lead-in lights to the airfield itself. The whole display was large and bright and could be seen from a considerable distance. I picked up the Wittering DREM system quite easily without a homing bearing, I landed and made my way to the control post. I was led from the tarmac to the control post by a young officer and discovered that the landing control officer at Wittering was operating from the block of headquarters offices in a room which was heavily curtained and brightly lit and in a position from which he could not either hear or see approaching aircraft. He was relying entirely on radio messages to follow what was happening outside. I did not consider this to be a very good arrangement. The station commander was in the control room, but he was not amenable to argument, he was very proud of the DREM system which had been developed at considerable cost at Wittering and could not believe that a simpler system operating with half-a-dozen lights on the airfield itself could possibly compete with it in any way at all.

I was up against what I later came to know as the NIH syndrome – that is 'Not invented here, can't be any good'. I tried to persuade the station commander at Wittering or someone at Wittering, a squadron commander or senior pilot, to come down to Duxford and see for himself that aircraft could be landed there under the Duxford system in quick succession without showing any naked lights. The station commander was just not prepared to believe that this could be possible and after a certain time I gave up the argument and returned to the tarmac to fly back to Duxford. When I arrived at the tarmac a young officer said to me, 'One of the squadron commanders is about to land in a twin-engine Beaufighter night-fighter.' Would I care to wait for a few minutes and see how the Wittering system worked in practice. I agreed to do so and watched with interest what happened next.

Much later I realised that I should have sent one of my pilots to sit in the co-pilot's seat of each bomber in the test together with my control vehicle complete with RT and controller. I set the shaded light flarepath, but the bomber station control system was inadequate, and the landing rate was too slow in the demonstration. However, Bomber Command would have been forced to adopt this new system if the Germans had not abruptly decided to discontinue the intruder operations during the winter of 1941–42. I believe this to have been a major blunder on the behalf of the Germans because these operations were very costly to the RAF until they ceased.

It was a great pity that Edward Jones at Turnhouse was the only other person to adopt my invisible flarepath as it would have saved many planes and their aircrew from being shot down by enemy intruders. It would have been especially valuable in Bomber Command where casualties from intruders were heavy as the Luftwaffe followed the streams of bombers home after their raids.

Until I arrived at Duxford in March 1941, I had never heard the suggestion made that carbon monoxide in cockpits might be a cause of fatal accidents. Alister Raby's draft *History of Duxford* gives two examples of this, but I can remember further details and other incidents.

The first example in the draft *History of Duxford* is on page 205 where it is state that a German 109 had crashed and, when the pilot's tissue was examined, it was found that carbon monoxide in the blood had been the cause. A little later, on 12 November when a Typhoon crashed, the pilot's blood was again tested for carbon monoxide, which was found to have been the cause of that crash also. Two fatal accidents in which the primary cause was carbon monoxide on different aircraft at the same station was a very extraordinary coincidence, or could it have been that once carbon monoxide had been established as the cause of one accident it led to the station medical officer (SMO) being on the lookout for a similar cause on subsequent occasions? It would appear so. My recollection of the whole sequence of events is more complex than that given in Raby's draft. In my recollection the first case where carbon monoxide was identified as the cause of pilot malfunction occurred before the 109 accident.

It was an occasion when a Hurricane pilot of 56 Squadron made a very bad landing. The landing did not damage the aircraft and the pilot's inclination was to go to his room, take an aspirin and recover from what he thought was a slight indisposition of some kind. However, his flight commander had seen the incident. He called him over and asked him to explain himself. The pilot said that he didn't think that there was anything wrong with him, a slight indisposition of some kind, a touch of 'flu or something of that kind, and he thought he would go to his room and sleep it off. The flight commander instructed him not to do that but to go to see the SMO and report to him as to what had happened. This put the SMO on the spot: the pilot had been sent to him because he had performed erratically in the air and it was up to him to try and find some medical reason for his lack of correlation and attention. He went through the normal tests of reflex actions and so on but found nothing abnormal. On the basis of leaving no stone unturned, he then took a sample of blood and sent it to a pathology lab for analysis. The answer came back next day. The lab report said that the pilot had an abnormal amount of carbon monoxide in his blood.

My reaction to this was to the send the Hurricane to the RAE at Farnborough for investigation. A pilot was told to fly it there wearing an oxygen mask, with his oxygen turned full on during the whole trip, so that he would be breathing pure oxygen from the oxygen supply and not any of the gas in the cockpit. A day or two later the report came from Farnborough that a cause had been found. A breather pipe connected the crankcase to the outside of the fuselage was found to be cracked. The pipe was replaced and inspection of that pipe was put on the maintenance schedule for daily inspection; that was the end of the matter as far as anyone knew at the time.

When the German 109 crashed, the SMO heard that it had simply dived into the ground. Remembering the Hurricane case, and what he had discovered there, he thought it would be worthwhile to take a test of the 109 pilot's blood. This proved positive and there was no doubt that carbon monoxide had been the cause of that crash also. By the time the Typhoon crash came on 12 November, the SMO at Duxford had in the back of his mind the strong probability of a link between carbon monoxide in the cockpit and accidents where an aeroplane dived straight into the ground. He therefore examined the blood and tissue of the Typhoon pilot's body and found a high proportion of carbon monoxide in that case as well.

By then evidence was accumulating as to how insidious and dangerous carbon monoxide really is. It gives absolutely no warning and does not give a pilot the opportunity of baling out. One minute he thinks that he is perfectly alright and behaves in a perfectly logical way and then simply goes to sleep. In the case of the German 109 and Typhoon the duty controller happened to tell me that he was directing the Typhoon round the circuit by radio. He had given the pilot an alteration of course and his instructions had been acknowledged in a perfectly normal tone of voice, but within one or two minutes the Observer Corps liaison officer sitting just below him in the operations room, looked up and said, 'The Typhoon has crashed.' The duty controller said, 'He can't have done, I've just spoken to him, he's perfectly alright.' But the liaison officer was correct. His information had come from an Observer Corps post. These were manned twenty-four hours a day during the war; those on duty there had nothing else to do except identify passing aircraft and plot their positions. They had recognised the Typhoon and seen it make the alteration of course that the controller had ordered. It had then entered a small cumulus cloud which would normally have taken it only a few seconds to pass through, but instead of coming out the other side of the cloud the right way up it had come out of the bottom of the cloud half inverted. Even then there would have been plenty of time for the pilot to have straightened out as he was at about 3,000 feet, instead of which he went straight on in a dive straight into the ground. Obviously, he was not conscious during that final stage.

Another possible fatality due to carbon monoxide was a Spitfire which crashed into the English Channel. This was piloted by Wing Commander Pool from RAF Wittering. His flight was told to practise mass-formation flying with my flight from Duxford. Only one of the two flight leaders was to take part and it was his turn. He flew to Duxford from Wittering and took off from Duxford but never returned.

Another possible carbon monoxide crash occurred on Christmas Eve 1941. I was told two of our Hurricanes were missing. One belonged to Czech pilot and I wonder if he tried to fly home, but his plane was never found.

Squadron pilots of 601 Squadron, the only RAF Squadron to be equipped with American-designed Bell P39 Airacobra aircraft. Taken at Duxford in August 1941. Arthur seated in front right. (*Photo courtesy of Imperial War Museum ref HU48131*)

Arthur wearing the AFC (Air Force Cross), awarded to him for his work on the Biggin Hill Experiment.

The pilot of the other Hurricane said over his radio that he had sighted the Duxford beacon and was told to change his radio frequency for landing but did not land. Around 2am the telephone rang next my bed and I was told he had crashed into a wood. He survived but could not remember any cause for the crash. I am sure that if my SMO had still been at Duxford he would have tested his blood for carbon monoxide but, unfortunately, he had been posted to Canada.

While I had been in bed with flu a senior medical officer, a wing commander, had come to the station

The Family 1941, Ann, Mary, holding baby Jean, Arthur, John.

and told the pilots that the reports of carbon monoxide poisoning were untrue rumours and bad for morale. I believe it was he who had had our SMO posted away.

Interestingly after that first interception in Biggin Hill, in 1941 at Duxford we were still dependent on the observer corps for plots of enemy aircraft in our sector. Night after night we used to blunder about in Hurricanes trying to intercept enemy aircraft which were being plotted through our sector by the observer corps. The only time we ever got reliable indications of where they were, or rather where they had been, was when we saw bomb flashes on the ground.

Chapter 18

Across Africa to Ceylon: The War in the Far East Against Japan, 1942–1943

In February 1942, Arthur was posted to Rangoon in Burma. He set off to take up this posting, flying solo, doing his own navigation in a Hawker Hurricane from one airstrip to another to refuel. On the way he needed to make a lengthier stop on the Gold Coast in Africa to have the inoculations needed for life in a tropical country. Luckily for him, the Japanese captured Rangoon while he was still in Africa, so his posting was amended and he was told to go to Ceylon instead, thus narrowly escaping becoming a prisoner of war.

The new posting was to the RAF HQ in Ceylon – No. 222 Group which had been formed in September 1941.

At this time, after naval losses at Pearl Harbor, off Malaya and in the Java Sea, the Allied forces were concerned about the growing strength of the Japanese Navy. They realised that the Indian Ocean had become vulnerable. Ceylon was seen as the gateway to Australia, India and the Middle East, the significance of which was later to make Churchill call the prospect of a Japanese attack on Ceylon 'the most dangerous moment of the war'. Ceylon at that time had a very sparse RAF set-up. The local headquarters had been positioned in Colombo to set up island refuelling bases and direct flying-boat operations with the purpose of protecting shipping against German commerce raiders. Ceylon had only two serviceable RAF airfields, one at China Bay and one near the naval base at Trincomalee. There was also a civil airport at Ratmalana.

Arthur was part of an urgent influx of high-ranking officers appointed to help prepare Ceylon for the Japanese threat. At the time Arthur arrived, the Commander in Chief, Air Vice-Marshal J.H. D'Albiac, also newly appointed, had just fifty serviceable Hurricanes (we assume the one Arthur flew over to Ceylon to be among them), fourteen Blenheims, six

Display of 30 Squadron's Hurricanes, Ratmalana, Ceylon, 1942. We assume Arthur is one of the officers passing in front of the Hurricanes. (*Photo courtesy of 'www.RAF-in-Combat.com'*)

Catalinas and a few Fulmars[1] at his disposal, against a potential attacking fleet of some 300 carrier-borne aircraft.

A letter to Air Vice Marshal J.H. D'Albiac from George Mavard shows that one of Arthur's first tasks was to set up his base in the 1937 Welcombe Hotel in Trincomalee.

> McDonald will tell you that he has decided to take over the Welcombe Hotel as a Fortress Headquarters and Operational Centre and, as a very few structural alterations are required from the Fighter Operations and Filter Room point of view, we should be functioning as a fully established Fighter Sector in the very near future. The only problem to be faced is one of communication and I have asked McDonald if he can let us have an experienced signals officer to take charge of the telephone and installations.[2]

We know that in Ceylon Arthur worked closely with radar using ground-controlled interception (GCI). According to the RAF historian

---

1. A Fleet Air Arm reconnaissance aircraft/fighter designed to fly from aircraft carriers. It carried a crew of two and had a Rolls Royce Merlin engine, optimised for low-altitude operations.
2. Extract from a document in the National Archive

The War in the Far East Against Japan, 1942–1943   181

Henry Probert, in his book *The Forgotten Air Force*, Churchill himself recognised the importance of radar in Ceylon's defences, asking for a personal briefing on progress. The Chief of the Air Staff at the time, Air Chief Marshal Sir Charles 'Peter' Portal, briefed Churchill that eight sets were needed and was hopeful that they would all be on the island by the end of March, although he was not sure they would all be operational. Probert explains that RAF personnel …

> … were tasked with collecting the necessary items and using ex-Singapore radar personnel … to set up an MRU (Mobile Reporting Unit) at Trincomalee. They succeeded – just – but a second installation at Colombo could not be made operational in time.

Other accounts from the time suggest the Colombo radar station was operational but was ineffective due to echoes, gaps and an inefficient watch-keeping rota.

The following extract in Arthur's own words about the Japanese attack in Ceylon's waters seems to confirm this:

> There was one (radar station) on the West Coast near Colombo and another on the East Coast near Trincomalee. During the raid on Colombo on Easter Sunday 1942, the one on the West Coast gave very little warning owing to the hilly nature of the surrounding country. During the raid on Trimcomalee a few days later, the East Coast one did better, but it failed to plot the Japanese aircraft which sank the *Hermes* and some other ships 60 miles south of Trimcomalee. Neither could give any warning of aircraft approaching Ceylon from the SE. I therefore tried the experiment of locating a GCI on a tea estate, on the edge of a cliff on the South East edge of the central plateau. The altitude was about 4,000 feet above sea level and the site looked down on to a flat plain below, stretching out to the coast about 30 miles away.
>
> This station gave excellent plots of every ship which passed round the SE corner of Ceylon on the way to or from Calcutta. These were plotted for a distance of about 120 miles and the speed of each could be worked out accurately. This information was passed to the Naval

182 *Helping Stop Hitler's Luftwaffe*

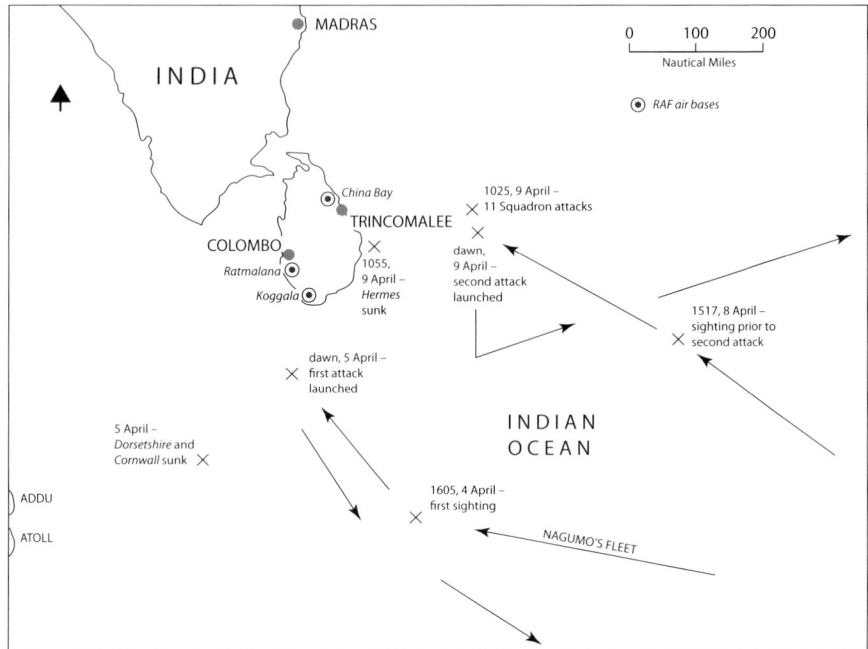

Map of Ceylon, April 1942, showing Japanese attacks. (*Courtesy of Henry Probert, The Forgotten Air Force*)

operators' room in Colombo and was most useful to them, as the SE coast of Ceylon is almost uninhabited and coast-watchers were few and far between.

We never discussed what effect this station would have had if there had been any further raids or an invasion attempt on Ceylon, as there [were] none.

We know little else about his time in Ceylon apart from the fact that, while he was there, he was able to further test the theory put forward by Dowding in his experiment on Salisbury Plain back in 1938 (See Chapter 15).

He did this by covering a local beach with upright wooden posts and then ordering his planes to bomb the beach trying to take out the posts. After this experimental operation the beach was covered in craters where bombs had fallen but not one post was damaged. This gave more evidence that bombers might have little impact on an invading army, as Arthur had witnessed in Dowding's experiment. For many years, visitors to these beaches may have been puzzled by the craters left by Arthur's experiment.

His time in Ceylon can be summed up by this extract from the Air Ministry's Weekly Newsletter

> 'In Ceylon for 12 months as chairman of the Inter-services Air Defence Committee, he applied his experience of interception to organising the fighter defences and co-ordinating the ground defences of the island. Two Japanese "feeler" raids which occurred soon after his arrival in March, 1942, were beaten and never repeated.'[3]

---

3. Air Ministry Weekly Newletter, page 2, this week's profile entitled, *FROM SUGAR ENGINEERING TO THE RAF,* April 1948

Chapter 19

The War in the Far East Against Japan, 1943–1945. Air Officer for Training, India

After Ceylon, Arthur was posted to India to take up the post of Air Officer for Training, responsible for the training of 20,000 Indians in a chain of RAF, training schools from Quetta to Colombo.

India's role in the war in the Far East against Japan was crucial; not only did it contribute over 2,000,000 men and women to the services,[1] but it was also the main staging post for the fighting in Burma. Arthur was based at the newly formed Air Headquarters in Delhi under the command of Air Marshal Sir Richard Peirse. It was Peirse's job to turn India's small RAF headquarters, manned by a handful of jaded, forgotten officers with outdated equipment, into an HQ responsible for co-ordinating the development of an RAF force in India capable of protecting an area four and a half times the size of Great Britain. Probert sums this up:

> One of Peirse's earliest tasks was to devise a new and expanded command structure. Up to March 1942 there had been only two Group Headquarters, No. 222 at Colombo and No. 1 (Indian) at Peshawar, controlling operations on the North-West Frontier …. The Air staff in New Delhi comprised just 10 officers, with 35 others to cover all the support roles; there were none elsewhere apart from 222 Group in Colombo. By the end of 1943 Peirse's own staff numbered 90 in all, and the AHQ and seven Group Headquarters staffs added another 104. A total officer staff of some 200 does not appear unduly generous given the immense task being undertaken, but the quality was good – far better than in Singapore – both in training and in range of experience.

---

1. The Indian Army of the Second World War was the largest volunteer army in history.

Arthur formed part of this team and was promoted to air commodore.

This was a time of great expansion for the RAF in India: the aircraft total went from 426 in April 1942 to 2,820 by November 1943. However, many of those aircraft were in transit or under repair so that the actual front-line squadrons had around 672 aircraft at their disposal. There was a large presence in India from the US Army Air Forces, numbering eighteen squadrons at that time. The other notable component of the air forces in India was the Indian Air Force.[2] At the end of 1943 it provided one of the operational Hurricane squadrons and several more squadrons were being trained. We believe this is where Arthur's role lay.

His RAF record of service shows that he took up the post of Air Commodore for Air Officer Training in India on 26 February 1943. Unlike the Indian Army, the Indian Air Force was completely Indian; after 1942 no RAF officers commanded IAF units. The problem was that there was a lack of suitably trained Indian officers.

In November 1943 a new organisation, Headquarters South East Asia Command, was formed to oversee the campaign in the Far East with Lord Mountbatten in charge and Peirse as the senior airman. Arthur was part of the air branch of this command HQ until his overseas posting finished in February 1945. During that time three major campaigns were undertaken which enabled the Fourteenth Army commander, General Sir William Slim, to reconquer most of Burma in 1945.

Arthur's letters home were heavily censored, but he was able to tell his family how he had an office in Government Buildings in New Delhi and, unusually, he flew his own aeroplane to visit the different training centres. A search in the National Archives in Kew produced several documents relating to his time in India that shine a light on some details of his work there.

The following extract comes from the minutes of a meeting about re-organising the structure of the Indian Observer Corps (IOC), which appears to have been one of Arthur's main focuses. In this, Arthur described how the IOC were changing from a static to a more mobile role, and illustrates how he was involved in organising the mobile wireless aircraft reporting units.

---

2. It was awarded the prefix 'Royal' by King George VI in 1945 in recognition of its wartime role.

The function of the training centres would be to provide Mobile Wireless Observer companies in any direction when required. For this, the air staff were much dependent on the army for assistance in army training and the Air Commodore wishes to thank army representatives for coming to assist at the current conference. ... Mobile Wireless Observer companies would be used as screens thrown out some fifty miles ahead of aerodromes to supplement other RAF methods of detection of hostile aircraft. They should be able to spot and report low-flying aircraft and thus play their part in helping get our fighters off the ground before hostile raids came in over the aerodromes.

It also shows how closely the army and RAF worked together in the campaign in the Far East.

This document can be found in the appendix along with a letter dated 27 March 1943 at the Indian Observer Corps in Rawalpindi written by Arthur as Air Commodore McDonald, Inspector, Indian Observer Corps.

India's role in the Far East campaign was crucial. Although, at the start of the campaign, the RAF in India had limited resources and suffered

Arthur in tropical uniform on 9 February 1945 in India.

badly from this, the Japanese army and air force were defeated and victory was won, thanks to the impressive alliance between ground forces and a now well-organised air force. As part of the combined efforts of the Allied forces, the RAF should be proud of what they achieved in what was their only major tropical campaign. Stanley Baldwin summed up the importance of the part the Indian Air Force played in this as follows: 'when victory is won India will owe a great debt of gratitude to her flying sons of the IAF.'

Field Marshal Lord Slim also refers to the importance of the Allied Air Forces' role in operations in the Far East:

> Our pattern of operations depended almost entirely on a very large measure of air supremacy. Until a degree of air superiority, amounting at least locally to dominance, had been secured, neither air supply, movement nor tactical support could be carried on with the certainty and regularity our operations demanded. The fighter and the bomber between them had to sweep the skies and push back the enemy landing grounds; the air battle had to be won first.[3]

---

3. Field Marshal Lord Slim, Fourteenth Army Commander, *Defeat into Victory*

Chapter 20

Photo Reconnaissance, 1945–1946

After a posting back at the Air Ministry, where Arthur was in charge of training, he spent an interesting year as Air Officer Commanding HQ Group 106, Benson, the Photo Reconnaissance Unit, at the very end of the war.

Arthur championed the importance of photo reconnaissance in the Second World War and wrote about how a civilian developed the workable system that gave the RAF such vital reconnaissance information during the war.

> Photo Reconnaissance was a private venture produced by an Australian business man by the name of Sidney Cotton. A rather fascinating story but it's never been published, except in a book by a woman Constance Babbington Smith,[1] who published a book called *Evidence in Camera*. Why (at the time of writing) it hasn't received any other publicity, and no films have been made about it I don't know, because I commanded the organisation at the end of the war and it was absolutely unique. None of the other combatant nations had anything like it at all.
>
> I don't want to go into a lot of detail, but what Cotton did was, first of all, he bought an American monoplane in the days when monoplanes were not very well known. He used to fly across Europe; this was before the war started, demonstrating this thing. The Germans were interested in it and some of their leaders would go up for flights in it. He fitted a camera underneath with a slide over the lens, the whole thing controlled by a switch in the cockpit; there were

---

1. Constance Babbington Smith was a member of the Royal Air Force's Women's Auxiliary Air Force and was a skilled photographic interpreter for their Central Interpretation Unit.

hundreds of other switches in the cockpit, of course, so it wasn't distinguishable and every now and again he would, even with some of the Nazis sitting beside him, flip these switches and … and he'd put the camera on and photograph strategic points of interest. When he came back and presented these photographs to the Air Ministry and the Admiralty, they were quite interested, but they said, 'Well of course when the war starts you won't be able to do that.'

He said, 'Oh, well yes, you can, you could use Spitfires.' Everybody laughed at that; they thought it was ridiculous. The Spitfire was a short-range interceptor fighter. It hadn't the range to go over Germany; anyway it had no navigational facilities whatever. So Cotton wouldn't be able to find the way. That was the senior view of the whole situation. But Cotton was a persistent man and he got together with some RAF types, one of them by the name of Winterbottom, and managed to persuade Dowding to lend him, or give him, three Spitfires – not three squadrons but just three individual Spitfire aeroplanes. This was just when the war

106 Group at Benson Photo Reconnaissance 1945, Arthur facing the camera. Crew member holding a reconnaissance camera.

was starting. They took these Spitfires and removed all the guns, all the ammunition racks, all the armour plate, threw the radio set away, stripped the whole thing completely out and lightened it a lot of course. That enabled them to put extra fuel in the wings, where the guns had come from, and they got a British firm to develop two cameras with 36-degree focal-length lens – big, three feet – just big enough to fill the space in the Spitfire, so that the film pack was behind the pilot's head and the lens was by the floor; they couldn't get in anything bigger than that. They started off and because these things were so light they could fly higher than the German fighters and in fact they had very low casualties. As for finding their way, it was discovered by practical experience that it could be done by the light of nature. If you are flying eight miles above the ground you can see the Alps and the North Sea coast at the same time. The pilots had, in fact, no difficulty in finding their targets and they brought back photographs to prove it.

Chapter 21

The 1948 Olympic Games, Torquay

From 1947 to 1948 I was commandant of the RAF Staff College. One of the things that happened while I was Commandant was really quite extraordinary. I was selected to represent Britain in the 1948 Olympic Games. This was for the single-handed yachting in the sailing Olympics which were held at Torquay.

This was absurd, I was a middle-aged Staff Officer sitting behind a commandant's desk at a Staff College in Andover. Mary and I had done quite a lot of dinghy sailing years before that, with considerable success, but at Andover I was interested in the job, my mind wasn't on sailing at all and I never thought about the Olympics. About three months before they came up, one of my friends came to me and said, 'You know the Olympics are in England this year?' I said, 'Oh yes, I have heard something about it, but don't think I'll be going along to Wembley, or wherever it is.' He said,' No, but the Sailing Olympics are in Torquay. The trials for the Single-Handed Class, which are to be sailed in Firefly 12-foot dinghies, are going to be held in Chichester Harbour the week after next. Why don't you have a go?' He knew we had had some success in yacht racing in years past. Well, I thought that this was absolutely absurd, but he said, 'Well, what are you doing that week anyway? We have a break in the course don't we?' and I said, 'Yes, we have, that is quite true.' I said ' I haven't got a Firefly, I've never had one, I've never sailed one,' but he said, 'Anyway, you must know people who have a Firefly, ring them up and borrow one.' He kept on at me until I said, 'Oh, alright! I'll do what you say.'

I started ringing people up that evening and I found someone who had a Firefly who wasn't using it at the time in question. He would lend it to me. He lived somewhere in West Sussex, I think, somewhere between Chichester and Andover. So, on Friday after work I went down there. His Firefly was on a trailer with a cover on it and mast lashed on top. So I just hooked it on to my car, arrived at Hayling Island Yacht Club as it was getting dark, parked it on top of the slip, went in and fixed up a room.

I went out next morning about an hour or forty-five minutes before the first race to have a look at what I'd got. Any old Firefly with a cover on it, I hadn't seen the inside of it at all. So I took the cover off and it was all there, the sails were there. I rigged it and put the sails up and cast off and started my first single-handed race that I ever raced, the first race I'd ever raced in a Firefly. It was all very interesting, one learned as one went on.

This went on for a whole week or eight days. I can't remember winning any races, I can't even remember doing particularly well. But it was a lot of fun, I thoroughly enjoyed it. At the end of the week I took the Firefly back to the owner, dropped it at his house and went back to Andover. I thought, 'That's that'.

A few weeks later I got a letter saying that I had been selected for the final trials down at Torquay on a certain date. This came as a considerable surprise, but I thought having got as far as this I might as well go a bit further.

I rang up the same chap who had previously lent me his Firefly, but he said that he couldn't lend me his as he was using it that week. I had to ring round a whole lot of other people. Eventually, I found someone with another Firefly who wasn't using it and he lent it to me and I took it down to Torquay and went off for the final trials.

I didn't think I had much hope of doing anything there, because amongst my competitors were some of the best small boat helmsmen in the country. They included Peter Scott who had been selected to represent UK in the Single-Handed Class in the 1936 Olympics, twelve years before, so he had experience of Olympic sailing in single-handed boats and he was one of my competitors. At any rate at the end of all this, to my absolute astonishment I was selected to represent the country. Having been selected and told that I was the one that the selectors had chosen, it wasn't for me to say, 'I think you are wrong.' It was their job; they had done it. Then I made a stupid error. I took the view that running a Staff College was more important than competing in the Olympic Games. In these days, of course, that would have been regarded as absolutely ridiculous, but that is the view I took. Anyway, I went back to Andover, and back to my office desk, in the interval between the trial and the Olympics. I should have been, of course, sailing round Torbay in a Firefly every day, day after day, hour after hour getting really used to it. So I went down there and for the Games themselves the management handed out twenty-two new Fireflys for the twenty-two competitors from twenty-two different countries. I had one of them and off I went.

Incidentally, I think, that possibly the only reason I got the selection was, in one of the trial races it blew quite hard and Peter Scott had been ahead of me as perhaps was to be expected, but when we came down to the gybe mark he capsized. As I passed him swimming he sportingly gave me advice, he said, 'Careful about the gybe! Careful about the gybe!' This was very sporting of him because I was competing with him for selection. The fact that he capsized and I didn't, I think probably was the deciding factor, but anyway that is all by the way.

In the Games themselves I did reasonably well to start with but I was never in the lead I don't think. Nor was a chap called Paul Elvstrom. I was forty-five years old and Elvstrom was twenty, he was the right age for that sort of thing, I was the wrong age. In the final race it blew hard and I hadn't done any practising in hard weather. Elvstrom had bought a Firefly the

As the oldest competitor Arthur was given the honour of swearing the Olympic oath at the opening of the Sailing Olympic Games at Torbay.

The Olympic Games 1948, Arthur preparing his boat with Paul Elvstrom who won the gold medal for the single-handed class. The oldest and youngest sailing competitor.

year before. He was a Dane, he lived on the Baltic, the tideless Baltic. He had this Firefly at the bottom of his garden and he used to sail it every day, single-handed in almost any weather. He'd got completely used to dealing with any kind of weather. He wasn't in the lead in the first few races at all, but in the final race he knew how to deal with the hard blow and a lot of us didn't.

Elvstrom won the Olympics in 1948 in the Single-Handed Class in the sailing, and I am told that if he hadn't won it he wasn't going to bother to go on racing small boats at all. Having won it, it fired his enthusiasm and he continued racing and he won three more gold medals, four gold medals in a row in intervals of four years. This was the first time that any individual

Arthur leading round the mark in one of the 1948 Olympic heats.

'At the helm', Arthur in his 12 ft Firefly in the Olympics.

Arthur's Olympic competitors' identity card.

in any sport had done that. He became the world's leading exponent of small boat racing.

As to myself, the selectors may not have been so very wrong after all, because I finished ninth out of twenty-two, the top half of the fleet. But for that unfortunate last race capsize I might have been better than that I suppose. It was a lot of fun and a very unlikely thing to have happened to a commandant of a Staff College.

Chapter 22

Later Career, 1948–1962

In his later career, Arthur was the last Commandant of the RAF Staff College in its location at Bulstrode Park from 1946 to 1948, and the first commandant of the college at its new location at Andover from 1948 to 1949; that was the post he held when he took part in the Olympics. We know in the former post he had general responsibility over 36–40 officers on the six-month course. He himself lectured on the principles of war and strategy and on photographic reconnaissance. The course was a broad one and more than half the officers were drawn from Allied and friendly nations, on one course alone twelve different nationalities were represented.

After this he rose even higher in the RAF ranks. His engineering skills would have served him well during a period at the renowned Boscombe

The Royal Air Force Fortieth Anniversary Dinner, Fighter Command, Bentley Priory, 1 April 1958. Arthur in bottom right of the photo.

Later Career, 1948–1962   197

Down Aeronautical and Armament Experimental Establishment as commandant from 1950 to 1952, after which he was Director General of Manning until his appointment to the Royal Pakistan Air Force.

In the appendices we have included letters from his wife Mary to illustrate his time as the last British Commander in Chief of the Royal Pakistan Air Force from 1955 to 1957.

From Pakistan he returned to the UK to become AOC-in-C of Technical Training Command, a post he held until 30 September 1959. In his final years in the Royal Air Force before retiring in 1962 he took on the role of Air Marshal for Personnel (AMP) at the Air Ministry. Serving in that post, he was the senior RAF officer responsible for personnel matters and was a member of the Air Force Board. His responsibilities covered all areas of recruiting, non-operational flying, management of careers, welfare of personnel, terms and conditions of service and the resettlement into civilian life of RAF regular, reserve and civilian staff wherever they might serve.

Control Room demonstration, Arthur seated far right.

Arthur making a speech wearing his insignia of the KCB, Knight Commander of the Bath.

He also continued to be a keen sailor throughout his time in the RAF. He was commodore of the RAF Yacht Club in 1948. He was also commodore of the RAF Sailing Association and was part of the three-man team who won the Royal Yacht Squadron Gold Cup in the 1954 Inter-services Sailing Championships. It was the first year that an RAF team had won the cup. He skippered the Mermaid-class boat alongside Squadron Leader R.P. Aylward and Flight Lieutenant S. R. Hawkey.

In retirement he was a very active member of the Royal Lymington Yacht Club. He served on the club's executive committee as Rear Commodore Sailing from 1963 to 1968. He raced a 1962 X class boat called *Mollymawk*, X135, of which he took ownership in 1973.[1]

---

1. This was one of 11 X-class boats built in 1962 out of a total of 202 boats built in Southern England since its conception in 1909.

Sir Arthur attending a Battle of Britain Service in London.

To celebrate his 90th birthday, a Mollymawk Trophy was launched for presentation to future XOD (X One Design) winners. He won the XOD Hotham cup three years running, in 1972, 73 and 74. He played a very active role in the X-class Technical Division from 1969 to 1988 where he championed technical innovation in the class rules. (For more details see his RLYC birthday address, Appendix 10)

He had an impressive collection of silverware from races he won during his retirement, and was still racing *Mollymawk* and his sailing yacht *Bacchante* in his late 80s! His motto when racing was 'luff in the puffs' which means when you get a gust of wind you sail closer to the wind.[2]

In retirement he also became Deputy Lieutenant for Hampshire in 1965.

---

2. In a letter to his brother Archie, Arthur writes 'a week before my 82nd birthday I won the Sail & Power Round the Island race for the 10th time.'

Appendix I

The Battle of the Saintes, 1782

(Including a first hand account of the battle written by Arthur's relative, William Spry)

The battle's name comes from the Caribbean islands of the Saintes. In 1782, the French hoped to capture the British island of Jamaica by using their fleet and an army in Martinique. The French were helping the American colonies in their revolutionary war against Britain, as well as helping Spain in their siege of Gibraltar. Jamaica was the largest and the most productive of all of Britain's sugar islands; the Trade Winds turned the sails of a huge number of windmills which crushed the sugar cane. Jamaican sugar was more profitable than all the imports from the thirteen American colonies.

The French Admiral François Joseph Paul, Comte de Grasse captured the island of St Kitts in February 1782, but the other Windward Islands, Antigua, St Lucia and Barbados, remained British.

On 7 April, de Grasse set sail from Martinique to meet 15,000 soldiers at Saint Domingue who were to land on Jamaica. The British Admiral Sir George Rodney, later 1st Baron Rodney, sailed from St Lucia the next day to chase him. Many of the Royal Navy ships were covered below the waterline by copper sheathing which meant that, in a good wind, they could sail much faster than the French and Spanish ships.

The Battle of the Saintes took place on 12 April. Besides the usual broadsides between lines of ships, some of the British cut through the gaps in the line of French and Spanish ships which made it difficult for the enemy to fire at them. This tactic, known as 'breaking the line', had been introduced by the Dutch in the seventeenth century and was later used by Nelson to devastating effect against the French and Spanish at the Battle of Trafalgar. However, many naval historians credit Rodney with its introduction.

In the Battle of the Saintes the loss of life among the French was much heavier than the British with thousands of French soldiers and sailors killed. When de Grasse surrendered, all his officers were dead or wounded, but de Grasse himself was not wounded at all. The British were shocked at the number of dead and dying on the deck of de Grasse's flag ship, *Ville de Paris*.

The French feared that if they did not sign a peace treaty the British would attack their sugar islands so they made peace along with Spain. So Gibraltar, St Kitts and Jamaica were saved by the Battle of the Saintes. Interestingly, Admiral de Grasse was taken as a prisoner to London where he played a part in the discussions that led to the Peace of Paris in 1783.[3]

Arthur's great-great-great grandfather, William Spry, was a Lieutenant on Admiral Rooney's Flagship, the *Formidable*, during the battle and wrote this first-hand account of the action that took place:

Formidable, at Sea
Hond Father and Mother,
On our arrival in the West Indies, which was February 14, we were informed that the island of Montserrat had been captured by the French and that they were in the greatest spirits imaginable. We have had nothing happen since my arrival worth relating till April 9th, when Capt Byron, of the Andromeda, brought us news (St. Lucia, which place we were then at) that the Count de Grasse, the French Admiral, had put to sea from Martinico with 32 sail of the line; it was supposed he intended to make an attack on the island of Jamaica. The instant St. George heard it, he swore on the quarter deck that he would put Jamaica out of their hands, and he immediately put to sea with 33 sail of the line, in pursuit of them.

On the 9th, at daylight, we got sight of them close under the island of Dominica, and at ten o'clock 20 of our ships came to an

---

3. In 1931 the US mail issued a stamp featuring Marshal Rochambeau, George Washington and Admiral de Grasse to commemorate the 150th anniversary of the Siege of Yorktown, which led to the surrender by Cornwallis of the British forces in the colonies. Grasse has been commemorated by two ships in the French Navy and three in the US Navy.

action with them. The Formidable was one of the 20. We fought them 42 minutes, when they made off, being to windward of us. We had 32 killed and seven wounded. One of our lieutenants was killed.

We kept sight of them till the 12th, when we held a most bloody action which lasted from seven o'clock in the morning until a quarter after six at night. However, we knocked out their fleet, and we can boldly venture to say it was the best day old England ever had, but I will not keep you in suspense by writing a long epistle, but will give you an account of the French ships we have taken and destroyed. "La Ville de Paris: 112 guns, 1,500 men. Taken." She stuck to the Formidable and we had 195 men killed, 180 wounded. The Count de Grasse was on board this ship. She is the finest that ever sailed from any port whatever, is much larger than the Formidable, and has upwards of a million of money on board. "La Glorieux: 74 guns, 900 men. Taken. "La Hector: 74 guns, 900 men. Taken. "L'Ardent: 74 guns, 900 men. Taken. "La Coeur: 74 guns, 700 men. Burnt. "La _____ : 94 guns, 900 men. Sunk."

The rest of the letter has been lost. The first *Formidable* was a 90 gun ship.

Appendix II

Ian Donald Roy McDonald Mc Dfc, Arthur's First Cousin and First World War Air Ace[1]

Arthur's cousin Capt Ian McDonald in 1918.

As part of the family history the story should be told of Arthur's first cousin, who also had a memorable but short career in the RAF.

Ian McDonald, only son of Arthur's uncle Donald, was five years older than Arthur and also attended Antigua Grammar School before completing his education in England. He joined the Royal Flying Corps at 17 and was credited with shooting down twenty enemy aircraft during the First World War when stationed in France with 24 Squadron. One of Ian's final victims during the First World War was the German air ace, Blue Max winner, Kurt Wusthoff, who was flying a Fokker D.VII when Ian, Horace Barton and George Johnson captured him in the air. During a dog fight with Ian's plane, a SE5, the German ran out of ammunition. He raised his hands in surrender and Ian pointed to his air base in Cachy in France to indicate that he wanted the German to land there. When the two planes were on the ground Wusthoff was

---

1. To be accorded the title 'ace', a pilot had to have shot down five enemy aircraft.

Captain Ian McDonald leaving Buckingham Palace after receiving medals on 3 July 1918. (*Photo courtesy of Robin McDonald*)

invited to dinner in Ian's mess before being taken to a Prisoner of War camp the following day.

He was awarded the Military Cross and the Distinguished Flying Cross,[2] which he received at Buckingham Palace on 3 July 1918.

After the war, he joined the RAF and was, for a time, a flying instructor at Cranwell. However, he craved a more active role and so applied for a posting to Mesopotamia (modern Iraq). During this posting Ian lost his life. On 22 September 1920 three de Havilland DH.9 bombers were told to drop supplies to the defence vessel *Greenfly*, which was stranded on a mudbank in the river at Samawahon. Ian volunteered to join them as an observer, although his own squadron was not flying that day. He took the second seat in one of the aircraft, but it was hit by small-arms fire and forced to ditch. Ian was seen to wade ashore where he was taken prisoner.

---

2. The Distinguished Flying Cross was introduced on 3 June 1918 to provide an RAF equivalent to the Military Cross for commissioned officers and warrant officers. Ian had already earned the MC with the Royal Flying Corps, which was part of the army.

The pilot of the aircraft was killed and, the following day, the crew of the gunboat were also killed. Leaflets were dropped offering a reward for Ian's safe return, but it was subsequently reported that he had been killed at Dangatora on the day of the incident.

Arthur was told how his cousin came to lose his life when he was visited in his home in Lymington decades later by the pilot leading the formation of DH.9 aircraft on this eventful day.

Douglas Whetton writing in *Aircraft Illustrated* in March 1970 went so far as to say:

> Of the many allied and Commonwealth pilots whose exploits in the two world wars have been lauded in the aviation press, one at least appears to have escaped serious attention; yet in the short time he was in action on the Western Front he scored twenty victories and played a major part in ending the war flying career of Lieutenant Kurt Wustoff of *Jagdstaffel* 15. His name and unit: Ian Donald Roy McDonald, 24 Squadron, Royal Flying Corps and Royal Air Force.

A First World War propeller from an SE.5a fighter that was once flown by Ian hangs over the altar on the right side of the cathedral in St John's, Antigua. He was the first and only air 'ace' produced by Antigua and there is a memorial to him in Basra, Iraq.

Here is an excerpt from a letter written by Arthur to Alvary Scott in October 1990, which provides an interesting sequel to Captain Ian McDonald's brief career in the RAF.

DH.9 Aeroplane, drawing from a birthday card.

I also enclose a copy of a drawing of a DH.9 aeroplane (DH for de Havilland, 9 for type no.). I thought you might find it interesting, as this particular type came into Ian's life and into mine. It is an exact and detailed representation of one of the day bombers produced by de Havilland in 1918–19. Further than that, serial no. J7086 reveals the fact that the drawing must have been made from a photograph of one particular DH.9 as the serial numbers were, of course, all different.

The drawing is a photocopy of a picture on the cover of a birthday card sent to me by one of my granddaughters, who must have picked it up at random on a bookstall, without having any idea of what it represented.

As soon as I saw it, I was struck by an extraordinary coincidence, in fact two coincidences. I had flown several hours on DH.9s at my training school at Sealand in 1924. I got out my old flying log-books and was amazed to find that the one I flew in 1924 was serial no. J7084, i.e. the one in the picture must have come off the production line next but one to the one I flew at Sealand.

Furthermore, the picture shows that 7086 has been modified for use in Iraq. The extra radiator under the engine and the spare wheel on the side prove that. So, 7084 must have been the last, or the last but one of a batch of DH.9s issued to flying training schools in England and 7086 must have been the first, or second, of a batch issued to the RAF in Iraq. I was told by the pilot who was leading the formation of aircraft in which Ian was flying when he was shot down, that it was a DH.9.

So it follows that is it remotely possible that the picture was drawn from a photograph of the actual aeroplane in which Ian was flying on that tragic day. Strange how these facts came to light sixty years after the event.

Appendix III

The Prelude to the Biggin Hill Experiment, the men who made it possible: H.E. Wimperis, Tizard, Watson-Watt and Dowding

In 1932 the prime minister, Stanley Baldwin, had told the House of Commons that 'the bomber will always get through'. In the 1934 air exercises he seemed to be right, as the fighter planes which took part were only able to intercept roughly half the bombers. One of the first to challenge this belief was H.E. Wimperis, who was Director of Scientific Research at the Air Ministry. His assistant, A.P. Rowe, sent him a memo saying, 'Unless Science evolved some new method of aiding air defence, we were likely to lose the next war.' Wimperis then wrote to the Secretary of State for Air, Lord Londonderry, and others, suggesting that a small committee should be set up with Sir Henry Tizard as the chairman, to discuss how science 'can be used to strengthen the present methods of defence against hostile aircraft'.

Wimperis wrote to Watson-Watt, who was the superintendent of the National Physical Laboratory's radio department. He asked Watson-Watt if a 'death ray' would be possible. Watson-Watt decided this would not work but asked Wilkins, who was his assistant, to work out what power would be required to produce a detectable signal from an aircraft. Wilkins did some calculations and told Wimperis that radio waves could be reflected off a metal plane and would show its position; defence methods had at last taken over those of attack. So he gave Wimperis a written paper on 'Detection and Location of Aircraft By Radio Methods' which was discussed by the Tizard Committee.

On 26 February 1935, Watson Watt and Wilkins with Rowe, the secretary of the Tizard Committee, met in a van and watched a cathode-ray oscilloscope as a metal bomber flew overhead through the radio waves from the BBC's transmitters at Daventry. They saw the green blobs on the screen move as the plane moved. Dowding was delighted and told Wimperis that he could have all the money he wanted within reason for developing this technique. A research station was set up with Watson-Watt in charge, first at Orfordness and then at Bawdsey Manor, to investigate and improve RDF (Radio Direction Finding, later called radar).

It was these developments that led to Arthur's team of pilots leading the trial that led to the first successful ground-to-air radar interception as described in Arthur's chapter on Biggin Hill. The trial, later to be known as the Biggin Hill Experiment, was initially given a timescale of two months, but it took a year between 1936 and 1937. By November 1937 Tizard could report that 85 per cent of the interceptions were successful and in December the Treasury released the funds to build the first five radar towers.

Dowding was the Air Member for Supply and Research and, in July 1936, he became the first Commander-in-Chief of Fighter Command. He arranged for phone lines to connect the radar towers with the filter room at his headquarters at Bentley Priory with more phone lines from the filter room to the groups and from there to the sector stations and, finally, to the fighter airfields.

When the war started there were twenty Chain Home radar stations but they could only detect planes before they crossed the coast. Watson-Watt developed Chain Home Low to detect enemy planes at low altitude, but during the Battle of Britain the operations rooms still depended on the 30,000 civilian members of the Observer Corps in over 1,000 posts phoning in their sightings. (The Observer Corps was granted the Royal prefix in April 1941.)

Appendix IV

The Biggin Hill Experiment: Further background information written by Arthur

I can confirm that several senior officers at Group and Command level thought that ground control of interception would not be practicable and that there was pressure from time to time to terminate the experiment and return 32 Squadron to normal training.

I am convinced that if we had not been able to achieve a high percentage of interceptions at an early stage, before DF fixing of fighters or radar plotting of fighters became available, the experiments would have been terminated and the CH chain would not have been installed in time.

From the start of the Biggin Hill Experiment, the signallers, under the direction of Walter Pretty, were working on the development of a system for plotting fighters by DF fixing but, as explained, progress was slow and it was not until May 1937 that the automatic time switch was devised and installed and DF fixing became the normal method of providing the fighter plots on the plotting table.

Therefore, from August 1936 to May 1937, we had to rely on DR plots for the fighters. To produce accurate plots for the fighters a number of problems had to be solved, which took time.

1. During the climb to operational height the true air speed of a fighter would be increasing, from minute to minute, because if the fighters climbed at a steady indicated air speed (120 FAS for Gauntlet) the true air speed would increase to almost 150mph at 15,000 feet. Plotters therefore had to learn how to increase the distance intervals between each minute plot and the restore throughout the climb.
2. Wind speed and direction usually varies with altitude. A wind of 20mph from south-west at surface might change to a wind of 40mph from the north, or north-west at 15,000 feet. Plotters had to learn how to make allowances for this change during the climb.

3. Forecast wind speed and direction at altitude was found to be inaccurate in many cases. We therefore had to find a method of measuring wind speed and direction at altitude. The most accurate method of measuring wind speed and direction was first used during the Biggin Hill Experiment and continued to be used whenever smoke puffs were visible from the ground, in clear weather.

There was a camera obscura in the AA Development Unit at Biggin Hill and one day, when we were discussing the difficulty of measuring wind speed and direction, it was pointed out to us that if we sent a pilot to fire a smoke puff from a Very pistol at any given height with in the field of view of the camera obscura then the operators of the camera obscura could plot the movement of the smoke puff across the screen of the obscura and work out form this wind speed and directions very accurately.

```
                    ......, .......,  Biggin Hill.
         To      :- The Secretary, Air Ministry (Director of Staff Duties)
         Ref.    :- BH/49/Air.
         Date    :- 6th. August, 1936.
                         --------------------
         Subject : Special Interception Exercises.
```

The first special interception exercises were started on Wednesday, 5th. August, 1936. These exercises were made as simple as possible in order to test out the general organisation and to try to establish what difficulties and inaccuracies would be experienced. The bombers were given definite set courses to steer, and definite times to start their courses; that is to say, the position of the bombers was always accurately known to the Operations Room Staff.

Three runs were made in the morning, and two in the afternoon, as follows :-

1. Bombers started from Foreness Point (Margate) on a course for Biggin Hill. Fighters were instructed to patrol Hornchurch.
Interception was not made owing to a slight inaccuracy in timing the start of the fighters. In this connection, it will be appreciated that with closing speeds in the region of 250 - 300 m.p.h., the slightest inaccuracy in timing will cause considerable error in the interception.

2. Bombers repeated previous course from Foreness Point. Fighters patrolled Tonbridge. Interception was effected with an error of approximately two miles.

3. Bombers again repeated course from Foreness Point. Fighters patrolled Gravesend. Fighters sighted the bombers two miles south of their course at estimated time of interception. (E.T.I.).

4. Bombers approached Ashford from Redhill. Fighters patrolled Gravesend and interception was effected at the E.T.I. over Penshurst.

5. Bombers approached Redhill from Ashford, fighters patrolling Uckfield. In this case the fighters crossed the line of attack, sighting the bombers some four miles to starboard on their course. It appears in this case that the bombers' airspeed was too slow, or, alternatively, that their was some deviation in the fighter's compass. This is being investigated.

In future, it is intended to carry out the exercises under more realistic conditions, basing the problem on the information which may be expected from R.D.F., and by despatching the fighters to a position a few miles in advance of the bombers' estimated position.

[signature]

Wing Commander, Commanding.

Letter to the Air Ministry from Station Commander Grenfell describing the first of the interception exercises on August 5th 1936. (*Document from a collection on the experiment stored in the National Archives at Kew*)

Copy

161 ST. JAMES' COURT, S.W.1.
5.10.36.

Dear Swinton,

I am exasperatingly immobilised with water on the knee, caused by neglecting a slight injury to a cartilage! At present I can only hobble about a few yards at a time with the aid of a stick, but I hope for better things soon.

As I have not been able to see you, I thought I would write to say:

(1) The Biggin Hill experiments have gone very well. They will have to go on for some time, as we have not reached the final realistic stage yet; but I am entirely satisfied with the progress except for one thing which is not their fault – namely that the radio direction finding is not nearly as good as it ought to be. Action is being taken about this in the Air Ministry.

It is pleasing to observe the growth of confidence at Biggin Hill. They really believe they can intercept now!

(2) The R.D.F. performance recently was most disappointing. When you were there it was just a fiasco, but it improved afterwards. They have the excuse that the masts were not ready to time, but nevertheless I think they ought to have done better. Things have been stirred up. My faith in <u>ultimate</u> success is not shaken, but we are some way off it yet.

(3) The silhouette experiments are all ready. They ought to be doing some tonight – but of course I have not been able to get down to see them yet. By the way, the War Office have been most helpful in every way, and up to time with their promises.

(4) The sound location experiments are practically complete. We have cleared up many doubtful points, and there is general agreement on what can, and what can't be done. We shall have to consider recommendations when the full report comes in.

(5) Wire barrage work has been going on steadily, but much more remains to be done, I fear.

There is a number of other things you would like to hear about sometime, but these are the principal points. My experience this summer has been of considerable value to me.

Yours

(SD.) H.T. TIZARD.

Letter to Lord Swinton from Tizard describing progress on the Biggin Hill Experiment on 5th October 1936. This outlines Tizard's view that the project needed time but that he firmly believed in a successful outcome. (*Document from a collection on the experiment stored in the National Archives at Kew*)

SECRET.

Interception of K.L.M. Aircraft from Biggin Hill.

1. The proposal to intercept civil air liners by the interception technique developed at Biggin Hill presents no serious difficulties provided positions of the aircraft can be obtained up to the ISLE OF SHEPPEY. It is understood that when the R.D.F. station at CANEWDON is in operation this condition will be satisfied.

2. Interception will probably take place at about 40 miles from Biggin Hill which is beyond the present R/T range at altitudes below 5,000 feet under normal conditions. The crystals for the stabilization of the R/T frequency should however be available shortly and the R/T range may be increased. Tests at the R.A.F. Station, TANGMERE indicate a range of 40 miles at 3,000 feet and 50 miles at 5,000 feet. There will therefore probably be no need for an advance R/T station for these experiments. Range tests to confirm this will be made at Biggin Hill as soon as the crystals are available.

3. Assuming the Fighter formation to be at "Readiness" at the beginning of the experiment, interception of aircraft at 5,000 feet would take place at the coast in about 20 minutes (including 5 minutes to "take-off") assuming no wind. If, therefore, 20 minutes warning is given, interception could be effected over the ISLE OF SHEPPEY by controlling the airspeed of the Fighters to allow for the prevailing wind.

4. Experiments using positions given by Bawdsey are not thought to be practicable, as the position of interception would be out of R/T range unless an advance R/T Station was provided, and further, because at 5,000 feet the Fighters would not be permitted to fly more than 5 miles outside the coast assuming no wind.

B. G. Dickins

Details of the planned interception of KLM Aircraft form Biggin Hill; memo written by the Scientific Officer working on the Experiment, Dr B.G. Dickens. (*Document from a collection on the experiment stored in the National Archives at Kew*)

Appendix V

The Battle Re-Thought: A Critique on the Symposium on the Battle of Britain in 1990, by Arthur

It seems strange that amongst all the senior officers and historians gathered together for the symposium on the Battle of Britain on 25 June 1990, not one appears to have ever heard of the Biggin Hill Experiment, of Sir Henry Tizard who organised and controlled it in 1936/37, or of the Dowding experiment which took place in 1938.

I find this astonishing because I am convinced that any detailed study and analysis of the Biggin Hill and Dowding experiments can lead to only one conclusion: that each of them was an essential prelude to victory in the Battle of Britain. In other words, if either of them had not taken place the battle would have been lost, and if neither had taken place the battle could scarcely have been fought.

Most historians agree that the system of ground control of fighters which we used in 1940 was a decisive factor in the outcome of the Battle of Britain and many quote Adolph Galland's tribute to it, but with different wording. The only wording which accurately describes the system appears in the book *Britain Alone* by Herbert Agar, published in 1972. This includes the sentence: 'The British fighter *was guided all the way from take-off his correct position for attack on the German formations.*' This was what Galland so much admired and envied.

Derek Wood heads his contribution to the symposium 'The Dowding System' and attempts to describe how it worked but omits any description of the key element in it, the ability to put fighter plots on the Operations Room table quickly and accurately. In the middle of page 6 of the proceedings of the symposium, Wood states 'in other words, he (the controller) has a moving picture' and goes on to describe at considerable length how bomber plots were obtained and put on the Operations Room table. To complete the picture, fighter plots are also required. Wood gives no definite information on how these were produced but hints that fighter plots may have been obtained by the Observer Corps. However, this suggestion does not bear examination. Observer Corps plots could not have been obtained, in cloudy weather, or at any time with sufficient speed and accuracy to lead to an interception.

Wood had obviously heard of something called 'Pip Squeak' and mentions it, as an afterthought, at the bottom of page 6 and describes it as a homing system, used to guide fighters back to base after combat. He seems to have confused it with the homing HF/DF stations located at many Fighter Command bases including Biggin Hill many years before 1936.

Wood clearly did not realise that 'Pip Squeak' was a complex HF/DF fixing system capable of putting fighter plots on the Operations Room table quickly and accurately and that it was developed as part of the Biggin Hill Experiment by Flight Lieutenant (later Air Marshal Sir Walter) Pretty as an essential part of the Biggin Hill Experiment, between 6 August 1936 and spring 1937.

Wood credits Dowding with having created the ground-control system of fighters used in 1940; but there is much evidence to the contrary. On page 86 of the proceedings of the symposium, Dennis Richards asked how far Dowding was really responsible for the system.

> It was normally accepted that when he was at the Air Ministry as Member for Supply and Research, from 1930 onwards, he approved the specifications for the Hurricane and Spitfire, but other things were rarely mentioned. Watson-Watt, in his book about radar, did not even list Dowding amongst the four most helpful people in the RAF who hurried it on. His number one figure was Sholto Douglas, and Freeman and Newell also rated well, but Dowding was well down the list – presumably because he was a cautious man who would not accept anything until it was proved in black and white. Park told Richards that when the RDF chain was established Dowding would still rely on standing patrols, and it wasn't until he (Park) actually connected the stations up with the Fighter Command headquarters, in the course of an exercise, and Dowding actually saw it working, that he said that this could become part of the system. He wasn't a chap who was rushing out in the forefront of technology.

On page 3 of the proceedings of the symposium Wood states, 'From 1936 the task of creating these defences (defences against air attack) was entrusted to Fighter Command and its Commander-in-Chief, Air Chief Marshal Dowding,' but Basil Collier, in his biography of Dowding, *Leader of the Few*, page 153, states that 'Dowding ceased in the summer of 1936 to be immediately concerned with the development of the early warning system and became the potential user.'

Also, Ronald Clark, Sir Henry Tizard's biographer, states:

> To tackle the problem (the problem of intercepting bomber raids on London) the Committee for the Scientific Survey of Air Defence was formed in 1935 with Professor Sir Henry Tizard as its Chairman .... He (Tizard) proposed a series of experiments to discover whether ground-control interception would be possible provided the newly discovered radar lived up to expectations. He persuaded the Air Ministry to allow him to use a flight of 32 Squadron and a flight of Hind day bombers for two months to carry out these trials.

It would thus appear that neither Derek Wood nor those at the symposium who supported his contention that Dowding created the fighter control system used in 1940 can have read Ronald Clark's biography of Tizard or Basil Collier's biography of Dowding. Had they done so they would have realised that it was not Dowding who had created the system of fighter control used in 1940 but that it was Tizard, through the medium of the Biggin Hill Experiment.

If the Biggin Hill Experiment was a well-kept secret, the Dowding experiment was even better kept. Whereas most authors of books on the Battle of Britain and its prelude make some reference to the fact that something happened at Biggin Hill in 1936 in connection with fighter control, none of them appear to have heard of the Dowding experiment at all. Nor have I been able to discover any retired RAF officer who had ever heard of it, with the exception of those on the Staff College course in 1938 who actually saw it. The only reference to it in print that I have so far discovered appears in Basil Collier's biography of Dowding entitled *Leader of the Few*: on page 110, Collier mentions the Dowding experiment but without putting a date to it. He describes it as an experiment to discover whether and to what extent the bomber force we were building up could destroy enemy aircraft on their airfields, and states: 'As on other occasions Dowding found his brother officers curiously loath to put matters to the test. At last, after a year of argument, he had his way.' A number of obsolete aircraft were dispersed around a dummy airfield and attacked by bomber formations in clear weather, with no opposition, and with all the weapons they possessed: large bombs, small bombs, incendiaries and machine guns at low altitude. At the end of the second day the majority were still serviceable!

The result of the Dowding experiment must have come as a complete surprise to all those in the Air Ministry who were planning the expansion of the Royal Air Force, as it demonstrated decisively that the bomber force which we were building up could not be relied to neutralise an enemy air force by destroying their aircraft on the ground.

Collier gives details of what the policy had been prior to the Dowding experiment. On page 161 he states: 'In 1922 Trenchard persuaded the Government to create a metropolitan air force. On the grounds that attack was the best form of defence he planned approximately two bombers to each fighter; a proportion reflected in all subsequent schemes of air expansion before the autumn of 1938.' Again, on page 162, Collier states: 'Happily, in the autumn of 1938, the Government had the courage to insist that fighters (production) should be preferred to bombers.' Also, on page 166, he states: 'The outlook improved still further in the autumn of that year (1938) when fighters were given priority over bombers.'

If Collier is correct it would appear that a vitally important change of policy took place in autumn 1938 when priority in production was switched from bombers to fighters. If this is so it is impossible to believe that Dowding could have won the Battle of Britain had that switch of priority not been made at that time. He had just enough fighters to win the battle; if the policy had not changed he would not have had enough. The margin was extremely narrow.

Although Collier mentions the Dowding experiment, he does not put a date to it. Perhaps he did not know the date, but it was in fact in late summer 1938, so it is a logical conclusion to draw that this vitally important switch of policy, which took place in autumn 1938, was the result of the experiment, and it is difficult to think of anything else which would have caused the Air Staff to make such a fundamental change of policy at that time.

In conclusion, it is suggested that although it is wrong to give Dowding the credit for the creation of the fighter control system which was such an important factor in winning the Battle of Britain, and was in fact Tizard's creation through the medium of the Biggin Hill Experiment, it is equally wrong not to give Dowding the credit for having persuaded the Government, through the medium of the Dowding experiment, to switch priority from bomber production to fighter production in autumn 1938.

This raises an interesting question. Why was Dowding never given any credit for this? Why have all reports on the Dowding experiment been swept under the carpet for so long? On page 34 of the proceedings of the symposium, Dr Vincent Orange would seem to provide the answer where he states:

> According to Bruce, Harold Balfour (Under-Secretary of State for Air) ... also thought it time for Hugh Dowding, Head of Fighter Command to go. This. I have no doubt, wrote Bruce on 5th November, arises from Dowding's incapacity to cooperate with anyone, which has probably aroused the antagonism of the Air Ministry. Quite apart from that antagonism, Dowding's command represented a recent – and bitterly unwelcome – focus on fighters and defence rather than bombers and offence, as the RAF's primary function.

In the above quote, 'recent' can only mean since autumn 1938 when the result of the Dowding experiment forced the Air Staff to acknowledge that, in the early stages of any war with Germany, offence would not provide the best defence against German bombing of British cities, which was so much feared at that time; that the security of the base was of paramount importance and this could only be achieved by the creation of a larger fighter force than had been planned prior to autumn 1938, when the Dowding experiment took place.

That this change of policy was 'bitterly unwelcome' to those brought up on the doctrine that offence is always the best defence, was probably only natural; but it does seem extraordinary that even after Dowding had won a decisive defensive battle on which the whole outcome of the war depended, he should have been criticised and penalised for forcing on the Air Staff a change of policy which had saved the country from irretrievable disaster.

The proceedings of the symposium leave unanswered a number of questions:

1. Could the Battle of Britain have been won without 'Pip Squeak'?
2. Was there any equivalent of 'Pip Squeak' before 1936? I can find no evidence that there was. In the Biggin Hill Experiment in August 1936 we had to rely on dead reckoning to provide fighter plots for the first seven months until Walter Pretty succeeded in making an automatic HF/DF system work with sufficient speed and accuracy to produce successful interceptions. The HF/DF station which had been in place at Biggin Hill for many years before 1936 proved useless for that purpose.
3. Was there a switch of priority from bomber production to fighter production in autumn 1938? Basil Collier says that there was. Could he have been wrong?
4. Could the Battle of Britain have been won if the switch of priority from bomber to fighter production had not taken place in 1938?
5. Was the switch of priority the result of the Dowding experiment? If not, what was the cause of it?

Appendix VI

Background Information on Ceylon During the War and Documents Relating to Arthur's Time in Ceylon and India

Churchill said that the situation in Ceylon in 1942 was 'the most dangerous moment in the war' and that 'we were saved from this disaster by an airman on reconnaissance who spotted the Japanese Fleet and, though shot down, was able to get a message through to Ceylon'. That airman was Squadron Leader Birchall. He and his crew became prisoners of war.

Due to Birchall's message to Ceylon, most of the seaworthy ships were able to leave the port of Colombo safely, and thirty-six Hurricanes and six Fulmars got airborne. However, twenty-seven of the aircraft were shot down. Luckily, the Japanese failed in their main objective to inflict a 'Pearl Harbor' on the British Fleet.

The Japanese Admiral Nagumo used his aircraft carriers to attack Trincomalee and China Bay as mentioned by Arthur in Chapter 17. On 9 April the British aircraft carrier *Hermes* was destroyed in twenty minutes. Unfortunately, the Hurricanes sixty miles away at China Bay did not know that she was in trouble as communications had broken down.

However, Nagumo dropped his attempt to fight in strength in the Indian Ocean. Two months later, Nagumo's aircraft carriers were destroyed by the Americans in the Battle of Midway.

Memo detailing Arthur's Appointment in Ceylon

```
Form 96A.
(Naval).                    MESSAGE FORM              Office Serial No.
                                                      No. of    Office Date Stamp
      IN                                              Groups
                                                      GR        6A
Preface OUT
                           (Above this line is for Signals use only.)
TO*     A.H.Q. INDIA.

FROM*   222 GROUP.         Originator's Number    Date      In reply to Number and Date
                              X.996                20/3.
(Write horizontally)
YOUR A.378 19/3 PARA 2 I AM SENDING BY W/CDR BAKER MY DETAILED

SUGGESTIONS FOR THE ORGANISATION OF THIS GROUP ⊙  I CONSIDER THAT IT

SHOULD BE CAST ON THE LINES OF A COMMAND H.Q. WITH THE DESIGNATION

R.A.F. CEYLON ⊙  THIS IS DESIRABLE TO ACHIEVE REASONABLE STATUS WITH

OTHER SERVICES ⊙  PARA 3 I HAVE APPOINTED WOOLLEY AS S.A.S.O. RANK

SHOULD BE AIR COMMODORE AND MACDONALD AS G/CAPT FOR FIGHTER DEFENCE ⊙

REQUIRE A G/CAPT OR W/CDR FOR G.R. WORK AND A GROUP CAPT S.A.O. ⊙

I CONSIDER IT IMPORTANT THAT OFFICERS SHOULD BE OF SENIOR RANK TO

MAINTAIN EQUILIBRIUM WITH THEIR OPPOSITE NUMBERS IN THE NAVY AND ARMY ⊙

PARA 4 DETAILS OF OTHER STAFF APPOINTMENTS FOLLOW WITH BAKER INCLUDING

PARTICULARS OF THOSE I CANNOT FILL ⊙  WILL DESPATCH ALL SURPLUS

PERSONNEL AT AN EARLY DATE ⊙  PARA 5 NOTED ⊙
```

IMPORTANT. TIME OF ORIGIN 1255/Z

Minutes from the IOC organisation conference mentioned in Chapter 19, March 1943.

INDIAN OBSERVER CORPS.

I.O.C RE- ORGANIZATION.

Minutes of a conference held at the office of Allahabad Observer Corps on the 15th March 1943.

Present:- Air Commodore J. A. Mcdonald R.A.F. Inspector I.O.C. (Chaiman)
Lieut. Col. F.T. Birdwood Asansol Obs. Corps.
Lieut. Col. H.R.Culley Offg. Condr. Allahabad Bgde. Area.
Major H.C. Graham D.A.Q.M.G., Lucknow District.
Major S. Hamidullah, Allahabad Obs. Corps.
Major W.D. Haigh, Garrison Engineer, Allahabad.
P/O G.E.Ridd R.A.F. Tech.Instructor No.2 Training Centre.
Col. W.N.Powell, M.C. Air Headquarters I.O.C. .... (Secretary)

Action.

1. The Air Commodore described the changed role of the Indian Observer Corps i.e., from a static role to a more mobile one. It was to include a series of mobile wireless aircraft reporting units available for duty in India, Assam and Burma and in relief of existing Wireless Observer Units (British). This change involved re-organization. As part of this re-organization, two training centres had been approved one at RAWALPINDI and the other at ALLAHABAD, and the present conference has been called to arrange the housing of personnel and accommodation for technical and operational training in respect of the latter of these training centres.

2. A description was then given of the installations needed for technical training, and the aid to be received from the Wireless school BOMBAY. V.C.O's would be sent there on courses of 3 or 4 months to qualify them as W/T Instructors.

3. At the same time, so far as existing static organization was concerned, the policy was to cut them down to small care and Maintenance Units, capable of being increased if the threat to India returned. The function of the Training centres would be to provide Mobile Wireless Observer companies in any direction when required. For this, the air staff were much dependent on the Army for assistance in Army training and the Air Commodore wished to thank Army representatives for coming to assist at the current conference.

4. Mobile wireless Observer companies would be used as screens thrown out some fifty miles ahead of aerodromes, to supplement other R.A.F. methods of detection of hostile aircraft. They should be able to spot and report low flying aircraft and thus play their part in helping get our fighters off the ground before hostile raids came in over the aerodromes.

5. Turning to the specific question of accommodation at ALLAHABAD for No. 2 Training Centre, it was confirmed that 1400 was the maximum limit of personnel requiring housing. This figure would be made up of the care and maintenance party for the Allahabad Observer Corps, the normal establishment of the training centre itself, together with up to four mobile wireless Observer companies at the centre at one time. It excluded, however, any companies which might be cut on operational training from the training centre. Between nine and twelve months were available for training 10 companies at ALLAHABAD, Existing personnel at ALLAHABAD with the exception of the care and maintenance party would be absorbed.

6. Discussing the accommodation question, it was confirmed that some men would be in tents, but that everything was satisfactory, subject to alterations and some new construction, costing of which was in progress. A sum of Rs 2,78,000 had been estimated, but it was expected that it would actually work out at less than Rs.1,30,000. This involved reference to G.H.Q. and to speed matters up it was proposed that one copy of the estimate should go direct to Delhi for information, while the balance followed the usual channel.

7. The question of living accommodation for the officers was then raised.

8. Air Commodore McDonald pointed out the necessity of as many of the senior personnel of the M.W.O. Coys as possible being trained at the R.A.F. Aircraft Recognition School. Already 14 E.C.Os. and V.C.Os. had been selected to attend a course to be held at ANDHERI on the 18th March, 1943. He then stated that officers who attended and passed these courses would be qualified Aircraft Recognition Instructors.

9. The use of M.W.O. Coys as a screen in front of fighter aerodromes and other targets was then described. The object of raising I.O.C. Wireless Units was to replace the R.A.F. Units at present in this country and to utilise them in Bengal, Assam and later in Burma. The Training Centres would probably be required for the remainder of the War and Companies might be required mobile operations as the course of War changed.

10. Wing Commander Stewart then suggested that the later part of operational training should be carried out in the vicinity of Peshawar where there was considerable flying activity. It was agreed that for the last fortnight of operational training a Wireless Company should move out to Peshawar Area fully equipped.
Lt. Col. M.A.Haines was asked to study the accommodation and rationing aspect of this move, and charging arrangements and report to Officer Commanding No.1. Training Centre.

11. Army Training was then considered. North Western Army were asked to arrange with Districts and Brigades concerned to assist in supplying instructors for musketry and loaning of arms for training purposes until the arms of the M.W.O. Coys have been issued and also to arrange M.T. instructors and hired transport for the training of up to 40 I.O.C. drivers at a time in M.T. driving. During this period the Officer Commanding No. Training Centre will ask for allotments for various courses e.g. musketry, driver mechanics, first aid and anti-gas.

12. It was decided that the following companies will move out to War Stations as under:-
No. 2 & 3 Companies by the first week of May '43.
No.1 Coy by the first week of June '43. (This Coy will move to Rawalpindi from Quetta on the first of April 1943)
No.4 Coy by the first week of July '43 and Nos. 9 & 10 Coys by the first week of August '43.

13. The immediate issue of all war equipment is to be taken up by Colonel Powell on his return to Delhi. The War Equipment Table, India Army Form F980 of Dec '42, issued under G.H.Q., M.G.O. Br. No.06234/5/MG.15-A dated 16-12-42 refers, advance copies of which are being forwarded to all concerned. The W.E.T. for arms is being issued as a separate amendment.

14. Accommodation for the I.O.C. Training Centre has been agreed to by H.Qrs. N.W.A. and priority for the necessary alterations to existing buildings allotted is being taken up with G.H.Q. (I) Q.M.G's Branch.

15. The proposed Trade Test for Ground Observers in M.W.O. Companies was considered. The grade pay being asked was agreed to, and the necessity for its inception was stressed.

16. In conclusion Air Commodore McDonald asked Area Commanders to give their views as to the formation of a H.Qrs. organisation for the administration of M.W.O.Coys in their War stations. The question of Plotters being part of their formation, and of a wireless detachment belonging to it, was also discussed. It was agreed that Plotters training would continue and at present 12 Plotters for each Coy have been ear-marked but will remain on I.O.C. static establishments as also do the personnel for Wireless Detachments.

DISTRIBUTION:-

Air Commodore McDonald.	....	3 Copies.
H.Qrs.N.W.Army, 'G' Br.	....	5 Copies for distribution to Peshist Baldis and Kodist.
Capt.J.C.Crocker,G.S.O II(AD) Pindist...		1 Copy.
Wing Commdr.R.W.Stewart, 223 Group R.A.F.		1 Copy.
Lt.Col.M.A.Haines,Comdt,N.W.F.P.Obs.Corps.		1 Copy.
Lt.Col.S.P.Williams,Comdt,Baluchistan Obs.Corps.		1 Copy.
Lt.Col.N.C.Verma,Comdt.,RWP.Obs.Corps Area.		1 Copy.
F/Lt.G.Wrentmore,I.O.C. W/T School,R'pindi.		1 Copy. (One extra copy
G.Hunt Esq.,E.T. Lahore.		1 Copy. for Dir.of TEI
S.P.Joseph Esq.,D.E.T. R'pindi.		1 Copy. LAHORE.

A letter written by Arthur illustrating the work he was involved in in India, organising the operational training layout.

To form 540 RAF Section   Indian Observer

Corps Training Centre   RAWALPINDI, MAY 1943

<u>SECRET</u>

From: Indian Observer Corps, Air Headquarters, India
To: Headquarters, 223 Group
Date: 1st May, 1943
Ref: 7071/3/IOC/SIGS

<u>OPERATIONAL TRAINING – IOC</u>

1. GENERAL.
   As the result of discussions at RAWALPINDI on April 28th 1943 between O.C. No. 223 Group and Inspector IOC, it has been decided to modify the Operational Training lay-out of the IOC Centre at RAWALPINDI in order firstly to get more benefit from the day and night flying training taking place in the RAWALPINDI/PESHAWAR area and secondly to produce more realistic conditions at the IOC posts where the IOC personnel are undergoing the final stages of their training preparatory to proceeding to their war stations.
2. The scheme of locating posts close in to the aerodromes at RAWALPINDI and PESHAWAR has been dropped for reasons discussed at the meeting referred to and a new lay-out of posts has been drawn up. This lay-out is shown in Appendix 'A'. Each of these posts is a permanent post retained from the IOC NWFP lay-out (now in the process of dismantling), and has permanent accommodation and telephone installed. The lay-out of posts was agreed on mutually as being the best suited to ensure posts getting the benefit of local flying at RAWALPINDI, RISALPUR and PESHAWAR aerodromes in order to practise and improve

aircraft identification and also the best lay-out to permit laying on exercises by arrangement to be made direct between the IOC Centre and the Operations Rooms at RAWALPINDI (CHAKLALA), RISALPUR and PESHAWAR.

3. The scheme for communication between the IOC Centre, its posts and the RAF aerodrome is as follows:-

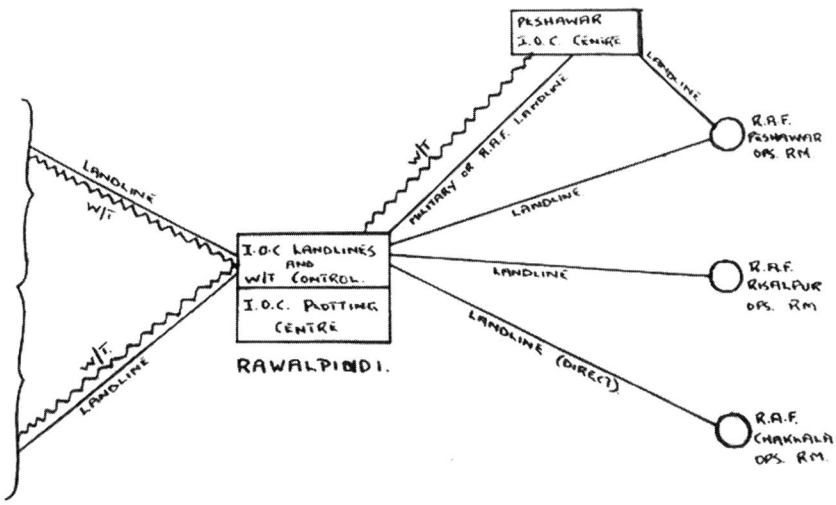

Author's sketch of the proposed IOC Rawalpindi communication network.

The IOC control arrangements (W/T and land line) will be housed alongside and in the same building as the main IOC Plotting Centre at RAWALPINDI. Then when an exercise is laid on, plots from the IOC posts will be passed into the Plotting Centre from the W/T Control where plots will be shown on the table and a track sheet recorded. This record will be sent to the O.T.U. on completion of the exercise and should serve as a guide on the accuracy of the pilot's track. With the scheme as laid out above it should be possible to vary the type of exercise to the mutual benefit of the RAF and IOC Mobile Wireless Observer Company system in BENGAL. It is hoped to have the system set up and in use in about a week.

4. The IOC posts will be occupied on a 24-hour watch basis for periods of approx. ten days at a stretch. During this period the

IOC Centre will be manned continuously with an Officer or Senior NCO in charge at the W/T and LL control point.

5. Your willingness to co-operate in the IOC Operational training and to instruct your units accordingly will be much appreciated at IOC Headquarters. You have already been of great assistance to the IOC training by permitting IOC personnel u/t to visit your aerodromes and see the outstanding characteristics of types of aircraft first hand. Your help in assisting at trade testing of the IOC Signals and Observer personnel is also much appreciated: this has been the subject of a separate instruction to the Training Centres.

(Signed) A. MCDONALD
Air Commodore,
For Air Officer Commanding-in-Chief,
Air Forces in India.

Appendix VII

Table of Aircraft, compiled by Arthur's Great Grandchild Joe Jameson

Type of plane	Image All images in the public domain unless otherwise indicated.	Years in service	Bi-plane Y/N	Engine type	Other notable features
Avro Mono 504K		1913–1940	yes	Gnome Rhône Monosoupape rotary engine producing 100bhp	Most produced aircraft of its era
Gloster Gamecock	Photo courtesy www.RAF-in-combat	1926–1931	yes	Bristol Jupiter	Short service due to high accident rate
Bristol Fighter		1916–1930s	yes	Rolls Royce Falcon V-12 engine	A two-seater fighter plane that was used for aerial reconnaissance.
de Havilland DH.9, also known as Airco, DH.9 and DH.9A		1917–1937	yes	Initially used an Adriatic Engine, which was unreliable so fitted with the more powerful Liberty L-12 in the DH.9A	First World War day bomber, which improved on its predecessor, the DH.4, by moving the pilot closer to the gunner/observer enabling better communication.

Page ref.	Type of plane	Image All images in the public domain unless otherwise indicated.	Years in service	Bi-plane Y/N	Engine type	Other notable features
61	Armstrong Whitworth Siddeley Siskin III		1923–1932	yes	Jaguar engine	The first all metal frame fighter in the RAF. They became popular in service as they were highly manoeuvrable
60	Supermarine Spitfire		1938–1948	no	Rolls Royce Merlin engine producing 1,030hp	The only British fighter produced continuously throughout WWII. Still in service until the 1950s
65	Sopwith Snipe		1918–1926	yes	BR2 (Bentley Rotary 2)	It was used by the Soviet Union post WW1
60	Hawker Hurricane		1937–1944	no	Rolls Royce Merlin	Inflicted 60% of the losses sustained by the Luftwaffe
76	Avro 504N	Photo courtesy of BAE Systems	1927–1944	yes	Armstrong Siddeley Lynx radial engine 160hp (120 kW)	Improved under-carriage. Built as a post war training plane
86	Dornier Do X		1929	no	12 Bristol Jupiter engines	A flying boat; only 3 were ever built.

Appendix VII   229

age f.	Type of plane	Image All images in the public domain unless otherwise indicated.	Years in service	Bi-plane Y/N	Engine type	Other notable features
4	Short Singapore III	Photo courtesy www.RAF-in-combat	1934–late 1930s 37 built	yes	Four 675hp Rolls Royce Kestrel IX mounted between wings in push-pull pairs	The RAF's main maritime patrol flying boat of the 1930s. It had a long-range fuel tank carried externally on the dorsal hull. They were flown with a crew of 6–7
3	Bristol Bulldog	Photo courtesy www.RAF-in-combat	1927–37	yes	Bristol Jupiter VII air-cooled radial engine	Over 10 different countries used them in the inter-war period. Over 400 were produced.
3	Gloster Gauntlet	Photo courtesy www.RAF-in-combat	1935–43	yes	Bristol Mercury VI engine	Made up 26 different squadrons in the RAF The aeroplane used for the Biggin Hill Experiment.
4	Gloster Gladiator		1936–53	yes	Bristol Mercury IX engine, 840hp	Some were used by Nazi Germany (in small numbers)

Appendix VIII

Commander-in-Chief, Pakistan Air Force, 1955–1957

Introduction by Ann, Arthur's eldest daughter

My father became Commander-in-Chief of the Royal Pakistan Air Force in 1955. Pakistan and India had become independent in 1947 and he was the last British Commander-in-Chief.

At the time, Karachi was the capital of West Pakistan and Dacca capital of East Pakistan, now Bangladesh. We lived at Air House in Karachi, easily recognised by a huge bomb embedded end-up outside the gates, and Pathan tribesmen on sentry duty.

Bomb outside Arthur's house in Karachi, Air House, placed there by AVM Atcherley. We believe this is a Grand Slam, a 10 tonne earthquake bomb, invented by Barnes Wallis in 1943 (only 99 were built, of which 42 were used)

Peter, my youngest brother, stayed in Karachi and attended the Karachi Grammar School. John, my eldest brother, but younger than me, was in the RAF, based mainly in Scotland, after finishing at Eton. Jean was at boarding school in England but came out to Pakistan for the holidays. When I completed my History degree I joined them and taught English and History at the Karachi Grammar School. My mother was teaching Science there. Due to all the diplomats in Karachi, the school had children from twenty-one nationalities and eight religions.

During our time in Pakistan we often went with my father on his visits to West and East Pakistan. On one visit to the Khyber Pass I remember seeing the badges of British regiments carved into the rocks and Pathan tribesmen stood on guard on the top of every hill. When we reached the border with Afghanistan, we were warned not to put even one foot over the border as they told us that, if we did, we would be taken prisoner and have to beg for our food, in chains!

We also visited the Darra arms factory where Pathan tribesmen turned motor axles into guns. They said they would not use modern machinery as it would cause unemployment. My son-in-law visited the same factory around forty years later and little had changed.

I remember a particular visit to Lahore with its ancient Zam Zama gun, described by Rudyard Kipling in his book *Kim*, and a great mosque built by one of the Moghul Emperors, Shah Jehan, in the fifteenth century, the largest mosque in India.

Being the capital, Karachi was full of parties for diplomats. The South East Asia Treaty Organisation, SEATO, had meetings there attended by rulers like the Shah of Persia and other important dignitaries.

When Arthur took over the role of Commander-in-Chief he built on the work done by his predecessor Air Vice Marshal L.W. Cannon to equip and develop the young air force of the newly born State of Pakistan. Arthur successfully supervised the integration of new equipment from Britain and the US, including securing technical training courses abroad for his local officers. An article mentioning Arthur's contribution to PAF in *Dawn*, the Karachi English speaking newspaper, sums it up by the following. 'It was due primarily to his careful planning, concerted hard work and dedicated professionalism that the modest air force became fully operational in a short span of time… he ensured through his foresight, dedication and loyalty that the PAF became self-reliant at all levels of

Arthur on his visit to Pakistan in 1984 when he was awarded the 'Crescent of Excellence' Medal.

command and leadership.' This self-reliance was vital because the Force dropped the prefix 'Royal' on 20 March 1956, during his command and became fully nationalised. His leadership enabled this transition to run smoothly.

Arthur was invited back to Pakistan with his predecessor, in 1984 by the Pakistan government to accept an award which acknowledged their contribution to the fledgling PAF.[1]

> Rawalpindi, Nov 10: A special investiture ceremony was held at Air Headquarters here on Saturday at which Air Chief Marshal Muhammad Anwar Shamin, Chief of the Air Staff, conferred the award of Hilal-i-Imtiaz (Military) on two former Commanders-in-Chief of the Pakistan Air Force, Air Marshal Sir AWB McDonald and Air Vice-Marshal LW Cannon, on behalf of the president of Pakistan.[2]

---

1. Pakistan sent its presidential jet to transport Arthur and Air Vice-Marshal Cannon to the investiture.
2. *Dawn*, Sunday, 11 November 1984, p. 3.

Arrival in Pakistan, Arthur, Mary, Air Vice Marshal Canon's Wife, Peter, Air Vice Marshal Canon disembarking the boat in Pakistan June 1955. The journey from England took 3 weeks via the Suez Canal.

Hilal-i-Imtiaz, translates as 'Crescent of Excellence', is the second highest award given out by the Pakistan government for outstanding service.

The following letters, written by Arthur's wife, Mary, to her father back home in England, give glimpses of their time in Pakistan.

Extract describing settling in from Mary's first letter home to her father:

Air House,
Karachi
June 15th, 1955

My dear Dad,

... Our arrival here seemed to me fantastic, but I am now beginning to get used to our future mode of life. The sentry at the gate presented arms, the guard inside were lined up (12 or so) and also presented arms. Outside the front door the 4 gardeners were lined up. The head one when asked said he had been here "half past three years".

Inside the front door were lined up on one side the butler and 3 bearers and washer up, on the other side the 3 sweepers, the dhobie (washerman) and the dhergie (sewing-man). The cook was absent as he had been sent to change his shirt. All these servants and their wives and children live in our servants' quarters in the compound. The 14 guards also live in the guard house inside our compound. There are 3 sentry boxes manned day and night on our 3 gates, a sergeant of the guard, and a sergeant and corporal drivers.

The guards are N.W. Frontier Forces, illiterate soldiers whose hobby is fighting. The Pakistani RPAS Provost Marshal told me we have them as guards to keep them occupied and out of trouble. Their sergeant proudly showed me their gunroom and ammunition this morning. I find it almost embarrassing to go into the garden, as a sentry presents arms or salutes every time I do so.

... Karachi is a most unattractive place, just a straggling town of 1½ million people in low buildings, few trees, no grass, no old buildings, and the country completely flat, and outside the town just red desert, desert, desert. Many of the 1½ million people are refugees living in tattered shacks of canvas and cardboard, with insufficient water and no sanitation. It must be the dryness and the heat of the sun that has prevented major epidemics. Some years there is as little as ½ inch of rain in the year, the annual average is about 9 in. which mostly falls in the first 3 weeks of July. This is the hottest month, though it is more humid for a short time after the monsoon.

The interest of the town lies in its inhabitants, domestic animals and methods of transport. Our house is on a tram route and the

Arthur taking the salute at Mauripur RPAF station, his headquarters. Standing beside him is Wing Cdr 'Auzzie' Khan, the station commander. Mauripur was the last active British unit on the Indian sub-continent.

trams are very noisy. Buses, camel carts, donkey carts, pony carts, bicycle and motor bicycle rickshaws are other methods of transport.

Arthur's HQ are some miles outside the town in the desert. There laden camels, and men riding on top of the loads can be seen setting off across the desert.

Water is only turned on in the mains for a few hours daily, but we have a tank and a pump, and two lorry loads of water is delivered daily. So water usually comes out of the taps.

The house is about the size of our Boscombe Down one and a similar size garden. There is a wide tiled semi-enclosed veranda the length of the front of the house upstairs and down. Peter has his Hornby trains out on it downstairs outside his bedroom.

There are 4 bedrooms, each with a modern tiled bathroom, and two dressing-rooms, and a vast drawing-room which is only used for winter parties. All parties at this time of year occur in the garden, and the trees are wired with lights. The lawns are quite brown as there is insufficient water for watering them at this time of year.

Arthur is now on a week's tour of his stations in W. Pakistan, with a party in a different RPAF mess each night, and inspections most mornings. He will be exhausted by the end of the week. Peter, Mrs Cannon and I are flying up to Peshawar on Friday to stay the night with the Pakistani Air Commodore commanding the Group up country. He has two boys of Peter's age. Lunch with the Governor, and dance in the Mess also.

Arthur takes over officially on Monday.

Arthur and I intend to cut down on the ridiculous round of parties …

They gave a farewell party of 300 here our 2nd night and we had attended the UK High Commissioner's party in honour of the Queen's birthday the day before, 1,000 guests 6:30 p.m. in the garden in full evening dress and mess kit in a gale of wind and sand.

Fortunately, in Arthur's interview with his boss, the Defence Minister and C-in-C. Army, Lieut. General Ayub Khan, the latter stressed that this was an austerity country and social life should not be too gay. I was never so relieved as to hear that that was policy – even if not practice. We shall try to put it into practice – when we

Anti aircraft gun Drigh Road, (PAF Base Faisal) Karachi.

get a chance. Printed invitation cards come in at the rate of 2 or 3 a day even now.

Our car has arrived but we have not yet seen it. It has gone to be under-sprayed.

Karachi is the largest airport in Asia and a cross-roads. I have already been out to the airport to meet a cousin of Arthur's and his wife en route for leave in England from Malaya. We last saw him in a rubber estate 21 years ago. The same evening, I was rung up by Gp Capt. Mungo Buxton (Jean's godfather) en route from Australia to England, and he came here from the RAF (not RPAF) staging post transit unit with a Wing Cdr. CO and I took him out to the civilian airport the other side of the town.

Must stop.
Much love, Mary.

Extract from letter dated 24 June 1955

We flew nearly 1,000 miles up the Indus, desert all the way except for some irrigated cultivation round the Indus and at Peshawar where there was a little green showing. We flew over barren brown-orange mountains as we approached Peshawar and for half hour it was very bumpy which Peter didn't like at all, and he cried out at each bump. He had been given some bromide tablets by the Doc. and he wasn't actually sick. On the way back we flew through a sandstorm and had to have the light on at 3:30 p.m. and fasten our safety belts. We were again thrown about and Peter didn't like it at all. He says he is never going to fly again. We travelled in great comfort, Arthur and AVM Cannon had gone up in the C-in-C's private plane, but we had the spare one which was just the same – all upholstered in pale blue leather, with four armchairs round a large table. It was cool at 7,000 ft. and we ceased sweating for a few hours. We travel with our own private bearer, as well as a steward, so Peter just rang the bell beside him for his toys to be brought. (I shall have to train him out here so that he does not expect that when he gets home.)

Peshawar was hot, about 106 degrees at midday, but there is a lovely swimming club there surrounded by green grass and green trees. The Pakistani Air Cdre we stayed with is President of the club so Peter lived in the water with his two boys of about the same age. Mrs Cannon and I on arrival had to go to lunch with the Governor of NW Frontier Province (also Arthur and AVM Cannon). We had a teetotal but very sumptuous lunch at Government House, red carpet and all.

I sat next the Governor, and found him quite easy to talk to. His youngest son, aged 16, is now in England being looked after by Field Marshal Auckinleck and going to Guys in 2 years' time to train as a doctor. The Governor, in appearance and conversation is a cultured European, yet he is a Pakistani who has never been out of undivided India. His second wife is now in strict purdah and never goes out of Govt. House ground even to shop. He buys her clothes for her. This is unusual in so cultured a family. She does not of course appear at meals.

The Air Cdre we stayed with took his wife out of purdah when he married her, she is still rather shy.

He attended a Mess dance at Peshawar. The Pakistani wives nearly all tend to sit together, very few dance or speak unless spoken to, but they are all very sweet and pretty in their saris and are gradually learning to emerge from their pupal state. They are shy of learning to dance, or swim or ride, it seems to them rather wicked, and their parents wouldn't approve. Most of the husbands are trying to encourage them to come out. The women are teetotal, but in spite of their religion most of the men drink whiskey except at very formal parties.

The one thing I notice in which the Pakistani women are in advance of us is the number of lady doctors, some of them RPAF or Naval wives with young children. One I met who is now studying medicine is the mother of 2 young children. Another I met, an RPAF wife, has two young children, is superintendent of a female hospital, and went to England to do a post-graduate course in medicine leaving a child of 3 out here, and having another one on her return.

The reason for this is the crying need for lady doctors, as none of the women, even the educated wives of fairly senior officers will allow a male doctor to attend them. They prefer to die.

AVM Cannon has had to provide RPAF lady doctors to attend the wives, and I saw two in their mess kit at the dance, pale blue saris over blue satin blouses with RPAF epaulettes and gold rank stripes (the latter exactly similar to Arthur's RAF ones).

I was also told that at one of the maternity hospitals when the lady doctor went sick and there was no other available, a male doctor was allowed to stand outside the door and shout instructions through the keyhole to the midwife.

Air House,
Karachi
June 29th 1955

My Dear Dad,

I have warned Jean that she will find Karachi very interesting but very irritating … It is certainly an experience not to be missed but at this time of year the climate is trying. This is the worst month though. It is always cool at the Yacht Club, as it is on the point in the harbour, exposed to all the winds that blow, and they do blow all the time (I have to wear an invisible hair net, even in the house). We go to the Yacht Club for a swim in the harbour most evenings, and after immersion in the sea our frayed tempers improve, and then the evening cools off and is pleasant…

Appendix VIII 239

Arthur's Vauxhall Vectra being loaded onto a Bristol Freighter. The car went with Arthur on trips to the North of Pakistan. (Arthur's car was a new Vauxhall Vectra that travelled out with them to Pakistan from England in the ship's hold. It flew with him on trips to the North of Pakistan as it was considered safer than using local cars because of the risk of terrorists attaching bombs to vehicles. Arthur had his own chauffeur who drove the car at all times. No one else was allowed to drive it, apart from Arthur himself).

Our Vauxhall is now in use and Arthur is very pleased with it, it is a pale soft green. I have not yet dared drive it as the Karachi traffic is fantastic. At least the camel carts continue to move in a straight line, but the pedestrians walk straight into the car, there are loose donkeys roaming the street, the bicycle rickshaws shoot all over the place, the bus drivers are very incompetent and erratic, there are trams and tramlines, much one-way traffic and little order of any kind. Arthur had told me that camel drivers went to sleep while driving their carts, but I did not realise he meant this literally. In the country we passed camel cart after camel cart, with the drivers lying down in the back of the cart wrapped up in a cloth as protection from the sun, and fast asleep. I presume they wake up when the camel arrives at its destination. (A. tells me it is considered a joke after dark to turn the camel round so that when the driver wakes up he finds he has returned to his point of departure.)

Extract from letter dated 18 August.

Last Sunday was a great day here, Independence Day, celebrated by a big parade of all the Armed Services. The Service Chiefs and the Defence Secretary stood on the dais with the Governor General and the Prime Minister. The Governor General arrived in a magnificent carriage escorted by his mounted bodyguard in scarlet and blue uniforms. The RPAF did a fly-past, as well as a march-past. The rains had started (at last) the day before, it was drizzling and the visibility was very poor. All the same the RPAF did a very good fly-past in tight formation, but the jets had to be left out. The musical drive by the bodyguard had to be cancelled as the ground was a quagmire. I had a front row VIP seat, and the children had front row seats in the children's enclosure. Jean was just well enough in time.

So far 'the rains' have been very little, just English rain and perhaps 1 inch in all. It has now cleared up but we are waiting for more. In 2 days our lawns started to turn green, and they are now brilliant green, and are being mowed. Last week they were a sandy waste. The gardener (mali) is looking much more cheerful. There are still two coolies employed doing nothing else but pouring watering-cans on the lawns and flower beds – what a way to employ two full-time robust young men. They water continuously from 6 a.m. until the water runs out at about 10 a.m., and then again in the afternoon. (We are not on a continuous water supply, and the RPAF buy two trucks of water for us daily to go in to our household tank.)

Little striped squirrels exactly like Chippy Hackee in Beatrix Potter's *Timmy Tiptoes* eat my Morny's bath soap every night – I must do something about it. They have learnt to open the shutters over the bathroom windows.

Hope you are better.
Much love, Mary.

Air House,
Karachi
Sept 25th 1955

My dear Dad,

The cooler weather you refer to will not come for another month. We are now having the hottest weather we have had out here at all.

Over 100° every day, 102° yesterday and 104° the day before. This is because the S.W. Monsoon wind has ceased, the sky is cloudless, and a hot wind (the beginning of the N.E. Monsoon) is blowing from the desert. It is like a hot blast from an oven when we go out in the car. The humidity has gone right down from 70% to 20%, and at least our clothes should no longer mildew. This hot weather when the S.W. Monsoon ceases is expected, and the Grammar School has just broken up for a fortnight's holiday for that reason. We are taking Peter up-country for 10 days at the end of this week. Karachi is now the hottest place in all of Pakistan.

Last night we slept with glasses of water beside us which we sprinkled on the sheets every few hours when we woke up from the heat, and with the ceiling fan at full speed, some coolness was produced by evaporation. We have moved Peter from his S.W. Monsoon bedroom to what was a storeroom that gets the N.E. wind.

I have taken on an amusing job, as tutor to a Pakistani, a qualified doctor and Chairman of the biggest pharmaceutical company in Asia (oriental drugs, not Western).[3] He is touring European pharmaceutical laboratories next year and wants to learn to speak fluent English. He advertised in the newspaper for a cultured European with Scientific background. He reads and understands English, but speaks very badly and is hampered by a stammer. He is a very intelligent self-made man who never went to school, and entered medical college self-taught. He has a library of 7,000 books, and I teach him in his English library – which includes all your Medical textbooks, all Winston Churchill's books, books on music and art, and a vast range of dictionaries, encyclopaedia, etc. Next door is the Urdu library. His medical training was done in Urdu, and his business in conducted entirely in Urdu. The only English he speaks is to me. His wife is in purdah so I have not seen her, and he has an 11-year-old daughter who will take up Chemistry. His brother, also in the firm, is doing a post-graduate course in pharmacy at Bonn University. He pays me 10Rs an hour and travelling expenses of 50Rs (about 17/6) per month. We aim at 5 lessons a week, of 1–1½ hours. All I have to do is to read to him and talk to him, later he will

---

3. Mary's employer was Dr Hakin Said.

read to me – when he is a little more fluent. So far we have read a chapter on popular atomic physics.

He is very Oriental, and I find it very interesting comparing Eastern and Western, views, though his halting English is rather a handicap at present.

On Saturdays and Sundays, he does not go to his factory or laboratories, but only to his Clinic – where he and his assistants see up to 500 patients between 6 a.m. and 5 p.m. Advice is free but they are given prescriptions for use at any chemist's shop or at his dispensary. The patients clock in from 4 a.m. onwards when they are given a time-card, so that they do not wait about all day. Most poor people in this country of course receive no medical attention at all – there is no State medical service. Only the Armed Forces and some other Govt. concerns such as the Railways provide free medical attention and hospital facilities for their employees. I was told by a British Brigadier recently that one small state up-country (Swat?), with a population of about 4 million, had as its only medical officer one veterinary surgeon.

Much love Mary

8,000 ft between Peshawar and Karachi

Oct 9th 1955

My dear Dad,

We are on our way back from a 10-day official tour of the N.W. Frontier Province. We stayed 3 nights in Peshawar, and did expeditions from there by car to the Khyber Pass (about 20 miles), and by air to Parachinar – a village in a green fertile valley in a piece of Pakistan jutting into Afghanistan.

On the bare rocky drive up the Khyber Pass we saw forts just like those sold with toy soldiers. At the top Arthur had to inspect a guard of honour of the Khyber rifles – local tribesmen trained as militia by regular officers. They were very smart though they had bobbed hair under their berets, and wore a local brand of sandals instead of boots. Their pipe band played somewhat incongruously 'Over the sea to Skye'. We were given lunch in the Khyber Officers' Mess, and entertained to coffee by the Political Agent (the representative of the

Appendix VIII 243

Arthur as C in C of the Pakistan Airforce shaking hands with Pathan tribesmen in the Khyber Pass.

Govt. responsible for law and order in the tribal areas). The militia out of uniform in white baggy trousers then did a tribal dance which included a lot of shaking of their blacked bobbed hair.

At Parachinar, 5,000 ft we were entertained at the Kerruce Officers' Mess and by the Parachinar Political Agent. He was a keen gardener and took us round his lovely garden, smooth green lawns with bright herbaceous borders of English flowers behind, and, as a background, mountains with a fresh sprinkling of snow. He spoke perfect English and was a very cultured person but looked most oriental, in a gold and blue turban, and long fierce black moustachios. We sat under a big chinar tree on his lawn and ate freshly roasted sweetcorn from his garden. He also drove us in a jeep to a fort on the Afghan border, a steel-plated bulletproof door was unlocked for us to enter and we drank beer on the balcony of the officers' mess with steel-plated window shutters behind us, and a machine gun manned and trained on the pass beside us. This pass, Peraksta?, was

This photo shows Arthur, thought to be in the garden at Air House, with the cook and other staff.

the one Roberts marched up to Kabul. Our jeep was accompanied by a truckload of armed tribesmen, and our aircraft was guarded by tribesmen lying on the ground with rifles trained on the grass airstrip. Everyone was armed, the villager herding his cattle, the servant carrying the coffee, all had bandoliers of bullets and rifles.

Forgot to mention a ceremony that occurred on the way up the Khyber where A. was met by a gathering of local chiefs. They made speeches in Pushtu which were translated by the Political Agent asking A to make the Air Force strong to fight against their enemies, and offering their services when required. (They all long to fight, it is their hobby.) A and I were then each presented with two live ornamental sheep which we had to touch on the head to signify we had accepted them. This is the custom, and as soon as we went the sheeps' throats were cut and all the tribesmen had a big feast. The local head-dress in NWFP is a straw cap surrounded by a blue cotton turban which hangs down as a scarf over the back of the neck. Even the Parachinar ('old chinar tree') Political Agent wore one but he had gold thread woven into the straw, and wore a European suit otherwise.

Garden of the Khyber Rifle Officers Mess on the top of the Khyber Pass. L to R: Air Cdre Rabb, Mrs Rabb, Political Agent, Mary, Colonel of the Khyber Rifles, Arthur and some officers of the Khyber Rifles. In front Said Rabb, Peter, Mahsood Rabb with Squadron Leader Butt, Arthur's personal Staff Officer kneeling behind the children.

Peter had got very tired and fed up with the official entertaining and travelling and asked to be left with the Rabb boys (Air Cdre Rabb's sons aged 11 and 9) in Peshawar. So we then left him there a week while we travelled on. Just as well we did because although we got up in to a cool climate eventually we were not long enough in one place to do Peter any good.

We flew from Peshawar to Rawalpindi (I should refer to your atlas at this point) and then drove in a staff car from there to Lower Topa near Murree, where we stayed the night with the English headmaster of a boarding-school there which is run by the RPAF for boys aged 13–16 who sign on to become aircraft apprentices.

After that they go to Karachi for their technical training. Lower Topa 7,000ft was cool and I had to borrow an overcoat to go to a cocktail party in the local officers' mess. We also just had time

Arthur being photographed by two of the boys at the RPAF boarding school at Murree.

to visit Mr (ex-Headmaster Christs Hospital) & Mrs Flecker at their school (public boarding) Lawrence College the other side of Murree. (By the way send me the initials of my godfather and tell me his connection with the Lawrences of India. Lawrence College was founded by one of them.)

We should have seen Nanga Parbat from the lawn of the headmaster's house but there was cloud on the distant mountains. However we saw it the next morning from another small hill station Nathiagali (also 7,000ft) about two hours' drive from Murree, and the official summer residence of the Governor of the NW Frontier Province. We drove from there down a mountain road for about another two hours to Abbottabad, a fine military town in an open valley at about 4,000ft and surrounded by mountains - a delightful place to be stationed. Murree is just a craggy hill station, steep pine-clad slopes. Abbottabad is surrounded by rolling grassy hills and pine trees, with the mountains in easy reach. We stayed there with the Scottish Brigadier (brought back from retirement in Scotland to command the Pakistan Military Academy, their Sandhurst). He has a lovely house and although a bachelor the house was the best run I have yet met out here, but he inherited it in apple pie order from the last British Commandant. That night we were entertained to cocktails by the General (Pakistani) commanding the Division there, and to dinner in an officers' mess, the PIFFER Mess, a famous one, with 29 VCs in a glass case won by members of the Mess, and Field Marshal Birdwood's uniforms and 35 medals.

The next day by staff car for 2 hours to the one-way jeep traffic up the Karghan valley, then a nightmare jeep ride up a rough rocky track the width of a jeep only, and a drop, not of 100s of feet, but of 1,000s of feet on the left hand side all the way. We had 6 jeeps with us to A's surprise. I think Air Cdre Webb was afraid he might lose his C-in-C in the wilds, so he sent a mobile wireless observation post with us with an officer and about 6 men to keep us in wireless communication with the outside world. A drove our jeep, he wasn't risking a strange driver on that track. We were humped about in the jeep for 2¼ hours and daren't look at the view, our eyes glued to the track all the time and I had to hold on to avoid being bumped out – though we were all ready to jump at any moment. (The police check post told us they had only lost 3 jeeps over the edge this year. One rolled a couple of thousand feet down into the river below, and the bodies were never recovered.) We eventually arrived at Shogran Forest Rest House at 7,000ft and we looked and felt as if we had done a 4-hour rough channel crossing. We should have gone on the next day further up the valley, but as it meant getting up at 5 a.m. to catch the one-way traffic and then sitting in a jeep again most of the day, we decided to stay where we were and have a few days' rest and walking the hills.

You would have loved Shogran, like Hindhead with everything multiplied by ten. From our rest house we looked over a grassy meadow through pine trees to a distant range of mountains, the highest 17,000ft and several glaciers in sight. Fresh snow fell on the 12–13,000ft mountains to one side of us while we were out walking. We were looked after by a very pleasant Forest Reserve Officer (Mr

Mohamed Ali), he knew the Latin names of all the trees and many of the flowers. Our second day there we walked two thousand feet up to 9,000ft (I did some of the way on a pony led by a local peasant). We walked through Pinus excelsa (the Blue Pine) and Cedrus deodar, the two commonest trees. Also a good deal of spruce abies, a very few deciduous trees, walnut, two or 3 sycamores, and a little poor ash. The evergreen trees he told us were 100–150ft high. There were many wild flowers even in October, the commonest a crimson geum and a bright blue and very prolific branching bugle? I also found pink, white and yellow balsas, gentians, dandelions, indigo wild strawberry, and many flowers I may be able to identify when I have time to refer to a flower book. We had fires in the evening and wore tweed suits and jerseys. We were out of reach of shops, but our food was tied up to the verandah and was bleating when we left for our walk. We had a very good roast lamb that night, and Irish stew the next day. Eggs, chickens, and rough bread, flat cakes baked from home-ground and home-grown maize were also available.

On the way back we walked 7 miles down the road to avoid the worst of the jeep journey.

We stayed with the Brigadier at Abbottabad again.

We flew over the flooded Indus at Multan yesterday, and saw flooded fields and houses sticking up out of the water. They have had a disastrous year with floods.

Love, Mary

Air House,
Karachi,
Nov 2nd 1955

My dear Dad,

We have had a very busy week-end as two Secretary of States came to Karachi. On Friday we went to a formal dinner at the Governor General's house to meet the Earl and Countess of Home, Secretary of State for Commonwealth Relations. He is on his way back from a 2 months' tour including Australia, New Zealand, Malaya, India and Pakistan. The dinner was terrific, off Crown Derby all specially made with crescent and stars. The anteroom was lined with the Governor General's bodyguard, also the stairs on the way up. Most impressive as they are all over 6ft 6 inch tall, dressed in scarlet uniforms with blue striped turbans, and they were holding their lances in front of them and standing like statues.

The guests assembled at 8:15 and whiskey and sherry was served and we all stood round and talked, attended to by the Military and Air Secretaries. Then we all stood round in a semi-circle and the Earl and Countess came in escorted by the UK High Commissioner and Lady Symon, and were introduced and shook hands all round. Then there was a fanfare of trumpets and the Governor General and his very beautiful new Begum came in and also shook hands all round. After that water only was served to drink. I sat between the Canadian High Commissioner, and the Pakistan Minister for Information who Ann will be delighted to hear also specialised in the Renaissance period at University.

After dinner the ladies drank coffee in the drawing-room and the Begum came round and talked to us in turn. Soon after the men came in, the Governor General and Begum went off, and shortly after that the Earl and High Commissioner. Then we were all free to go.

The next day Lord and Lady Home were due to visit the Yacht Club at tea-time. Arthur and I took them for a sail in the Governor General's yacht. Arthur asked the Military Secretary at the dinner if he could sail it. It has not been used for 6 months but is kept in commission. The Governor General has now given his permission to sail it.

I discovered that Lady Home is daughter of Alington, ex-headmaster of Eton, and knew Peggy's Christian name.

They were easy to talk to and were suffering from too intensive a tour, no rest, and speeches to make and broadcasts to give wherever he went. On Sunday he was taken out to a beach for 'a rest' but while there he had to prepare 5 speeches and a broadcast.

Sunday afternoon the Secretary of State for Air and his wife, Lord and Lady de L'Isle and Dudley, refuelled at Mauirpur on their way to Delhi, also on a Commonwealth tour of the RAF. We gave them tea at the Officers' Mess, and Lord Home wanted to have a private talk with the other Lord, so that was arranged. Lord and Lady de L'Isle will be staying in Karachi on their way back. Last night we had to put up an Air Commodore and Wing Cdr. Passing through. So we are weary.

Much love, Mary

Air House,
Karachi,
Nov 28th 1955

My dear Dad,

We had a very successful trip to E. Pakistan…

We stayed one night in Lahore on the way, and had two hours sightseeing. It is the old capital of the Punjab and has many ancient Moghul buildings. We saw the remains of the large Fort built by Akbar about 1500 and something, and the Mosque built by Aurangzeb the 6th Moghul Emperor (Akbar being the 3rd). Also we saw the Shalimar gardens built by Jehangir, Akbar's son. He was a great gardener and also built the Shalimar Gardens in Kashmir.

We had two hours in Delhi the next morning, and were taken for a drive round the magnificent Indian Government office buildings in New Delhi, in which Arthur worked during the war. Then we had coffee under an immense tree in the lovely garden of Air Marshal Mukenjee, C-in-C Indian Air Force. There to meet us was Miss MacMahon and her brother, who is Senior Trade Commissioner in Delhi. She was our John's form mistress in III A at the mall. Her brother was at the Imperial Defence College with Arthur.

We drove under Marshal Hulganin's triumphal arches and strings of flags. He had arrived the night before. Air Marshal Mukenjee gave us permission to do a circuit over the Taj Mahal at Agra, but unfortunately the permission was then cancelled, because Marshal Hulganin was circling over it at that moment.

We then flew over the fertile W. Indian plain, hundreds of miles of patchwork fields, with villages here and there – no waste-land at all, a few trees in the villages, otherwise all fields. Then down the valley of the Ganges all day until we landed at Dacca at 7 p.m. For several hours we could see the snows of the Himalayas looking like a layer of stratum cloud above the mists of the distance. I argued with Arthur to start with and said they were clouds, until I saw peaks on the upper surface. We were too far away to see anything except mist below the snow.

At Dacca we stayed at Government House, and that evening went to a buffet dinner in the garden of RPAF officers' mess. Now that the nights are cooler there is a heavy dew, so dinner parties are held under vast brightly coloured awnings called shamiars.

The next morning Arthur inspected the RPAF at Dacca, and then we flew 100 miles to the port of E. Pakistan, Chittagong, where he again inspected RPAF, followed by an official lunch. From the air over Dacca one can see what a vast amount of water there is in E. Pakistan, all the mouths of the Ganges joined to the mouths of the Brahmaputra, and between bright green and golden fields – all rice. When the sun shines at the right angle the water sparkles between the rice stems, and one can see that even the fields are mostly water. They had just started to harvest the rice, and we could watch them cutting it as we landed and took off. Some of the rice fields, those being harvested, were dry, and some were brown earth spotted from the air with rice stacks.

All of E. Pakistan is green, green fields and green trees. It rains for 6 months of the year, and Chittagong's annual rainfall is over 100 inches, and there is an area N. of Chittagong with over 300 inches. It is a pity E. and W. Pakistan cannot share their water, then it would be a fertile country.

We flew back to Dacca that night, and dined with the Governor of E. Pakistan (ruler of 45 million people). His wife is in purdah.

Next day we flew back to Chittagong and had a most interesting trip in a river launch up the river (name forgotten) on which Chittagong is situated, 50 miles up to see a modern paper mill. The river was wider than the Thames at Westminster, but silts up frequently, and we were unlucky and our launch stuck 5 miles from our destination. We transferred to a sampan for a mile or two, but that was so slow rowing against the stream that we eventually got out and walked along the river bank in the heat of the day. The paper mill was most interesting, we saw bamboo go in one end and paper come out the other. The paper was made entirely from bamboo pulp.

On our way home we touched down at Calcutta for a check, but did not go outside the airport.

Arthur goes up-country again at the end of this week on a 10 days' annual inspection. I am staying with Peter who is about to start his annual exams.

Much love, Mary.

Air House,
Karachi,
December 7th, 1955

My dear Dad,

Descriptions of my morning routine for your amusement:

7.25 a.m. see Peter off to school. 7.45 a.m. fill the washing-machine and set it going. Send for the cook, and give him orders for the day written down in capital printed letter, and he dictates to me his previous day's shopping account (he wears an astrakhan Jinnah cap, an un-ironed very off-white shirt outside ditto trousers). I provide him with clean white aprons (which I wash) for cooking in.

Then I issue the day's tea and sugar, and any other groceries required from my locked store cupboard. The servants insist on a daily issue of tea and sugar, otherwise it disappears. So, I count it out in teaspoons, a tiresome waste of time. The cook measures out the sugar he needs.

Then to the kitchen, across the other side of the backyard, to see the drinking-water boil and the milk brought to the boil 3 times.

Then the cook calls the 3rd Sweeper, Inyat Myshi (he is dressed in a very dirty turban, large gold rings hang from his ear, his shirt and trousers are the usual colour of sweepers' clothes, which is the colour of dirt as they are never washed). He salutes smartly 'Salaam Memsahib' and escorts me to the servants' latrines, which are always spotless, and liberally sprinkled with bleaching powder, which is issued by the RPAF. He then leads me to the servants' refuse bin and raises the lid for me to see that there are no flies and that it has been emptied. After which he raises the metal trap arrangements, as if they are not inspected, they become blocked up with the ashes with which they scour their saucepans. All of this is done to a chorus of 'Salem Mum-Sahib, Salaam Memsahib', from the seven little daughters of Mungli the 1st Sweeper. They are pretty little girls but very dirty, completely unwashed, wearing ragged garments of no colour at all except dark dirt. However, they are always happy and playing out in the sunshine, minding the baby for their mother who goes out to work (the Sweepers are Hindus, so she is not in purdah). Goodness knows what they live on, but I have now discovered why Mungli sits on the back-door steps during meals. He is waiting for the food Peter wastes on his plate.

In the meantime, my Smith's Timer having rung the alarm, Anwar (the washer-upper) will have turned off the washing-machine, and be removing the clothes to the line. (Anwar also wears an astrakhan cap and white shirt and trousers.)

The sergeant of the guards will then salute smartly, and want to know (via an interpreter) if I am inspecting their quarters that day. Their quarters are now so clean I rarely inspect them.

Air House,
Karachi,
January 15th, 1956

My dear Dad,

I am sorry not to have found time to write while the children have been here.

Ann and Jean should have arrived in London yesterday afternoon by BOAC, as PIA now only runs monthly and would have made them too late. They were both due back on the 11th. John has got a passage in an RAF Hastings leaving tomorrow morning, which gives him several days to spare before his leave expires.

They have been very lucky seeing so much of the country in a short time. They had 3 nights in Peshawar, going up the Khyber Pass, up the Kohat Pass visiting the arms factory near Kohat where rifles and revolvers are made by hand by the tribesmen complete with label saying "Made in England", or in one case "Made in USA". We saw them boring the barrels by hand, turning a bicycle wheel which acts as a fly wheel, and boring it with a steel rod attached to a weight which keeps the pressure constant, the whole contraption turned by hand. The metal obtained for making them is mostly stolen, and the RPAF Station Commander of Kohat has great difficulty in preventing pieces off his fire extinguishers and so on being removed. Peter thoroughly enjoyed turning their handles for them, and the head Malik suggested we might leave Peter with them to work their machines. We were entertained to tea and biscuits by the Maliks in the factory, and John was presented with a dagger (Arthur had been presented with one on a previous occasion). The little village sells nothing but lethal weapons, rows of rifles hanging up. All the tribesmen from whom the local levies are recruited are supplied by them. The Govt. pays the local tribesmen to keep the peace, and they provide the sentries and their arms.

We had breakfast with the Peshawar Vale Hunt under the orange trees laden with ripe fruit in the garden of the head Malik of a nearby village. Curried chicken, meat fried on skewers, and meat rissoles full of chillies for breakfast, all cooked by villagers in the garden.

Peter, Mary, Ann and Arthur at the Darra Arms Factory on the road to the Khyber Pass.

Mary checking the riffling in the Darra Arms Factory.

We drove the 100 odd miles from Peshawar to Rawalpindi through lovely fertile country beside the Kabul river, crossing the river by the famous Attock Bridge where the Kabul river joins the Indus. The bridge can be closed by large steel doors, and is the only means of crossing the river for a hundred miles or so, and is the way the NFWP tribesmen got in to Kashmir last time there was trouble.

About 20 miles before we got to Rawalpindi we visited the ruins of the city of Taxila, dating from the time of Alexander the Great. After an official lunch at Rawalpindi where we met some of the Army generals ('Pindi is Army HQ) Arthur and John drove up to Murree to see the 2 ft of snow up there. (The weaker sex were too weary, but did a little shopping in the bazaars. They had also shopped in the old city of Peshawar, where even Pakistani RPAF, wives would not venture to shop without an escort.)

The last sentence reminds me that on our way up the Kohat Pass through Afridi tribal areas, the Kohat RPAF Station Commander told us that the whole area had been alerted the day before of our impending arrival, and all undesirable tribesmen had been confined to their houses. We were escorted by a jeep-load of RPAF police armed with Sten guns.

It was cold in Peshawar at night and very cold in Rawalpindi. At the party in the RPAF mess in the evening I wore my fur coat in front of the fire. The building with their high ceilings and many doors are designed for the long hot summer, not the short winter. We stayed there in a vast rambling Circuit House (Govt. VIP Rest House for Ministers, Judges etc.). The Mir of Hunza was supposed to be sharing it with us, but he did not turn up.

Then to Lahore, one night in the Circuit House there, an afternoon visiting Akbar's 17th century Fort and Aurangzeb's 18th Century Mosque, and Jehangir's tomb. Parties in the evening. A visit to the State museum the next morning where we saw seals and pottery 4–5,000 years old from Mohen Jo Daro (the ancient Indus Valley civilization, only discovered fairly recently). A visit to the School of Art where we saw the ex-Court artist of Paticla painting Moghul miniatures, and bought two. Then lunch with the Governor of West Pakistan at Government House in a magnificent dining-room which was once a 17th century Moghul tomb. The Governor's wife is in purdah. The Mir of Hunza and his Rhanee were the other principal guests. She only spoke Pushtu, and sat between Arthur and an Urdu-English speaking RPAF officer, so had to remain silent throughout the meal, but she looked very aristocratic. The Mir spoke some English. Hunza can only be reached by pony, there is no other access.

Air House,
Karachi, Pakistan,
March 3rd, 1956

My dear Dad,

Thank you very much for the cheque for £5 for my birthday which arrived most punctually on the morning of my birthday. I shall buy myself another Dacca muslin evening stole with half of it, in view of the fact that we have to attend one banquet and one dinner at the Governor General's, one dinner at the Admiral's with the G.G. as guest, and one dinner at the Australian High Commissioner's to meet Mr Casey with the G.G. again as guest, all in the space of

5 days. During the same 5 days we also attend a reception by the Prime Minister, a reception by the Ministry of Foreign Affairs, a Torchlight Tattoo by the Army, an Air Display by the RPAF, and entertain in our own home a '5 star general', Sir William Dickson, Marshal of the RAF and Chairman of the Joint Chiefs of Staffs Committee, and a Naval captain on his staff.

In case this should sound even more bewildering to you than it does to me, we are about to have a SEATO conference of the council of SEATO in Karachi. Sir Anthony Eden and Mr Selwyn Lloyd are attending. The UK delegation is 45 members, the USA I think 60 odd and then there are all the others, Thailand, Persia, France, Australia and so on.

In addition, the Shahinshah of Persia is choosing this week to visit Karachi, so the Banquet at G.G. house is for the Shahinshah and his Queen. The dinner is to meet members of the SEATO conference. The dinner at the Admiral's is because he is running the conference.

As far as Arthur is concerned it has started already as he and the Admiral have to meet all the Service delegates at the Civil airport, and he has just gone off tonight (Sat.) in gaberdine and medals to meet the first two. Tomorrow he meets the Iranian War Minister and Sir William Dickson.

Sir William Dickson sent a cable accepting Arthur's invitation to stay at Air House, and asking that no formal evening parties should be arranged for him personally on medical advice.

Little does he know what has been arranged for him officially. Let us hope he will be able to get out of some of them.

Peter is very blooming and happy, singing about the house, and very busy with his rabbits and his furnace. We get a child in to spend the day with him every Saturday - always younger than himself, but he seems to enjoy being boss and being looked up to by his young friends, after being ordered about as 4th of the family. Bunny Raza is the only friend he has who is older than himself, except for Judith Lane the Wing Cdr's daughter out at Mauripur whom he stayed with once, but she is too far out of Karachi to be much use normally. He gets on very well with the Raza boys (12 and 9) his only near neighbours, and we share cars for school journeys so he sees them twice daily in the car, and they often come to tea.

Some local colour - Elphinstone St., the 'west end' of Karachi if it deserves such a title is plagued by beggars. As you get out of your car begging bowls are pushed in front of you by cripples, and naked stumps of arms are paraded before you, while other beggars crawl along the pavement. I have just discovered from Hakin Said (Dr Said) my employer, that these beggars are all on contract to the contractor of beggars for that area. He pays them a wage, and they give their earnings to him. Presumably he turns them off his street if they don't earn enough.

Must stop as A. should soon be back for dinner.

Much love, Mary.

Air House,
Karachi,
March 17th, 1956

My dear Dad,

Thank you for your letters of March 4th and March 11th. I am sorry not to have written for about a fortnight.

We had a very exhausting though interesting time last week with the SEATO conference, and a state visit of the Shahinshah of Iran and his Queen. We are just recovering but now the Turkish Prime Minister arrives on an official visit tomorrow, and that means another round of parties.

Sir William Dickson, Marshal of the RAF, Chairman of the UK Joint Chiefs of Staffs Committee, and Chairman of the Military delegates to SEATO, stayed with us, and a Naval Captain on his staff. He is a very nice person, but is suffering from stomach ulcers, and arrived feeling very poorly. He went to bed early most nights, missing the official parties.

Arthur and I get asked to most of the high level parties, dinner with the G.G. to meet the delegates, and a reception and banquet to meet the Shahinshah all in one week.

At the dinner Arthur, doing his duty, saw a group of rather sad looking individuals sitting in a group in the garden, and went up and made conversation to them. The palest and saddest of all A. addressed, and asked him if he was a SEATO delegate. He turned out to be Monsieur Pireau, the French Foreign Minister.

At the banquet we chatted to Mr Macdonald, the New Zealand Foreign Minister, and Prince Wan the Thailand one, a very cheery individual.

We went out to dinner with the Australian High Commissioner to meet Mr Casey their Foreign Minister, and I was the only woman guest and had to sit on the right of the Governor General, the principal guest. The other women had all fallen out, and gone to a female dinner party given by the Finance Minister's wife to meet Mrs Foster Dulles.

The RPAF gave a very good air display which went without a hitch, timed to a second, and with aerobatics in jet planes. It was watched by all the SEATO delegates, and Arthur was congratulated by many of them on it. At the display I sat next to the Vice-President of the Philippines. Mrs Foster Dulles was on his other side, and I talked to her too.

On my other side I had the RPAF Air Cdre responsible for organising the flying, and beyond him was the Prime Minister, Arthur, and the Governor General.

The Prime Minister reviewed the aeroplanes on the ground before it started, standing in a car with Arthur.

At the reception the Military Secretary presented me to the Queen, and then asked me to sit down in an armchair next her. She was sitting on a sofa with the G.G.'s wife, Begum Iskandar Mirza.

I was embarrassed as no-one else was sitting at all. I waited for the Queen or the Begum to speak, but both sat in silence (probably of exhaustion~ already having had an official reception at the airport at 11 a.m., drive through the city in state, official lunch, official tea-party and the reception was then to be followed by banquet and a military tattoo). Mrs Amjad Ali (the Finance Minister's wife) told me she changed into 5 different saris that day, and Sir Alexander Symon (UK High Commissioner) told me last night that he changed 7 times that day.

The Ambassadors and High Commissioners all had to stand out in the full sun at 11 a.m. in their top hats and long black European coats to be presented to the Shah at the airport. Arthur had to stand on the dais with the other two Service Chiefs. He has to do it again tomorrow morning (Sunday) for the Turkish Prime Minister. Then we have to go to dinner with the G.G. tomorrow Sunday night.

The G.G. becomes the President on Friday, and he, his Begum and the Governors of the two provinces are then no longer to be addressed as 'Your Excellency'. All the crowns come off the Service caps and badges.

Much love, Mary.

Air House,
Karachi,
November 1st 1956

My dear Dad,

The news today is very bad. I wonder if Eden's Govt will fall this afternoon. It would seem the best thing that could happen. Britain and France versus the rest of the world is a poor alliance. We feel very uncomfortable and apologetic out here. There are to be anti-British demonstrations in Karachi tomorrow, so the Grammar School is to be closed tomorrow. The Russian big annual reception tonight (to which the British Diplomatic Corps had been invited and commanded by the High Commissioner to attend) has been cancelled. Racing at the Yacht Club tomorrow may be cancelled.

We have been asked to meet Lord and Lady Attlee at a Reception on Sunday.

November 3rd

Sorry not to have got this off before.

The Govt did not fall.

We stayed in the house all yesterday, but Peter went out to work with Arthur to get books out of the RAF library, and use office typewriter, so Ann and I had a peaceful morning. I am sure that Arthur's staff did not. Sailing was cancelled, and so was the farewell Ball at the Staging Post.

There was a procession yesterday to the Prime Minister's house to protest against the British and French action, and they also went to the UK High Commissioner's and the French Embassy. No disorders. There are groups of armed police about as a precautionary measure. Shops were closed in protest.

We still feel the use of force was wrong, and especially after the dispute had gone to the United Nations.

Much love, Mary

Air House,
Karachi,
November 8th, 1956

My dear Dad,

Thank you for your letter of Nov. 4th. Do not worry about us in Karachi. Reading the London *Times* and the *Karachi Times* of Monday this week, 6 policemen were injured in Karachi but 8 were injured in Trafalgar Square. So Arthur said I should write to you and tell you to keep away from the dangers of London.

The demonstrations here have been mostly students. There were some stones thrown at the UK High Commissioner's Office and at UK cars outside, and one was overturned. Otherwise the demonstrations have mostly been in the City, and outside the Prime Minister's house. The press is very anti-British, but the local press is very irresponsible at the best of times. I enclose a cutting from *Dawn* at the start of the hostilities, to give you an idea of local feeling. Everyone is very polite and pleasant to us, but we attend parties with some embarrassment, and I find small talk less easy under the circumstances. Senior officers and Govt officials continue to come up to us and make pleasant conversation.

Ann is the only one who has to keep her end up, as one of her Pakistani 17-year-old VI form boys is an ardent Nationalist, and she has difficult political discussions with him under normal conditions.

British people have kept away from the bazaars and crowded parts of the town; the Diplomatic and better class residential district is in a suburb. We are on the fringe only of the town ourselves, 3 houses out of the Municipal area, in the old cantonment area. (Our address is really Air House, E.I. Line, the latter standing for European Infantry Lines I believe). I have not allowed Ann or Peter to go shopping since the trouble started. Our house of course is almost a fortress with 16 armed guards. They have a locked armoury all complete.

Racing at the Yacht Club was only cancelled for one day, and only UK parties have been cancelled.

We have seen no crowds or disturbance.

Now that a cease-fire has been agreed upon, we wait to see what happens next.

For the first time since we came here we have been using the special radio set (short-wave) we brought with us. We get the BBC news quite well on it.

In the Air 7,000 ft between Karachi and Lahore

November 19th, 1956

My dear Dad,

We are now on our way to Dacca and Chittagong (East Pakistan). We were to have spent tonight in Delhi, but unfortunately Marshal Bulganin and an official party of Russians arrived in Delhi yesterday, and Arthur did not want to get mixed up with their official reception. So instead we are staying tonight with the RPAF Station Commander at Lahore, and going on to Delhi tomorrow morning. We have to touch down there as a military aircraft, and will have about two hours there and are lunching with the C-in-C of the Indian Air Force, Air Marshal Mukenjee. We were to have stayed with him. We get to Dacca tomorrow evening and have two nights there at Government House, dining with the Governor one night, and at the RPAF Mess the other night. We fly back all-night Tuesday night, touching down at Calcutta at 10 p.m., and arriving back in Karachi at 7 a.m. Arthur and I each have a curtained off cubicle with a bunk, bed-linen and blankets, electric fans and reading lamps. I doubt if I shall sleep, Bristol freighters are very noisy aircraft. We have to shout when speaking to each other, and conversation is not really practicable. At the moment Arthur is drawing plans of a new yacht for the RAF staging post, and has plans, graph paper and slide rule, etc. spread out in front of him on a large table. Sq. Ldr. Qudus (Public Relations) and Sq Ldr. Butt (Staff Officer) are playing cards on a small table opposite, and Group Captain Nurkhand, who is also accompanying us, is reading.

I hope to get a glimpse of Lahore this afternoon, before the usual round of official parties. I am to be driven round for an hour. Lahore has some fine old Moghul buildings and is a I believe a quite attractive old town unlike Karachi. It was too near the border of India to be made the modern capital.

We have had a round of parties this week, the American General (full General) Orval Cook in command of the American Forces in Europe under Gruenther was visiting Karachi, the Admiral's wife and I sat on either side of him at a lunch. Then the C-in-C of the Indonesian Navy and his wife were also on a visit and an Australian frigate was in. Parties by the Australian High Commissioner (dinner), RPN Navy (cocktails) on board Australian frigate, American Military Aid and so on.

I forgot to tell you that my employer has been paying me Rs 40 per lesson (i.e. over £3). There have been so many parties this week though that I have not been able to fit a lesson in.

Visit of Chou En Lai (Zhou Enlai) first premier of People's Republic of China in December 1956.

I still find it warm enough in the evening to sit at a dinner party in the open-air with bare shoulders and no wrap, though now I always take stole with me, some evenings I have needed one. The max. and min. temperatures are now about 89 degrees and 63 degrees.

Air Commodore Raza's wife was bitten on the thigh by a shark or barracuda last Sunday – very bad luck as it is the first time anyone we know of has been bitten and she was swimming with her children on a popular bathing beach with Europeans swimming all round her. She is one of the very few Pakistani ladies who swim, in fact the only one I know of who wears a swim-suit. (She is a westernised Xtian). The few others who swim, or rather bathe, immerse themselves in their saris, when there are no men about. Irene Raza had to have stiches in one thigh, and is still in bed, but getting better. We are not supposed to have sharks here. Whatever fish it was had jaws wide enough to bite on both sides of the thigh. She knocked into the fish first, I told her she mustn't go kicking fishes about or of course they will bite back. She was in her depth.

Last time I visited her the Group Captain Director of Medical Services and Mauripur RPAF lady doctor arrived to dress her thigh. The lady doctor would do the dressing, male doctors are very

Arthur shaking hands with Shukri al-Quwatli, President of Syria on his visit to Pakistan in January 1957.

nervous of seeing lady patients. It amused me when Mirza applied a stethoscope to Jean, he inserted it carefully between the done-up buttons of her pyjama coat, so as not to expose her chest. Pakistani ladies often prefer to die rather than be seen by a male doctor. I was told one lady saw a male doctor in her burqa and put her tongue out for examination through a slit in the burqa and expected a diagnosis on that.

There has been nothing to look at since we left Karachi except desert peppered with scrub, and two or three glimpses of the Indus, and an occasional road. Now we have just reached an irrigated area, with check-board fields below us, mostly brown but a little green showing. With such a low rainfall (annual average 6 in. in Karachi) all agriculture depends on irrigation. The soil is very fertile (away from the salt spray of Karachi), immense new barrages are being built, and I have heard it said that if the Indus was never allowed to reach the sea, a large part of W. Pakistan could be brought under cultivation.

Much love, Mary.

Air House
Karachi
March 10th 1957

My dear Dad,

We went to Lahore for the Horse Show last weekend, the great social event of the season. The President, Prime Minister, and many of the Ambassadors, High Commissioners and other VIPs had gone up there for part of the week's festivities. We saw a full morning's programme including tent-pegging, horse jumping, parade of prize-winning cattle, sheep, horses and dogs, and the massed bands. The bands included 750 pipers and drummers all playing at once. No brass or other instruments, the Army bands here are all bagpipes and drums, and the pipers wear regimental tartans and colours. I think nowhere else in the world would one hear 750 pipes and drums playing at once, and marching and counter-marching – first the pipes in front, drums distant, and then the drums marching through and the pipes becoming distant.

There were dances every night, we went to two – the polo ball and a dance at the Gymkhana Club. The President was at both.

On the final afternoon there was an exhibition polo match between the Pakistan Army and a visiting Indian Army team, a very good match drawn 6 all. It was spoilt for the spectators by a dust storm that came up just before the start and blew throughout the match, the temperature dropping about 20°. We were in cotton dresses, and my teeth were chattering by the end. Ann caught a bad cold, and Peter went to bed with a temp. of 102° a few days later. Visibility became so bad we could not see across the field, and our nose, mouth and eyes were full of sand.

Swat Hotel,
Saidu Sharif,
Swat.
March 29th 1957

My dear Dad,

I am afraid you will have had a big gap in my letters, as I did not get one off from Karachi before we left for this week's holiday. We had had a very strenuous time in Karachi with Republic Day celebrations coinciding with the visit of a British Vice Admiral, the Commander-in-Chief East Indies. We had also had a visitor from the Air Ministry staying in the house for a fortnight.

On Republic Day (the first anniversary) there was the Armed Forces parade in the morning, including a fly-past of jet aircraft. In the evening we went to the President's reception, and after that the Prime Minister's dinner. The next day (Sunday) there was a sailing race in the morning at the Yacht Club v. the visiting British Navy, then the Admiral and various other people had lunch with us, and in the evening the PAF at Mauripur gave a Republic Day dance. We had to stay at that until 2 a.m., as the Prime Minister came on after a dinner before taking off from Mauripur at 2 a.m. for East Pakistan. The next day we flew up to Peshawar, spent the night there, and then drove on here the next day, about 130 miles drive.

Swat is a lovely state, especially at this time of year. The capital Saidu Sharif (a village really in size) is at 3,000 ft and rather like an

Alpine resort in spring. Snow-covered mountains in the background, steep bare hills surrounding the flat fertile valley of the Swat river. The colours are magnificent, as the wheat fields (with wheat about 1 foot high) are a brilliant green, the common weed in the wheat fields is a wild pink tulip. There are vivid yellow fields of mustard, and the fruit trees are in blossom – pink and white blossom of apricots, pears and plum. Pale green willow trees grow beside the streams, while the avenues of trees along the main roads are Persian lilac still quite bare of leaf. The Swat river flows in rapids over a pebbly bed, and timber is being carried down from higher up the valley.

The wheat will be harvested in June, and then a second crop of rice with be grown. Swat oranges are extra sweet, and it is also famous for its honey.

There are no railways, no aerodromes, and no cinemas in Swat. They have electricity from the hydro-electric works further down the Swat river in Malakand. We visited the works on our way here.

Arthur skiing in Pakistan.

We had dinner with the Wali of Swat, a very enlightened ruler, and a very charming person. He runs his State so well that the Government of Pakistan do not need to interfere with him. He is so light-skinned and so Western in manner that he could easily be mistaken for a European. His wife is in purdah.

The Akond of Swat should really be spelt Ak-hund. You may remember Edward Lear's *Nonsense Song*. He was the Wali's great grandfather, and a great religious leader. In his time Swat was not a state, and was inhabited by a number of wild tribes. They led a nomadic existence, because every 5 years they drew lots for all the fertile land, and all land changed ownership, so that it was not worth-while for anyone to build a house or even plant trees.

The hotel is very comfortable, European style run by the State to encourage tourists.

Arthur brought skis hoping to find a suitable skiing place for the Pakistan Air Force. We drove up two passes to 7,000 ft and found patches of snow, and Peter much enjoyed making a snowman. He could not, however, get within reach of snow-slopes. One road finished below the snowline, and the other was blocked by landslides.

It seems likely we may come home at the end of July. Arthur has been told he is wanted in December for his next post, having finished his leave, and he is due for about 4 months leave.

Air House
Karachi
April 23rd 1957

My dear Dad,

Arthur is going to England for a week next Sunday to attend the Commonwealth Naval Conference, accompanying Admiral Chandri. He also hopes he may be able to find out something about his next posting. All the family hope so.

Peter was very pleased to appear in a yachting article in the local press. He has often appeared in the results of the races, but this time they suggested that he would follow in his father's footstep and take part in the 1968 Olympics. He is certainly doing very well at sailing, and is quite fearless in a boat, though usually over cautious in other things. The article said correctly that he was the only child racing.

The new Yacht Club over at Bunker Island is a great success. We moved there after Xmas, the Pakistan Navy having taken over the old premises to build a new wharf. (It was inside their dockyard at any rate.) Now we have to go over by launch, but the service is so regular and frequent that it is little disadvantage. Bunker Island was a small uninhabited island near the harbour mouth, which had once been used as coal bunkers for ships. Much work has had to be done on it, building concrete embankments and steps down to the water, a slipway, club-house, servants' quarters, boat-building, sail and store rooms. It is now nearly complete, the final entertainment this weekend being the divers cutting off underwater, with the acetylene and oxygen, some old rusty iron piles which were in the way.

Peter is so keen on sailing that we spend every Sunday there, instead of going to the beaches. The swimming off the concrete steps is much better at this time of year than on the beaches where it is too dangerous for anything but splashing about in the surf. Sailing, of course, is all inside the harbour and up the creeks. Only in one or two races during the calm winter months do we go outside the harbour mouth.

Arthur's successor has now been published in the paper – Air Commodore Asghar Khan, and that he takes over at the end of July. So the date of our return is now fairly definite.

Much love, Mary

When it was time for the family to return to England in July 1957 the Suez Canal was closed, due to the 1956 Suez Crisis. As the return trip would have taken six weeks via the Cape of Good Hope, they flew back using PIA (Pakistan International Airlines). The plane had to stop several times for refuelling on the way and broke down en route. They had to wait in Baghdad for a couple of days, we believe, for a new engine to be flown out. Breakdown was not unusual at that time, leading Mary to comment, 'If you have time to spare travel by air!', as planes of the period were so unreliable.

Appendix IX

RAF Service History

Arthur William Baynes McDonald **b**: 14 Jun 1903; **r**: 20 Apr 1962; **d**: 26 Jul 1996

KCB - 1 Jan 1958 (**CB** - 1 Jan 1949), **AFC** - 1 Jan 1938, **MiD** - 11 Jun 1942, **MiD** - 8 Jun 1944, **MiD** – 1 Jan 1945, **MiD** - 14 Jun 1945, **MA** (Peterhouse College, Cambridge) - 1931, **CEng**, **FRAeS** - 1959, **DL** (Hampshire) - 14 Jul 1965.

Plt Off (P): 15 Mar 1924, **Plt Off**: 15 Sep 1924, **Fg Off**: 15 Oct 1925, **Flt Lt**: 13 Nov 1929, **Sqn Ldr**: 1 Dec 1936, **(T) Wg Cdr**: 1 Jan 1940, **(T) Gp Capt**: 1 Dec 1941, **Wg Cdr**: 14 Apr 1942 [1 Jan 1940], **Act A/Cdre**: 26 Feb 1943, **Gp Capt (WS)**: 26 Aug 1943, **Gp Capt**: 1 Oct 1946, **A/Cdre**: 1 Jan 1949, **AVM**: 1 Jul 1952, **Act AM**: 10 Jan 1958, **AM**: 1 Jul 1958.

15 Mar 1924:	**Granted a Short Service Commission** (Five years on the active list)
15 Mar 1924:	U/T Pilot, No. 5 FTS
16 Feb 1925:	Pilot, No. 41 Sqn (Siskins – Northolt)
1 Jul 1925:	Pilot, No. 23 Sqn.
30 Jul 1927:	Attended Engineering Officers' Course, Inland Area Depot.
1 Sep 1928:	**Granted a Permanent Commission in the rank of Flying Officer.**
8 Jul 1929:	Attended Peterhouse College, Cambridge/ Cambridge UAS.
5 Aug–27 Sep 1931:	**Placed on half-pay list, scale B for return to Antigua**
1 Nov 1931:	Attended Imperial College of Science & Technology, London
24 July 1932:	No. 24 Sqn
23 Sep 1932:	Staff, RAF Base, Singapore

Appendix IX

22 Nov 1935:	Supernumerary, RAF Depot
19 Mar 1936:	Flight Commander, No. 32 Sqn, Biggin Hill
22 Mar 1937:	Officer Commanding, No. 79 Sqn, Biggin Hill
12 Apr 1937:	Officer Commanding, No. 32 Sqn, Biggin Hill
24 Jan 1938:	Attended Course No. 16, RAF Staff College, Andover
31 Dec 1938:	Staff, Directorate of Repair and Maintenance.
1 Jan 1940:	Assistant Director of Repair and Servicing (1) Air Member for Development and Production
28 Aug 1940:	Engineering Officer, No. 6/56 Operational Training Unit, Sutton Bridge
21 Jan 1941:	Church Fenton
24 Mar 1941:	Duxford, Wing Commander, then Group Captain.
19 Feb 1942:	HQ 221 Group, Burma (Burma captured before he arrived)
25 Mar 1942:	222 Group, Air Defence Commander, Ceylon. (Ops fight)
26 Feb 1943:	AHQ, Air Headquarters Malaya, India, Air Commander, Air Officer training
16 Nov 1943:	Air Officer Training, HQ Air Command, South-East Asia.
16 Apr 1945:	AOC, No. 106 Group, (Photo Reconnaissance) Group, Benson Air Officer Commanding
14 Oct 1947:	Commandant, RAF Staff College – Bulstrode (later Andover)
11 Jan 1949:	Imperial Defence College.
1 Jan 1950:	Commandant, Boscombe Down, Aircraft & Armament Experimental Establishment.
8 Sep 1952:	Air Member for Personnel, Director General of Manning, AVM
20 Jun 1955:	Commander in Chief, Royal Pakistan Air Force.
10 Jan 1958:	AOC-in-C., Technical Training Command, Henlow
1 Oct 1959:	Air Member for Personnel.
20 April 1962:	Retired
1965:	Deputy Lieutenant for Hampshire

Appendix X

Address Made at the Celebration of Sir Arthur's 90th Birthday, 16 June 1993

Royal Lymington Yacht Club

Ladies and Gentlemen:

It is my privilege to have been asked to say a few words at this celebration of Arthur's ninetieth birthday.

We all think we know him well, but it is not until one starts to delve deeper into his past that one begins to discover the great scope of his activities and of his achievements. He suffers from iceberg syndrome – one part shows and three parts remain below the surface. It is really not possible to do justice to a span of ninety years in the space of a few minutes, but I will try.

Arthur was born in South Africa on 14 June 1903, but his early childhood was spent in Antigua, where his father was Chief Medical Officer of the Leeward Islands. He was educated at the Antigua Grammar School. At about that time the original version of the film *Ben Hur* was distributed. The boys all went to see it, so of course in their break period they had to organise a chariot race, which became rather noisy. The Head emerged and told them to keep quiet, but after a while the competition hotted up again – as these things do. Out came the Head again, very angry, latched on to one small boy and told him to report to his study in half an hour. The other boys told him, 'Watch out, you'll be for it.' The wretched boy duly reported and without more ado got four cuts of the cane. The Head then asked him, 'What's your name? I don't know your face.' The boy replied, 'I haven't joined the school yet sir – I shall be a new boy tomorrow!' This was Arthur's first experience of a pre-emptive strike!

His formal education continued at Epsom college, and at the age of 16½ he went to work as an apprentice at the Antigua sugar factory. Fed up with his princely salary of £40 a year for a 66-hour week, he quit in 1924, came back to England, joined the RAF and trained as a pilot. Recognising his obvious mechanical bent, the RAF sent him to Peterhouse College, Cambridge, where he obtained an honours degree in engineering. He also happened to meet a science student from Girton, a girl called Mary Gray, whom he married, making her one of the few married women to graduate. They have four children, two sons and two daughters.

Arthur's initial appointment was an Air Engineer at Singapore, and there he first developed his interest in sailing. At this stage it became evident to the powers that be that his forte lay in the field of technical innovation, and he was at the heart of many developments, notably Radar interception. In 1937 he led a formation of Gloster Gauntlet biplane fighters to intercept a Dutch airliner flying from Amsterdam to Croydon, at 6,000 feet above ten-tenths cloud, the first time anything of the sort had ever been done. And it was at this time that he helped develop the jargon still used by fighter pilots, such as 'scramble,' 'angels,' 'bandits,' for brevity and security, the terms familiar to all of us from wartime movies. Everyone must now realise the value of these developments in the war years that followed.

Just before the war, in 1937, Arthur's interest in dinghy racing really took off. He bought a beaten-up old 12-foot National dinghy, No. N23, called *Farandole*, applied scientific method and aerodynamic principles to the rig, and a fortnight later won the Burton Cup! He chalked up an impressive score of successes with *Farandole*, fourth in the Burton in 1946 and second in 1948, and he represented the UK in Fireflies in the Torbay Olympics in 1948. Although he did not win a medal he was clearly a notable helmsman in the dinghy racing scene at the time, and had become well aware of the value of the kicking strap.

There followed some impressive career appointments at the very summit of the RAF, which would have left him very little spare time for sailing, including two years as the last British Commander in

Chief of the Royal Pakistan Air Force, and culminating in 1959 when he was appointed Air Member for Personnel on the Air Council.

When retirement came in 1962 he promptly joined the RLYC. 1962 also happened to a be a vintage year for the X-class because Hampers built nine X-boats, one of which was X135, *Mollymawk*. *Mollymawk* was owned by Brigadier Towell, who took Arthur on as a partner on condition that he taught Towell's son to sail. Arthur took over as sole owner in 1973 and in 1974 was partnered by Colonel Christopher Biddle, and they won the Cock Boat Cup. Arthur was elected Vice-Captain of the Lymington Division in 1969, and the same year was appointed to the X-class Technical Committee, where he stayed until 1988. He has worked tirelessly in favour of technical innovation in the class rules, notably on rigging, sail controls and spars. He experimented with spinnakers, making use of Mary's sewing machine, and he must have found a lot of this work frustrating in the innate conservative environment of a class which has been in existence and thriving since 1911. No detail escaped his attention. I remember that when he was Captain he gave me a trial run in *Mollymawk* in 1977, and I was interested and a little surprised to find several gadgets powered by knicker elastic, including a sort of brake to stop the spinnaker halyard running too fast.

His attention was not confined to boats; he is an acknowledged expert on the racing rules and a frequent member of protest committees and he played a large part in the evolution over the years of our sailing instructions. It was he who solved the little nasty over the definition or rounding and passing marks!

Arthur has done a lot of work on instrumentation of wind speed and direction indicators on the starting platform, and recently developed a system of red, green and amber lights for defining the starting line – perhaps a spin-off from the work he did during the war on lighting systems for landing night-fighters. The project is proving very successful and continues to be developed.

In this appreciation of Arthur's sailing career, it would be wrong to dwell only on physical or technical accomplishments. Mention must be made of his sportsmanlike attitude towards competitive sailing, which has won him so much respect from his competitors and to some extent rubbed off on them. His approach has been the antithesis of the no-holds-barred, money-no-object viewpoint.

And so here we are celebrating his ninetieth birthday. He may be less robust but his mind is as active and his standards as high as ever. We hope to see him and Mary out in *Mollymawk* for a long time to come. But with all he has done for the X-class through the years he has left us one major objective still to be achieved – metal masts!

Ladies and Gentlemen, I give you a toast – Arthur McDonald, sailor, sportsman and innovator.[4]

---

4 We were unable to find out who made this speech for Arthur but our thanks go out to him for an excellent summary of Arthur's life.

Appendix XI

Sailing Highlights in Retirement, Royal Lymington Yacht Club,

by Jez Dean, one of Arthur's Grandsons

Grandad was an expert sailor, bringing to bear both a technical understanding of sail power, and aeronautical skills from his time in the RAF. He enjoyed adding innovations to his yachts ahead of the mainstream.

I remember his early adoption of propellers using self-opening blades to reduce drag when under sail on his yacht *Bacchante*. In racing he often combined technical improvements to his XOD (X One Design) yacht along with detailed experience of the wind, tide and solent allowing him to maximise each tack even over obstacles like Bembridge Ledge or the mud flats near Lymington. He enjoyed racing X135 division Y yacht *Mollymawk*, built in 1962, often partnered by his wife Mary and later by other club members.

He once made a spinnaker net out of a plastic laundry basket to rapidly deploy and capture the spinnaker, saving time on tacks while racing.

He combined his knowledge of sailing and aeronautics in formula to calculate power/weight characteristics and apply these as handicaps with motor and sail durations to race times to obtain overall ranking of yachts in the Royal Lymington Yacht Club (RLymYC) Round the Island Sail and Power Race for many years. The Ware and Power Cups, in this annual race around the Isle of Wight, provide a unique opportunity for 50–50 type cruising yachts to compete by using their advantage of power in combination with sail. This was a race Arthur particularly enjoyed, winning the cup on numerous occasions, initially in a yacht called *Theodora* and then later in his yacht *Bacchante*.

After races he often helped judge and arbitrate decisions concerning right of way protests from race competitors in a jovial but clear way and was respected amongst club members.

He also enjoyed deploying and maintaining the wind speed indicator on the club launch platform near the river entrance. This provided a visual wind speed indication based on rate of flashes visible via binoculars from the club house on land.

Arthur was a lead innovator as this extract from the Club's 1978 bulletin shows

> 'Our Easter dinghy meeting organisation steadily improves and adapts. This year Sir Arthur McDonald introduced what one competitor called the "Railway Line System" – so called because, if on a railway there is a crash you stop sending trains down the line until the crash is cleared; so with Sir Arthur's system on a very windy Easter no class is started from the Club line until the previous class has been seen to be surviving or has been rescued at the river mouth. The system relies on entirely reliable radio communication and a highly effective rescue organisation.'

Arthur was Vice Captain and then Captain of the 'X' One Design Class for 8 years between 1968 and 1976 and continued as Chairman of the Technical Committee for many years. As detailed in the 1976 Club bulletin;

> 'After 8 years as Captain and Vice-Captain Sir Arthur McDonald is giving up the Captaincy of the Division, although of course, he still remains Chairman of the "X" Class Technical Committee. Space does not allow a full account of what the Division owes him during his long term of office. His racing record can be seen on the boards of the club stairway and can be read in past and present bulletins but the example and leadership he has shown in everything connected with the Division is what he will be remembered for. He always found time to help and encourage newcomers and say "Well done!", when deserved. He was a first-class Committee Chairman and above all a second Sambrook Sturgess on the racing rules. His knowledge on this vital subject he is now taking pains to pass on to all members.'

Bibliography

Photo reconnaissance
Babbington Smith, Constance, *Evidence in Camera*, QBC, UK, 1957

Radar and the Biggin Hill Experiment
Agar, Herbert, *Britain Alone: June 1940–June 1941,* The Bodley Head, London, 1972
Clark, Ronald W., *Tizard*, Methuen and Co. Ltd, London, 1965
Collier, Basil, *Leader of the Few: The Authorized Biography of Air Chief Marshal the Lord Dowding*, Jarrolds, London, 1957
Latham, Colin & Stobbs, Anne, Radar*; A Wartime Miracle,* Sutton Publishing Ltd, Cheltenham, 1996
Ogley, Bob, *Biggin on the Bump,* Froglets Publications Ltd, Westerham 1990
Probert, Henry, Cox, Sebastian (Eds), *The Battle Re-Thought, A Symposium on the Battle of Britain,* sponsored jointly by the Royal Air Force Historical Society and the Royal Air Force Staff College, Bracknell, 1990
Raby, Alister, draft *History of Duxford*
Rowe, A.P., *One Story of Radar*, Cambridge University Press, Cambridge, 2015
Wallace, Graham, *RAF Biggin Hill*, Putnam & Co, London, 1957
Watson-Watt, Sir Robert, *Three Steps to Victory*, Odhams Press, London, 1957
Wood, Derek, *The Narrow Margin: The Battle of Britain & the Rise of Air Power, 1930-1940*, McGraw Hill, London, 1961

The War in the Far East
Cossey, Bob, *An Eye in the Sky*, Pen & Sword, Barnsley, 2018
Dent, Elizabeth, *Clipped Wings, Cpl Peter Walker's Illustrated Diary of his RAF Service in India & Burma 1942–1946,* Writersworld, Oxfordshire, 2017
Probert, Henry, *The Forgotten Air Force, the Royal Air Force in the War Against Japan 1941–1945,* Brassey's, London, 1995
Slim, William, Field Marshal the Viscount, *Defeat into Victory,* Cassell, London, 1956
Wood, Derek (Ed), *The RAF and Far East War 1941–1945,* Bracknell Paper No 6 A Symposium on the Far East War,* Royal Airforce Historical Association, London, 1995

Antigua and family background
Seheult, Thelma, *Beloved … The Memoir,* Paria Publishing Company Ltd, 2016

Sailing
Fox, Uffa, *Racing, Cruising and Design*, Peter Davies, London, 1938
Fox, Uffa, *Uffa Fox's Second Book,* Peter Davies, London, 1947
Fox, Uffa, *Sail and Power,* Peter Davies, London, 1947

Index

5 Flying Training School, 38
6-metre, international class, racing yachts, 99–100
11 Group, 143
14-foot International Club, 118
23 Squadron, 63, 65–74
32 Squadron, 133–47, 209, 216
41 Squadron, 61–4
79 Squadron, 142
106 Group, 188–90
222 Group, 179–83, 184

Abbotabad, Pakistan, 225, 227
Adastral House, 161–2
Afghanistan, 231, 242
Africa, 1–2, 64, 154, 179
Agar, Herbert, 147, 214
Agra, India, 249
Air Headquarters, Delhi, 184, 224
Air House, Karachi, 230, 233–6, 240–42, 252–3
Air Ministry, London, 37, 48, 77, 83, 86, 90, 145, 150, 153–4, 158–62, 183, 188–9, 197, 207, 211– 18, 266
Air Speed Indicator, ASI, 140–1
Akond of Swat, 268
Akbar, Pakistan, 250, 256
Ali, Mrs Amjad, 259
Alington, Cyril, Eton Headmaster, 249
Andover, 130–1, 148–57, 191–2, 196
annual air exercises, 72
anoxia, 51, 52–9
Anson, 64
anti-aircraft guns, 73–4, 152, 169
Antigua, 1–2, 25–37, 83–6, 88–9, 101, 104, 200–202, 203–206, 272–3
   Antigua Grammar School, 5, 12–16, 203, 268

Antigua Sugar Factory, 26–30, 34–5, 76, 273
English Harbour, 5–6, 12, 31, 88
Fort James, 88
High-Point, 17
Holberton Hospital, 11
Nelson's Dock Yard, 6
St Johns, 12, 86,
St John's Harbour, 31, 88
armistice, 25
Armstrong Whitworth Siskin, aircraft, 61, 228
Arzilla, Antigua to London cargo ship, 20–2
astro-navigation, 60
Attlee, Lord and Lady, 260
Attock Bridge, Pakistan, 255
Auckinleck, Field Marshal, 237
Aurangzeb the 6th Moghul Emperor, 250, 256
Avenger, International 14-foot dinghy, 122
Avro 504K, 38–40, 65, 227
Avro 504N, 76, 228
ayalı, 97–8
Aylward, Squadron Leader R.P., 198

Bacchante, Arthur's sailing yacht, 199, 276
bagasse, fuel, 29
Baldwin, Stanley, 136, 187, 207
Balfour, Harold, 218
Baltic, 194
Bangladesh, 230
Barbados, 5, 12, 18, 200
Bassingbourne, 170
Batavia, Java, 106–109
Battle of Britain, 9, 60, 138, 140, 147, 152–4, 199, 208, 214–19

Bawdsey, 8, 136, 143–4, 208
B-class boats, Singapore, 99–100
Beaufighter, 173
Ben Hur, 14, 272
Benson, the Photo Reconnaissance Unit, 188–90
Bentley Priory, 146, 196, 208
Bentley Rotary 65, 228
Berkeley Square, 158, 160–1
Berlin, 129, 159–60
Bernese Oberland, 79
Biddle, Colonel Christopher, 274
Biggin Hill, 9, 118, 122, 133–48, 163, 165, 177–8, 207–13, 214–19, 227
  Experiment, 9, 118, 122, 133–48, 163, 165, 177–8, 207–13, 214–19, 227
  Operations Room, 143
Birchall, Squadron Leader, 220
Birdwood, Field Marshal, 247
Birkenhead, 55–6
Blenheims, 179
Bombay, 63, 90–1
Bomber Command, 152, 154, 173
Boscombe Down, 196–7 235
Bradshaws, 61
Breda, Treaty of, 17, 88
Bristol Bulldog, 133, 229
Bristol Fighter, 45, 50–59, 227
Britain Alone, 147, 214
Britannia, The Royal Yacht, 124
Broadhurst, Harry, 150–1
Brooklands Flying Club, 76–7, 155
Browning machine guns, 134
Bulat, 101–104 116
Bulstrode Park, 196
Bunker Island, Pakistan, 269
Burling, Bill, 111–13
Burton Championship, 125–8
Burton Cup, 125–32, 158, 273

Calcutta, India, 63, 181, 252, 262
Cambridge, 78–9, 82–3, 86, 133
camera obscura, 141, 210
Can Can, National 12-foot dinghy, 121
Cannon, Air Vice Marshal L.W., 231–2, 235–8

carbon monoxide, 9, 22, 174–8
Catalina, aircraft, 180
cathode ray tube, 145
Caton, 91
centrifugal force, 49
Ceylon, 179–83, 220–1
Chain Home, 144, 208
Chamberlain, Neville, 159
Chandri, Admiral, 268
Chartwell, 146
Cherry Hinton Road, 82
Cherwell, Lord, 42
Chichester Harbour, 125–6, 191
Chile, 18
China Bay, Ceylon, 179, 182, 220
Chinese junks, 90
Chittagong, Pakistan, 251
Choba, Arthur's first National 12-foot dinghy 120–1
Christchurch, 22–3
Churchill, Winston, 110, 146, 179–81, 241
Clark, Ronald, 147, 216
Codrington College, Barbados, 12
Cohu, John Mesurio, 80, 90–1
Collier, Basil, 215–18
Collishaw, Raymond, 69–71
Colombo, Ceylon, 63, 179–84, 220
Colonial Office, 1, 11
Coltishall, RAF base, 170–2
Committee for Scientific Survey of Air Defence, 136
Commonwealth, 89, 110, 206, 248–9, 268
Constantinescu, interupter gear, 68
Cookie, 94–7, 116
Cornwall, 160
Coronel, Battle of, 18
Cotton, Sidney, 188–9
Coventry, 73
Coward, Noel, 30
Cowes, 120
Craddock, Admiral, 18
Cranwell, RAF college, 36–7, 203
Crasher Craig, 48
Curry, Charles, 126

Index 281

D'Albiac, Air Vice Marshal J.H., 179–80
Dacca, East Pakistan, 230, 251, 256, 262
Darra arms factory, 231, 254–5
Daventry, RAF base, 8, 136, 207
de Grasse, Admiral Francois Joseph Paul, 200–203
de Havilland DH.9, aircraft, 54–9, 204–206, 227
de L'Isle, Lord and Lady, 249–50
Dead Reckoning, 139–40, 145, 219
Delhi, India, 63–4, 184, 185, 249–50, 262
Deputy Lieutenant for Hampshire, 188
DC-3, intercepted Dutch airliner, 142, 144, 213
Dickens, Dr B.G., an Air Ministry Scientist, 137, 139, 213
Dickson, Sir William, 257
Dolphin Square, London, 161
Dornier Do X, aircraft, 86
Douglas, Sholto, 215
Douhet, Giulio, Italian General, 152
Dowding, Air Chief Marshal Sir Hugh 152–4, 182, 189, 207–208, 215–16, 219
Dowding Experiment, 152–4, 182, 214, 216–19
DREM Airfield Lighting System, 172
Dubois, Monsieur, 9–10
Duncan, Isa, 34
Dunkirk, 149
Dutch Islands, 103–104
Duxford, 163–78
Duxford Invisible Flare Path, 163–73

East Anglia, 172
East Fortune, 172
Eastern Front, 24
Eden, Sir Anthony, 257, 260
Edward VII, 124
Elvstrom, Paul, 193–94
Emden, SMS, German commerce raider, 107–109, 116
English Harbour, Antigua, 5–6, 12, 31, 88

Epsom College, 24, 273
Eton, 231, 249
Evidence in Camera, 186

Farandole, N23, Arthur's National 12-foot dinghy 121–32, 158, 273
Farnborough, 43, 137–8, 175
School of Aviation Medicine, 57
Fighter Command, 60, 135, 140, 143, 145–6, 151, 196, 208, 215–18
Firefly 12-foot dinghies, 191–5
First World War, 17, 20, 22–5, 44–5, 54, 56, 61, 65, 67–70, 89, 134–6, 150–1, 205
Flecker, Oswald, 246
Fleet Air Arm, 164, 180
Flying Training School, No. 5, 38, 63, 206
Formidable, Royal Navy Flagship, 201–202
Fort James, Antigua, 88
Fox, Uffa, 118, 121, 127
Fraser's Hill, Singapore, 92, 109–10
Frazer Nash, sports car, 75
Freeman, Air Marshal Sir Wilfred, 215
Fulmar, aircraft, 180, 220

Galland, Adolph, 147, 214
George V, 124
George VI, 185
Germany, 17, 86, 107, 135, 146, 150, 159, 189, 218, 229
Girton College, Cambridge, 78
Gloster Gamecock, aircraft, 42–3, 67–73, 227
Gauntlet, 133–45, 229, 273
Gladiator, 134, 229
Gnome Rhone Monosoupape engine, 36, 65
Good Hope, British warship, 18
Good Hope, Cape of, 269
Göring, Hermann, 149
Graf von Spee, Vice-Admiral Maximilian, 18
Grantchester Road, 78
Gray, Mary, 26, 273

Great Bird Island, Antigua, 84–6
Greig, D'Arcy, 43–4
Grenfell, Wing Commander Eustice Osborne, 137–9, 211
ground controlled interception, GCI, 140–7, 180, 207–19
Gsteig, Switzerland, 80–1

Haig, Douglas, 24
Halley's Comet, 7–8
Hammersmith Bridge, 119–20
Hampshire, 199
Harrogate, 156, 160–1
Hart, Wing Commander Raymond, 143
Haw Haw, Lord, 160
Hawker Hinds, day bombers, 137, 139, 216
Hawkey, Flight Lieutenant S.R., 198
Hayling Island, 125, 192
Hazlitt, William, 83
Henlow, RAF base, 61–70, 75–82, 133, 154
High Frequency/Direction Finding, HF/DF, 139–46, 215, 219
High-Point, Antigua, 17
Hilal-i-Imtiaz, Star of Excellence Award, Pakistan, 232
Hindhead, 78, 83, 247
Hitchin, RAF base, 62
Hitler, Adolf, 128, 149
Holberton Hospital, Antigua, 11
Holt Allen Combine, 119
Holt, Jack, 119
Home, Earl and Countess of, 248–50
Horseheath, 168–70
Hulganin, Marshal, 250
Hurricane, aircraft, 60, 64, 74, 142, 150, 168, 170–2, 175–8, 179–80, 185, 215, 220, 228
Hyde Park, 72, 159

Imperial College, London, 86–7, 133
Inanda, Antigua to London cargo ship, 83, 86
India, 63–4, 90, 179, 184–7, 220–6, 230–1, 237, 246, 248, 250, 263

Indian Air Force, 185–7, 250, 262
Indian Army, 184–5, 266
Indian Observer Corps (IOC), 185–6, 222–6
Indus, 236, 248, 255–6, 265
interrupter gear, 68, 134
Isa, motor boat, Antigua, 31–5, 38, 84

Jamaica, 200–201
Japan, 91, 179, 184
Japanese, 88–9, 110, 179–83, 187, 220
Java, 106–109, 179
Jones, Edward 172–3
Junkers 88s, Luftwaffe twin engine plane, 171

Kabul, Pakistan, 243, 255
Karachi, Pakistan, 230–69
 Karachi Grammar School, 231
Karghan Valley, Pakistan, 247
Kathleen, 6-metre yacht, Singapore, 100
Kenley, RAF Base, 42–5, 70–2
Kennedy, Coverley, 117
Kennedy, Ludovic, 117
Kensington Gardens, 87
Khan, Air Commodore Asghar, 269
Khan, Wing Commander 'Auzzie', 234
Khan, Lieutenant General Ayub, 235
Khyber Pass, Pakistan, 231, 242–5, 253–4
Kipling, Rudyard, 231
Klerksdorp, South Africa, 2
Kohat Pass, Pakistan, 90–1, 253–5

Lahore, Pakistan, 231, 250, 256, 262–3, 265
Lawrences of India, 246
Lee Enfield rifle, 17
Lindemann, Frederick, Alexander, Lord Cherwell 42
Liverpool, 55, 70
Lloyd, Selwyn, 257
London, 2, 18, 20–1, 48, 61, 70, 72–3, 78–9, 86–7, 129, 131, 135, 143, 146, 152, 158–62, 199, 202, 216, 253, 261
London, Frank, Singapore Yacht Club Commodore, 100

Index 283

Londonderry, Lord Charles Vane-Tempest-Stewart, Secretary of State for Air, 1931-1935, 207
Lower Topa, Pakistan, 245
Luftwaffe, 74, 154, 159, 166–7, 170–3
Lydeat, 2
Lymington, 5, 7, 20, 35, 91, 198, 204, 272–4, 276

Mackintosh, 80
MacMahon, Miss and Master, 250
Maginot Line, 150
Malaya, 104, 106–10 179, 236, 248
Marine Corps, 151
Martinique, 6, 200
Mauripur, Pakistan, 234, 257, 264, 266
Mavard, George, 180
Maxim guns, 67
McDonald, Ann, now Dean, 97, 116, 177, 230, 249, 251, 261, 266
McDonald, Ian Donald Roy MC DFC, 203–205
McDonald, Jean, now Williams, 231, 236, 238, 240, 253, 265
McDonald, John, 4, 130, 177, 231, 250, 253–5
McDonald, Peter, 231, 235–7, 241, 245, 252–4, 257, 260–1, 266, 268–9
McDonald & Company, 2
Meakin, Alfred, 22–3
Mechanical Sciences Tripos, 81
Merilees Watson, 26
Merlin, B-class yacht, B10, Singapore 100–103, 112–13, 116
Merlin engine, 180
Mermaid Class boats, 198
Midway, Battle of, 220
Mir of Hunza, 256
Mirza, Begum Iskandar, 259
Mobile Wireless Observer companies, 186, 225
Mollymawk, Arthur's X-class racing yacht, 198–9, 274–6
Mono Avro, aircraft, 38–40, 65, 227
Mono Soupape, engine, 38, 65
Morris, Stuart, 125–6

Morse Code, 24, 60
Mukenjee, Air Marshal, 250, 262
Murree, Pakistan, 245–6, 255

Nagumo, Japanese Admiral, 182, 220
Nanga Parbat, mountain, Pakistan, 246
Nathiagali, Hill Station, Pakistan, 246
National 12-foot dinghy, 119–32
National Archive, 180, 185, 211–13
Navy;
    Australian, 109
    French, 201
    German, 107
    Indonesia, 263
    Japanese, 179
    Pakistan, 263, 269
    Royal, *see* Royal Navy
    US, *see* US Navy
Nelson's Dock Yard, Antigua, 6
Nelson, Horatio, 6, 31, 200
Newell, Cyril, 215
Nicholson, Charles, 121
Nicholsons of Gosport, 125
night raiders, 74
Normandy, 154
Northolt, RAF base, 61–2, 65

Observer Corps, Royal, 167, 175, 178, 208, 215
Officers' Training Corps, 24
Olympic Games, 191–5
Omdurman, Battle of, 67, 134
Operations Room, 137–46, 170, 175, 208, 214–15, 225
opium, 91
Orange, Dr Vincent, 218
Orfordness, 8, 208

Pakistan, 230–69
    East Pakistan, 230–1, 250–1, 262, 266
    Pakistan Air Force (PAF), 230–2, 236, 254, 265, 268, 274
    Pakistan Army, 266
    Pakistan Independence Day, 221
    Pakistan Republic Day, 243
    West Pakistan, 265

Parachinar, Pakistan, 242–4
Park, Air Chief Marshal Sir Keith, 215
Parkstone Yacht Club, 120
Parsons Green, 21, 23
Pathan tribesmen, 230–1, 243–4
Pearl Harbor, 179, 220
Peirse, Air Marshal Sir Richard, 184–5
Pembroke Lodge, Prep School, 23
Penang, Malaya, 116
  Harbour, 108
Pennington marshes, Lymington, 7
Peshawar, Pakistan, 184, 224–5, 235–7, 242–5, 253–6, 266
Peterhouse College, Cambridge, 82, 273
photo reconnaissance, 151, 188–90
Pip-Squeak, 140–1, 147, 216, 219
Pireau, Monsieur, 259
Pool, Wing Commander, 176
Port Stanley, Falkland Islands, 18
Portal, Peter, 181
Pretty, Flight Lieutenant Walter, B.G., 137, 140, 209, 216, 219
Prince of Wales Cup, 125
Probert, Henry, 181–2, 184
Punei, racing boat, Singapore, 113
purdah, 237, 241, 251, 253, 256, 268
Putney Bridge, 120, 127

radar, 8–10, 136–47, 167, 180–1, 208, 215–16, 273
radial engine, 76, 228–9
RAF, 9, 35–7, 40, 42, 48, 54, 56, 58, 60, 67, 75–6, 78, 80, 82–7, 90, 111, 114, 133–4, 153–7, 161, 166–8, 170, 173, 176, 179–83, 184–6, 196–8, 203–206, 215–18, 228–9, 270, 273, 276
RAF Sailing Association, 198
RAF Staff College, 153, 191, 196
RAF Yacht Club, 198
Raby, Alister, 174
Ragg, Squadron Leader R.L., 137–9
Railway Line System, 277
Ranelagh Sailing Club, 120, 127–31
Rangoon, 64, 180
Ratsey and Lapthorne, sailmakers, 125
Ratsey, Colin, 125
Rawalpindi, P & O, 116–17

Rawalpindi, Pakistan, 186, 224–6, 232, 245, 255–6
Richards, Dennis, 215
Richards, Vivian, 16
Richardson, 134–6
Richthofen, Manfred von, 44
Rodney, Sir George, 200–202
Rolls Royce engines, 50, 53, 180, 227–9
Round the Island Race, Singapore, 105–106
Round the Island Sail and Power Race, Lymington, 106, 276
Rowe, Albert Percival, 207
Royal Army Medical Corps, 2, 20
Royal Batavia Yacht Club, 107
Royal Lymington Yacht Club, 198, 272, 276
Royal Navy, 31, 117, 150, 164, 200, 266
Royal Observer Corps, 167
Royal Pakistan Air Force, 197, 230–68, 274
Royal Singapore Yacht Club, 98–100 106, 112
Royal Yacht Squadron Gold Cup, 198
Royal Yachting Association, 113
rugby, 23–4, 79

S.E.A.T.O. conference, 231
Said, Hakin, 241, 258
Saidu Sharif, 266
Saintes, Battle of the, 6, 200–202
Salisbury Plain, 151–2, 182
Scott, Alvary, 205
Scott, Peter, 192–3
Sealand, RAF base, 38–44, 51–2, 55–7, 60–3, 65, 206
Second World War, 10, 60, 74, 117, 128–9, 136, 150, 154, 166, 184, 188
Seletar, RAF base, Singapore, 92–3, 111–16
Seydlitz, SMS, 19
Shah Jehan, 231
Shahinshah of Iran, 258
Shahinshah of Persia, 257
Shalimar Gardens, 250
Shamin, Air Chief Marshal Muhammad Anwar, 232

Shogran, 247
Short Brothers, 114
　Short Singapore, aircraft 114–15, 228
Signals, 24, 61, 77, 110, 137, 180, 226
Singapore, 81, 87–110
skiing, 79–81, 267–8
Slim, General Sir William, 185, 187
Smith, Constance Babbington, 188
Senior Medical Officer, SMO, 174–5, 177–8
Sopwith Camel, aircraft, 65
　Pup, 65
　Snipe, 65–6, 228
South Africa, 1–2, 272
Southbourne, 22–3
Spitfire, aircraft, 60, 64, 150, 176, 189–90, 215, 228
Spry, William, 201–202
St Bartholomew's Hospital, London, 2
St Cergue, Jura Mountains, 81
St Johns, Antigua, 12, 86,
St John's Harbour, Antigua 31, 88
St Kitts, West Indies, 1–12, 200
steam engine, 3, 35, 89
Stevens, F.P., 73–4
Strait of Johore, Singapore, 89
Sturdee, Admiral, 19
sugar-cane, 3, 5, 27–8, 35, 200
Surrey, 78, 162
Sutton Bridge, 67–70, 73–4, 172
Swat, Pakistan, 242, 266–8
Swinton, Lord Philip Cunliffe-Lister, Secretary of State for Air, 1935-1938, 146, 212
Symon, Sir Alexander, 259
　Lady, 249

Taj Mahal, 250
Tate and Lyle, 28
'The Phoney War', 162
The Tatler, 36
Theodora, Arthur's yacht, Lymington, 276
Thorneycroft, 112
Tiger beer, 91
Titanic, 8–10
Tizard, Sir Henry, 136–47, 207–208, 212, 214–18

Torquay, 128, 158, 191–5
total eclipse of the sun, 70
TR9, radio set, 135
Trade Wind, 5–6, 12, 17, 26, 35, 200
Trafalgar Square, 261
Trafalgar, Battle of, 200
Trenchard, Air Marshal, Sir Hugh, 217
Trincomalee, Ceylon, 179–82, 220
Twickenham, 162
Typhoon, aircraft, 174–6

US Army Air Forces, 185
US Navy, 151, 201

Vickers .303-inch machine guns, 67, 69, 134
Victory, HMS, Nelson's flagship, 150
Virgin Islands, 12

Wali of Swat, Pakistan, 267
Watson-Watt, Robert, 207–208
Welcombe Hotel, Ceylon, 180
Wendover, 161
West Indies, 1, 3, 20, 28, 34
Western Front, 24, 45, 70, 151, 205
Weymouth, 132
Whetton, Douglas, 204
White Hare Ski Club, 81
White Swan, yacht in Singapore, 99
Wilkins, Arnold, 207
Wimperis, Harry, E., 207–208
windmills for sugar cane crushing, 4–5, 17, 35, 52, 200
Wittering, RAF base, 170, 172–3, 176
Wood, Derek, 214–16
Worham, Henry, 98

XOD, X One Design, racing yachts, 199, 276

Yacht Racing Association, 113, 118
Yachting World Trophy, 125

Zam Zama gun, 231

List of boats and ships

6-metre, international class, racing yachts, 99–100

Arzilla, Antigua to London cargo ship 20–2

Avenger, International 14-foot dinghy 122

Bacchante, Arthur's yacht, 199, 276
B-class boats, Singapore, 99–100
Britannia, The Royal Yacht, 124

Can Can, National 12-foot dinghy, 121
Chinese junks, 90
Chobaj, Arthur's first National 12-foot dinghy, 120–1

Emden, SMS, German commerce raider, 107–109, 116

Farandole, N23, Arthur's National 12-foot dinghy 121–32, 158, 273
Firefly 12-foot dinghies, 191–5
Formidable, Royal Navy Flagship, 201–202

Good Hope, British warship, 18

Inanda, Antigua to London cargo ship, 83, 86
Isa, motor boat, Antigua, 31–5, 38, 84

Kathleen, 6-metre yacht, Singapore, 100

Merlin, B-class yacht, B10, Singapore, 100–103, 112–13, 116
Mermaid Class boats, 198
Mollymawk, X-class racing yacht, 198–9, 274–6

National 12-foot, racing dinghies, 119–32

Punei, racing boat, Singapore, 113

Rawalpindi, P&O, 116–17

Seydlitz, SMS, 19

Theodora, yacht, 276
Titanic, RMS, 8–10

Victory, HMS, Nelson's flagship, 150

White Swan, yacht in Singapore, 99

XOD, X One Design, 199, 276

List of Key Aircraft

Armstrong Whitworth Siskin, aircraft, 61, 228
Avro 504K, 38–40, 65, 227
Avro 504N, 76, 228

Beaufighter, 173
Blenheims, 179

Catalinas, 180

de Havilland DH.9, 54–9, 204–206, 227
DC-3, intercepted KLM Dutch airliner, I42, 144, 213
Dornier Do. X, 86

Fulmars, 180, 220

Gloster Gamecock, 42–3, 67–73, 227
Gauntlet, 133–45, 229, 273
Gladiator, 134, 229

Hawker Hinds, day bombers, 137, 139, 216
Hurricane, 60, 64, 74, 142, 150, 168, 170–2, 175–8, 179–80, 185, 215, 220, 228

Junkers 88s, 171

Mono Avro, 38–40, 65, 227

Short Singapore, 114–15, 228
Sopwith Camel, 65
  Pup, 65
  Snipe, 65–6, 228
Spitfire, 60, 64, 150, 176, 189–90, 215, 228

Typhoon, 174–6